C. F. Peter Collingridge

The Civil Principality of the Vicar of Christ

C. F. Peter Collingridge

The Civil Principality of the Vicar of Christ

ISBN/EAN: 9783744659291

Printed in Europe, USA, Canada, Australia, Japan

Cover: Foto ©Lupo / pixelio.de

More available books at **www.hansebooks.com**

Et Potestas temporalis definienda est.

THE CIVIL PRINCIPALITY

OF THE VICAR OF CHRIST:

A POINT OF DOCTRINE CALLING FOR DEFINITION.

BEING A SERIES OF PAPERS

CONCLUDING WITH

A PETITIONARY APPEAL TO THE BISHOPS AND THEOLOGIANS OF THE BRITISH ISLES AND OF THE ENGLISH-SPEAKING WORLD, FOR THE THEOLOGICAL DISCUSSION AND DEFINITION OF THE CIVIL PRINCIPALITY OF THE VICAR OF CHRIST.

BY THE

REV. C. F. PETER COLLINGRIDGE.

"Dabit illi Dominus sedem David patris ejus et regnabit in domo Jacob in æternum."

LONDON: BURNS & OATES, LIMITED.
NEW YORK, CINCINNATI, CHICAGO: BENZIGER BROTHERS.

Imprimatur:

HENRICUS EDUARDUS,

Card. Archiep. Westmon.

Die 18 *Sept.,* 1889.

CONTENTS.

THIS DISCOURSE, FULL OF ASSOCIATION WITH HIM,
IS INSCRIBED
TO THE MEMORY OF ALFRED,
A DEAR BROTHER,
WHO HAVING OFFERED TO GOD FOR SERVICE IN THE SANCTUARY
A HEART ADMIRABLE FOR PURITY, DETACHMENT, AND
CONFORMITY TO THE DIVINE WILL,
VOLUNTEERED IN A TIME OF DANGER FOR THE
DEFENCE OF THE PRINCELY RIGHTS OF THE VICAR OF CHRIST,
FIRMLY RESOLVING
THAT SHOULD NO SACRIFICE OF BLOOD BE REQUIRED,
HIS FIRST OBLATION SHOULD BE CONSUMMATED.
THE SACRIFICE
IN THE CAUSE OF THE HOLY SEE WAS ACCEPTED.
HE DIED OF HIS WOUNDS AT NEROLA,
OCTOBER 18TH, 1867.

L. J. C.

INTRODUCTION.

DIVINE PROVIDENCE, which maintains the order of the universe. extends

3. If so, is the Civil Principality then first founded on a mere human right, springing from cession, gift, or growth of favouring circumstances ?

4. Could any divine sanction, bestowed after the foundation of the Church, on a mere human institution, change its nature ?

5. Are we taught that the Civil Principality is inalienable under all possible circumstances ?

6. Is sovereign power founded on mere human right inalienable under all possible circumstances ?

WARNING AGAINST POLITICS.

It might appear unnecessary to caution the reader that a subject which professedly transcends ordinary politics is not immediately concerned with political parties nor with forms of government. The warning, however, seems called for, since offence has already been taken, apparently on political grounds. Such is the only conclusion to be drawn from a letter of the late Vicomte de Bonald. The letter received from that gentleman, besides marking his own and his Bishop's interest in the subject, so far as it had then been treated, suggests the influence that caused the miscarriage of an attempted French edition. If certain Royalists find the subject not to square precisely with their views, why should not Republicans ? The writer trusts to the unbiased judgment of those who place the interests of " the kingdom of God " above the affairs of men.

The reader is requested to take notice of the *excerpta* from Pontifical Acts in last pages.

Any communication on this subject may be addressed to C. F. P. C., at 28 Orchard Street, London, W.

Palm Sunday, 1894.

INTRODUCTION.

DIVINE PROVIDENCE, which maintains the order of the universe, extends to the physical world, to the moral world, and to the supernatural world. We are taught by the words of the late Pope Pius IX., and by the declaration of the Bishops of the world assembled around him in 1862 (see Appendix) that the Roman Pontiff obtained the Civil Principality by a peculiar design of Divine Providence, and that the temporal sovereignty did not accrue to him by the effect of hazard, but was granted to him by a special disposition of God. Such is the grave and authentic teaching of the Church of God, which deserves the greatest attention at the present day. The measured terms of the Pontifical utterance and of the Bishop's declaration are very striking ; but, what is more so, is the vast import of that conjoint teaching and its infolded character.

Twenty-nine years have elapsed since the Church raised her voice in that solemn manner, during which long period we have been schooled by the sad lesson of events. Is it presumptuous to inquire whether, if there be any analogy between the Civil Principality of the Vicar of Christ and other points of Catholic doctrine, which have at last been put into a clear light, we may not legitimately expect a further elucidation of this teaching.

1. Are we to understand by the solemn teaching of the Church in 1862 that a peculiar design or ruling of Divine Providence raises the Civil Principality above the ordinary moral order of society, and transfers it to the supernatural order ? Or are we free to hold that, in spite of such "particular design of Divine Providence," and "special disposition of God," the Civil Principality remains subject to the natural laws which govern the moral world, and hence to the ebb and flow of the affairs of men ?

2. Are we to understand that the Civil Principality is something less than a direct gift of God ?

3. If so, is the Civil Principality then first founded on a mere human right, springing from cession, gift, or growth of favouring circumstances ?

4. Could any divine sanction, bestowed after the foundation of the Church, on a mere human institution, change its nature ?

5. Are we taught that the Civil Principality is inalienable under all possible circumstances ?

6. Is sovereign power founded on mere human right inalienable under all possible circumstances ?

7. Are we taught that the Civil Principality is a right inherent to the office of the Vicar of Christ, or may we hold that it is adventitious?

8. When we are taught that the temporal sovereignty was not added to the Holy See by an effect of hazard, but was granted by a special disposition of God, are we to understand that the Roman Pontiff's right did not arise from human activity or natural causation, but is founded on God's own gift and institution?

9. Can an absolutely inalienable sovereign right have any other than a divine foundation?

10. Is it conceivable that the Civil Principality should be inherent to the office of the Vicar of Christ, and thus constitute an inalienable temporal right without a distinctly divine foundation?

11. Supposing the spiritual and universal supremacy of the Roman Pontiff necessarily implies a *de jure* inalienable temporal sovereignty, is it conceivable that God failed to grant such a right from the beginning?

12. If the existence of the Roman Pontiff's temporal right may be inferred from the necessity of the temporal power, should not the basis of that right be discoverable?

13. Which is more conducive to the interests of the Faith, and to those of the Church, merely to infer the existence of the Pontiff's temporal right, or to discover it plainly by indicating its foundation?

14. In what sense does the Civil Principality belong to the Catholic world? How, when, and from whom did Christians acquire that right?

15. The territory over which any sovereignty is exercised must be determinable, because no territory is geographically indeterminable. Therefore the "temporal possessions" of the Roman Pontiff must be determinable as to extent. By what standard are we to judge of such extent?

16. If the gift of temporal sovereignty to the Roman Pontiff be divine, it was contemporaneous with the foundation of the Church. For the Divine plan was then complete, and nothing has been added to it since. On what occasion, then, was the gift bestowed?

17. Should we be afraid to invoke more light on this subject, or is it a matter of indifference to acquire a more definite idea of the Civil Principality?

May we not legitimately inquire concerning the bestowal of temporal power on the Roman Pontiff: "*Quis, quid, ubi, quibus auxiliis, cur, quomodo, quando?*"

These are questions which I have feebly attempted to solve in this little work, which was published from the beginning with a practical object in view. It can possess no claim save to invite the clergy and all friends of the Holy See to a closer study of the foundation of the temporal power of the Pope, in the hope that not mere secular loyalty will be encouraged towards the Pontiff-king, but that a more sublime and potent feeling may be appealed to, namely, our Faith. For "this is the victory which overcometh the world, our Faith."

C. F. P. C.

St. James's, Colchester,

November 3rd, 1890.

Dear Father Collingridge,

I have read your paper upon the Temporal Power of the Holy See with much interest. I recommend you to publish it. The subject has been abundantly treated from the historical, the political, and the economic points of view, as it regards the interests of Christendom. It has not however been so fully brought before the public from the scriptural and theological standpoint. You have attempted to analyse and draw out the meaning which lies hidden in the words of Sacred Scripture and in events recorded in the Gospel. Thus your study cannot fail to interest a great number of Catholic minds. The more you can show that the Prerogatives of the Roman Pontiff are in reality inherited from Blessed Peter, who in his turn received them from His Divine Master upon being associated with Him as His Vicar and Representative on earth, the more you will raise the esteem in which those Prerogatives are held by Catholics.

The principal text on which you comment—that of Matthew xvii. 25, 26—is carefully examined by Suarez in his " Defence of the Faith against Anglican Errors," where he asks the question, Why does Christ associate Peter with Himself in the freedom of the children of kings and in the payment of the stater ?

This great theologian, who speaks for the whole school, says that Christ declared Peter to be exempt from

tribute just as He Himself was ; and that we are to understand that Christ granted this privilege of exemption to
Peter because Peter was to be the Prince and Head of
the Church and the Vicar of Jesus Christ Himself.

This privilege was therefore not *personal* to Peter
alone, but *real*, and attached to the dignity and office
which passes on to his successors in virtue of Divine
power and of the peculiar institution and will of Christ.
If tribute be the sign of temporal dependence and subjection, he who is not really subject to the payment
of tribute is not really under temporal subjection. He
is independent : if independent he is Sovereign. The
principle, therefore, of the temporal independence of
the Pope appears to be contained in the text of the
Gospel just referred to.

That there may be, and are, differences of opinion
among theologians as to the precise meaning of certain
texts and facts, is no reason why we should not put
forward for acceptance the sense and the consequences
which we, after careful study of such texts or facts,
consider to be evidently contained in them.

This you have done with becoming modesty, and I
therefore think that your little treatise cannot fail to
render a real service to the great cause of the Papacy.

Wishing you every blessing,

I am, your faithful and devoted servant,

✠ HERBERT,
Bishop of Salford.

THE CIVIL PRINCIPALITY OR TEMPORAL PRINCEDOM OF THE VICAR OF CHRIST, FORESHADOWED IN THE OLD TESTAMENT AND VINDICATED IN THE NEW.

." Then the children are free."—St. Matthew xvii.

Dear Brethren,—I have frequently in past discourses reminded you of the event which took place in Rome on the 20th of September of the year 1870, of which I was an eye-witness ; how the Vicar of Christ was then violently despoiled of the last remnant of territorial independence constituting what is called the Civil Principality. I have quoted the page of history in proof that the Civil Principality was acknowledged as a right of the successors of Peter so soon as rulers and subjects embracing the Christian Faith understood the unique, supreme, and universal position of the Vicar of Our Lord, and that in all Christian ages both Kings and their subjects have in their conduct towards the Pontiffs, more eloquently than in words, manifested their implicit Faith in his civil independence and temporal sovereignty.

I have now to inquire whether this great historical fact which, like a ray of Heavenly guidance, is cast down the Christian ages with only here and there an exceptional diminution of splendour, is merely the outcome of the goodwill of Christian nations, or a provisional state allowed by Divine Providence to be followed by some more enlightened agreement with modern rulers of the Nineteenth Century, or whether it is not rather the work of the Invisible Head of the Church, securing to His Vicar the exercise of a right once Divinely bestowed upon Him in the person of Peter. If once we become convinced that his Civil Principality or Temporal Princedom is a gift of Jesus Christ and an essential part of the Divine Plan for the Church Militant, we shall not be surprised, as unbelievers have sometimes been, at the luminous fact just alluded to, namely : that except in times of persecution, which God's providence over His Church does not permit to last long, the Roman Pontiffs have ever enjoyed territorial independence with all Kingly rights. I maintain then that *the Civil Principality or Temporal Princedom is a gift of Jesus Christ, and a Divine institution foreshadowed in the Old Testament and vindicated in the New.* To defend this thesis, dear brethren, I will confine myself to texts that are clear in themselves or susceptible of plain deductions, and shall have recourse to two principal arguments.

First : That the order of Christ, which is that of Melchisedech, to which the Roman Pontiffs belong, constitutes them Kings and therefore gives them a territorial independence.

Second : That the Roman Pontiffs were actually associated in the person of Peter in the supreme independence of the Son of Man, and therefore in His earthly Freedom.

I.—That the order of Christ, which is that of Melchisedech, to which the Roman Pontiffs belong, constitutes them Kings and therefore gives them a territorial independence.

THE ORDER OF MELCHISEDECH.

Let us examine the essential features of the order of Melchisedech by which it is distinguished from the Levitical order. We read in Genesis, chapter xiv., that " Melchisedech, the King of Salem, bringing forth bread and wine, for he was a priest of the most High God, blessed " Abraham. In the Psalms we read the following words of King David in reference to his Divine descendant and successor : " Thou art a priest for ever according to the order of Melchisedech." These words are quoted in the Epistle to the Hebrews. From the commentary of St. Paul and from the tradition of the Church we gather these essential features of the new order which distinguish it from the old.

1. That it is the fulfilment of the old which it abolishes.

2. That the Pontiff thereof belongs to no particular tribe.

3. That his oblation is that of bread and wine.
4. That besides being priest he is King.

Each of these essential features must now come under our particular notice :—

First : The first feature or characteristic of the order of Melchisedech seems also to be the one which the Apostle St. Paul writing from Italy insists on principally. For the Hebrews clung to the old order of things. If the Levitical order were changed, then the law, then the inheritance of the sceptre, then the whole national organization must be at least altered. St. Paul insisted that the new order put an end to the old, that Christ constituted "priest for ever according to the order of Melchisedech" had entered the true sanctuary, Heaven, which He had opened not with the blood of animals, but with His own, and once for all ; that the typical sanctuary of the temple, with the annual visit of the Pontiff carrying the typical blood was therefore put an end to.

Again according to the Apostle, Melchisedech had by legal prescription neither "beginning of days nor end of life" which was typical of the eternal priesthood of Christ, whereas the Jewish Pontiff had a limited term of office, which was ominous of the limited duration of the Levitical order.

Second : The second essential feature of the order of Melchisedech which distinguishes it from the order of Aaron consists in this, that the Pontiff thereof belongs to no particular tribe, but may be chosen from any nation, whereas the Jewish Pontiff was taken from the tribe of Levi and the family of Aaron. Which St. Paul expresses by saying that Melchisedech was "without father, without mother, without genealogy." The same idea is expressed by the Apostle, when speaking of Christ, the eternal Priest, he shows Him to belong to the tribe of Juda, "of which no one gave attendance at the altar," which translation of Priesthood brought about therefore a translation of the law.

Third: The third essential feature of the same order is that the Pontiff's oblation is that of bread and wine. This essential characteristic of the everlasting order of Priesthood, although not so interesting to the Jewish priests or nation as the foregoing, is the most striking for us. In Abraham's day God raised up a Priest to offer bread and wine, a typical oblation on the same spot where Christ instituted the Eucharistic sacrifice. The blood of animals slain on the Levitical altar foreshadowed the coming Sacrifice of the Son of God, but the oblation of bread and wine by Melchisedech was typical of the unseen presence of the Divine Victim on the Christian altar.

Fourth: Having outlined these distinguishing features of the order of Melchisedech, I now come to the one with which I am most concerned in this discourse, namely, that the Pontiff of the order of Melchisedech, besides being Priest is also King.

St. Paul quotes from Genesis: "For this Melchisedech was King of Salem, priest of the most High God . . . who first by interpretation of his name is King of Justice, and then also King of Salem, that is King of Peace." This then is also an essential feature of the order of Melchisedech which distinguishes from the order of Aaron. For in the former the priestly and Kingly dignities are combined in the one person, whereas in the latter the Law makes no provision for the sceptre on behalf of the priesthood, but according to the national prophecy of Jacob it is to be held principally by another tribe, that of Juda, and in fact was held as an hereditary right, by the successors of David, the first King of the said tribe. It may possibly be objected, but was Melchisedech any more than a nominal King? Had he a kingdom or real territorial independence? If anyone were bold enough to make such an objection, it would suffice to answer, that history has nowhere put on record the existence of a king of no place, or of an honorary king or of a king in partibus; that such an empty title would not be mentioned in Scripture nor repeated by the Apostle when insisting on the character of the priest, whose order was typical of, or rather identical with, Christ's. That Melchisedech without his kingship would be unrecognisable, and that his kingship is as essential as his Priesthood in order to his being recognised. But there is a plainer answer. Melchisedech was King of Salem just as truly as Bara was King of Sodom or Bersa King of Gomorrha. And Salem is the ancient name of the city of Jerusalem. Melchisedech then was truly King and in the enjoyment of a real territory and capital, whose name explains why its Pontiff-King took no part in the wars of the other Kings, but considered it his part to bless the righteous and victorious Abraham. All possible doubt as to the Kingly character of Melchisedech being removed, it remains clear that an essential feature of his order, which is the order of Christ, is the combination of the Pontifical and Kingly characters and dignities. And this feature is nowhere found in the Levitical order. The Priests for a time combined the office of Prince or Chief Ruler with the sacerdotal office, but besides the fact that such authority was delegated from the Jews, never was a High Priest saluted or recognised as King. Having passed in review the essential features of the eternal Priesthood of Melchisedech and dwelt particularly on his combined dignity as Pontiff-King, we may now, dear brethren, turn with love and reverence to Christ and to His Vicar and view these essential features in the head of the everlasting Priesthood.

CHRIST IS PONTIFF-KING.

We have it from David's inspired pen: "Thou art a Priest for ever according to the order of Melchisedech." But some timid inquirer might suggest the question: Did Christ really possess all the essential features or characteristic powers of the order of Melchisedech? To which common sense at once replies: Certainly. For a portion of the features or characteristic powers of an order are not that order, which must be taken in its integrity or

forfeit all reality. Remove from the order of Melchise
dech its Kingly character and it becomes unrecognisable
and drops out of existence. Since Christ then belongs to
the order of Melchisedech, and Melchisedech is Pontiff-
King, so is Christ Pontiff-King. It is impossible that
the other characteristics of the order should apply to
Christ, this remarkable one alone excepted.

PETER, AFTER ASSOCIATION WITH CHRIST, WAS PONTIFF-KING.

The above reasoning applies also to the Vicar of
Christ. If the order of Christ be that of Melchisedech,
then is the order of the New Testament identical with it.
The order of Christ has its succession of Pontiffs like the
order of Aaron. To these Christ transmits His Priesthood, not through genealogical succession, but individually,
and with all its characteristic powers. If Christ transmitted the Priesthood without the Kingly character, He
would not transmit the Priesthood of Melchisedech. The
order of Melchisedech, destined to be everlasting, is that
of the Catholic Church. The plenitude of characteristic
powers must reside in the Pontiff, for the Pontiff's
character determines that of the whole body and Hierarchy.
Christ then could not confer, or rather transfer, the plenitude of spiritual power to Peter, His first Vicar, without
endowing him also with the Kingly character and dignity,
which carries with it territorial independence. Therefore
the order of Christ, which is that of Melchisedech, to which
the Roman Pontiffs belong, constitutes them Kings and
therefore gives them a territorial independence.

If this be revealed truth we should be able to trace
the Kingly dignity of Christ and of His Vicar and
ascertain how they came by it. And there is plenty of
evidence at hand for the purpose. We shall trace elsewhere Christ's Kingly dignity as a necessity in the order
of society created by God. We shall trace it in prophecy.
We shall gather it from contemporary witnesses, and
from the lips of the Saviour Himself. But before
examining this most consoling evidence in the times we

live in, we may, as a preliminary question connected with the order of Melchisedech, trace the Kingly character of the Redeemer in what I believe to be the reason of one of the great contrasts between the two orders and the two laws, namely, the divided authority of the old law and the united authority of the new.

For this reason or mystical meaning I go to St. Paul. He declares that "all these things happened to them in figure." If all, therefore probably this divided authority under a single legislation.

CHRIST'S KINGLY DIGNITY TRACED TO REASON OF DIVIDED AUTHORITY OF OLD LAW AND UNITED AUTHORITY OF NEW.

And what was such divided authority moulding the one people under the same Divine legislation a figure of? It seems to me it was a figure of what was wanted and to come ; the union of the two elements of the sacred humanity together and to the second Divine Person and of their respective functions for the redemption of mankind. " Drop down dew, ye Heavens, from above, and let the clouds rain the just ; (His holy soul) let the earth be opened, and bud forth a Saviour (His sacred body)."

Look back then, dear brethren, sixteen centuries before the coming of Christ to the early days of our race and behold God, ever the Saviour of men, preparing the Redemption to come. Out of the twelve tribes, the offspring of Jacob, two, I cannot find better words, are preeminently pre-destined. Listen to the prophetical blessing bestowed respectively upon Juda and upon Levi. " Thou hast couched as a lion and lioness, who shall rouse him ? " says the Patriarch blessing his son Juda, " the sceptre shall not be taken away from Juda nor a ruler from his thigh, till He come that is to be sent, and He shall be the expectation of nations."

Here is a blessing all temporal, physical and political, winding up with a prophecy of the sleep and the resurrection of the body of the Redeemer taken from the tribe of Juda. He alone slept as a lion in His death, and none could rouse Him but His own Divine Person.

But of Levi the Patriarch says : " I will divide them in Jacob and scatter them in Israel." There is no temporal blessing, but rather a temporal curse for Levi's posterity. The Levites are to inherit no tribal portion of the promised land, but then God draws good out of evil and through Jacob bestows a spiritual blessing in compensation for the temporal punishment or deprivation. For the Levitical tribe will be the soul of their brethren in Israel, scattered indeed throughout the whole national body. And when the limbs are broken away and the heart and head alone remain in the enduring tribe of Juda, that Levitical soul will cling to what remains and with Juda will live on in mutual preservation. The two tribes receive opposite blessings, the one to carry and represent the earthly or temporal life of the coming Saviour, the other to energize with His spiritual life. The former to transmit the blood, to hand down the sceptre, to defend His temporal interests, to fix His country and birthplace and determine His earthly rights and social position. The latter to anticipate the work of His soul, to forego earthly rights, to bow before His Heavenly Father, to offer up His blood for the various wants of mankind in typical sacrifices. Such anticipation and separation of His temporal and spiritual life and of their respective functions in the national life of the people of God was not the work of man. It was the love of the second Divine Person preluding the work of Redemption that did it. And as long as He had not assumed a united body and soul in the mystery of the Incarnation, so long did the temporal and spiritual elements remain separate in the life and government of His people. But when the sacred humanity of the Son of God appeared and Christ had reached the plenitude of His age, it was fitting also that the theocracy should cease to contain two separate elements of government and distinct sources of authority under the single Divine legislation. And if such be the reason of a divided authority under the old law, then do we understand why Christ holds both the sceptre and the priesthood in the perfection of the new. " For the priesthood being translated, it is necessary that a translation also be made of the Law."

II.—That the Roman Pontiffs were actually associated in the person of Peter in the supreme independence of the Son of Man, and therefore in His earthly freedom.

CHRIST'S KINGSHIP A SOCIAL NECESSITY.

God alone, my dear brethren, is supremely independent. Independence, in other words, is a Divine attribute. It means exemption from control, power, direction, influence, or support. Christ being God enjoys this supreme independence. But Christ led also a human life. He was truly man. He had a country with a definite lawful position therein like other men. For this is essential to man. God, who hath created society, is likewise the author of the lawful position of citizens and of the lawful position of rulers. And there is none other created by God. Christ therefore in His own country could only be lawful subject or lawful Prince. Let us suppose for one moment that He was lawful subject. If so, He was bound to the Levitical Priesthood as well as to the political power, bound to pay tribute to the temple and bound to pay tribute to Cæsar, bound therefore to contribute to the preservation of the Old Law and forbidden to procure its abolition. It will be seen at once that there is utter incompatibility between His subjection as man and His independence as God. In other words, it is inconceivable that the Son of Man on account of His Sovereign Divine Power and independence among His fellow-men should not be possessed likewise of Sovereign earthly power and independence and therefore of the lawful position of King. For the former could not be exercised or vindicated by the God-Man without the latter.

Divine Vindication of the Kingly Right of Christ and His Chief Apostle.

We are now about to consider how Christ vindicated for Himself and for His Chief Apostle this right to supreme earthly freedom. But we must bear in mind that as Our Lord transmitted the identical Divine truth under various parables because of its various aspects, so did He transfer or intimate the transference of His supreme power to His Vicar under various comparisons or images because of its various relations.

Thus the Chief Apostle received communication of the spiritual firmness symbolized by the rock as a foundation for the spiritual structure of the Church. He received the spiritual care of the whole flock in the command to feed both sheep and lambs. He received the universal spiritual power of binding and loosing with the metaphorical keys. And as a remedy against Satanic sifting of the Church, he received the power and was imposed the duty of confirming the whole Hierarchy in the Faith resulting from the prayer for the infallibility of himself in particular and his successors. On all these occasions the Chief Apostle received communication of the Supreme Power that was in Christ. But Supreme Power besides these positive relations has negative ones. Supreme Power is also supreme independence. In God it is inherent and absolute. In man, who is finite, it must be delegated and relative. In Christ there was inherent and absolute independence, which called for a corresponding supreme earthly freedom. The supreme spiritual power transmitted to the Chief Apostle has also its counterpart in supreme earthly independence. Independence of spiritual control and influence, independence of temporal control and influence. I will then introduce you, dear brethren, to a most wonderful and pleasing scene wherein you will discover the supreme rights of the Son of Man and the association of Peter in the same rights. It is only another of those occasions wherein the Chief Apostle's supremacy is declared and vindicated.

We read in St. Matthew, chapter xvii. : " And when they were come to Capharnaum, they that received the didrachmas came to Peter, and said to him : Doth not your master pay the didrachma ? He said : Yes. And when he was come into the house, Jesus prevented him saying : What is thy opinion, Simon ? Of whom do the Kings of the earth take tribute or custom ? Of their own children, or of strangers ? And he said : Of strangers. Jesus said to him : Then the children are free. But that we may not scandalize them, go thou to the sea, and cast in a hook ; and that fish which shall first come up, take ; and when thou hast opened its mouth thou shalt find a stater ; take that, and give it to them for Me and thee."

In this scene on the shore of the lake depicted by the inspired pen you behold the most admirable manifestation of the Divine Power of Christ, yet with a definite ulterior object. For why, may we ask reverently, was the Divine Power exerted on this occasion ? Was it principally in self-manifestation or not rather to shield the human rights of the Son of Man ? For on the same occasion you have recorded the declaration of the supreme earthly right of Jesus Christ and of His Vicar : " Then the children are free." Christ instructed His Chief Apostle as to the supremacy of His freedom before vindicating it. Before Peter had time to report to his Divine Master the reply he unwarily gave to the taxgatherers or to carry Him their request, Christ anticipated His Chief Apostle on the very subject and elicited from him the opinion that the children of the Kings of the earth are free from the payment of tribute or custom. Here then is a comparison instituted between the Kings of the earth and their children on the one hand and the Lord of the temple, for which the tax was gathered, and Jesus Christ and His Chief Apostle on the other. If the Kings of the earth do not take tribute or custom from their own children, neither does the Lord God from His Divine Son made man nor from the Apostle associated in His freedom. Here it will be useful to

2

bear in mind what has been said of the necessarily
definite and lawful position of Christ as man within
His own country. The Jews who believed Christ to
be God, believed in His supreme right, for who will
deny or misconstrue the supreme Divine right? But
the earthly right of Christ as man was liable to be
misunderstood and in fact was on this occasion being
invaded. Rather than this should be the Son of God
resolved to pay as God :* " Volle pagare da Dio." The
first fish that comes to the hook is the treasurer of the
Son of God for this occasion. The human purse
carried by Judas is dispensed with, not because Judas
will betray his Divine Master, but because Christ
on this occasion hath resolved not to pay as man.
Now I reason thus : If Christ were subject as
man at this period of His life, His Divine freedom
would not exempt Him from the duty of a subject.
Christ did not so teach, who deemed it became Him " to
fulfil all justice," whom " it behoved in all things to be
made like His brethren," who was " one tempted in all
things like as we are, yet without sin," who before His
public ministry, that is, before He came into the exercise
of His supreme rights, was subject to His parents, who,
even on the threshold of His public ministry, acknowledged the authority over Him of John the Baptist.
Christ nevertheless had recourse to a miracle on this
great occasion to avoid yielding the obedience of an
earthly subject. If so, and who can deny it, what lesson
could more significantly set forth the sovereign earthly
right of the Son of Man? The Lord who loved to waive
every right, to take the place of a servant at the feet of
His Apostles, to appear not only as a subject, but as an
outcast, was also the Divine teacher of man and the
Founder of the New Law and the Introducer of the new
Priestly order. Hence the reason for declaring and
vindicating His earthly supremacy and that of His Chief
Apostle.

---

* Mastai Ferretti. Gli evangelisti uniti.

Association of Peter in Christ's Kingly Right.

We have seen, dear brethren, from what has been said: First—That the exercise of Divine independence and Power in Christ is inconceivable without corresponding earthly freedom and supremacy; and Second—That Christ on a celebrated occasion vindicated not His right as God, since He paid as God, but His supreme earthly right as man and Son of the Lord of the temple.

As St. Peter is associated in the declaration and vindication of the earthly right of the Son of the Lord of the temple, let us now look more closely into that association.

If you remember the words of the text from St. Matthew, it will occur to you, dear brethren, that Peter is not merely the instrument of Christ for the performance of the miracle, but that he is a sharer, first, in the material object of it, second, in the benefit of it, and third, in the purpose of it.

First: He is a sharer in the material object of the miracle. The Chief Apostle, and he alone, is called upon to give for himself what he gives for Christ. "Give it to them for Me and thee." The stater or silver tetradrachm being equal to twice the didrachma and therefore to twice the tax for one person, Peter obtained as well as his Divine Master the wherewith to apparently pay the tax. The amount is not levied on his earnings, he loses nothing by paying the tribute, subtracts nothing from his means, whatever they were or might have been. Which amounts to saying, that neither Peter nor his Divine Master have been taxed. Those who receive the didrachma, receive from Peter a silver coin equal to the taxation of two persons, but neither from Peter nor from Christ do they get it as a tribute, for neither have really been taxed. Peter therefore is here associated with Christ in his remaining untaxed according to the meaning and intent of the law and therefore in His earthly freedom.

Second: Peter is a sharer in the benefit of the miracle: the avoiding of scandal. "That we may not scandalize them, go thou to the sea. . ." Those who received the tribute, as well as those who employed them, were quite unprepared to admit Christ's right of exemption or that of His Chief Apostle. They were no doubt also unfit as yet to be enlightened on the subject. There was nothing therefore to do but to yield to their demand or to present the appearance of doing so, if the appearance of insubordination were to be avoided. Peter is associated with his Divine Master in avoiding the appearance of insubordination, by presenting the appearance of earthly subjection. Now, a good subject should not only wish to avoid the scandal of refusing to pay tribute, but he should be also willing to pay what he is bound. But Peter is associated with Christ in a proceeding which reveals no anxiety to pay the tribute, but only to avoid the scandal. Therefore Peter is associated with Christ in his exemption from tribute. Therefore the Chief Apostle is no longer subject to the temple or Jewish Priesthood or Levitical law, but he is raised from subjection to the old order to partnership in the new.

Third: Peter is associated with Christ in the purpose for which the miracle was wrought, namely the safe guarding of the supreme spiritual and temporal earthly freedom of those who are compared to, although they rank higher than, the children of the Kings of the earth. The vindicating of this freedom for His Apostle was so important in the Divine plan, that it must be secured, cost what it might. There would be scandal! Then let scandal be removed by a Divine payment. It only cost Christ a few words and some prayer to bestow upon His Chief Apostle the plenitude of spiritual power and the perfection of Doctrinal Infallibility in the church, but to vindicate his supreme independence it cost nothing less than a miracle. But I foresee a possible objection. I may be told: your reasoning proves no doubt the spiritual independence and supremacy of the Vicar of

Christ, and so far his earthly freedom, but you have yet to show that his temporal or political freedom was declared or vindicated on the occasion.

To which I reply that Peter was associated in the same freedom which Christ, his Master, vindicated for Himself. But Christ could not vindicate spiritual supremacy and exemption, without at the same time vindicating temporal supremacy and exemption. For according to St. Paul : " The priesthood being translated, it is necessary that a translation also be made of the Law." Claiming independence of one therefore was claiming independence of the other. And for the same reason the tribute to be paid to the temple, although purely spiritual so far as it was paid for the Divine worship and spiritual rule, was temporal and political insomuch as it was enforced by the co-ordinate authorities of the Priesthood and the sceptre under the one national legislation of Israel. Therefore refusing as man to pay the tribute to the temple and associating Peter in the same right is tantamount to vindicating for the Chief Apostle both spiritual and political independence. But supreme spiritual independence constitutes Peter Supreme Pontiff, and supreme political independence constitutes him King. Therefore like his Divine Master he is Pontiff-King.

Possibly my supposed objector might still feel inclined to insist, saying : No doubt Christ as man could not have been a subject in His Country, but must have held both spiritual and temporal supreme power, since He translated both the Priesthood and the Law, but what proves that He on the occasion associated Peter in both supreme powers? Well, two reasons: First—Because He declared and vindicated His supreme freedom as man in respect to both spiritual and political authorities on the same important occasion, and simultaneously associated His Chief Apostle in the declaration and vindication of the identical freedom. " Then the children are free," and " give it to them for Me and for thee." Second—Because if Peter and his successors were not associated both in spiritual and

3

temporal independence, then there would not be translation both of the Priesthood and of the Law, but only of the Priesthood to the New Testament. Then the plenitude of authority inherited by Christ from the Old Law would not have passed to the New. Christ, to whom as man is given all power in Heaven and on earth, inherited all the spiritual and temporal authority with which God had invested the leaders of His people. Such authority was divided by the Mosaic legislation between the heir to the sceptre and the heir to the priestly rule. Christ abolished the co-ordinate authorities with their imperfections and their shadows by gathering God's one authority over body and soul, over time and eternity, to Himself. He combined, or more truly united, in Himself the authority of the Jewish sceptre and the authority of the Levitical priesthood, and translated the united authority under the order of Melchisedech to the future rulers of His Church in the person of His Chief Apostle. Therefore the Roman Pontiffs were actually associated in the person of Peter in the supreme independence of the Son of Man, and therefore in His earthly and temporal freedom.

HOW FACTS CORRESPOND WITH RIGHTS.

In the first argument it was proved that the order of Christ which is that of Melchisedech, to which the Roman Pontiffs belong, constitutes them Kings and therefore gives them a territorial independence. In both arguments, which rest on different texts of Scripture and are quite independent, a distinct principle is conveyed, namely : the Kingly right of Christ and of the Supreme Pontiff of the New Law. But rights so far as they are acknowledged become embodied in facts. The facts therefore should square with the Kingly right both of Christ and His Vicar. The History of the Catholic Church will supply the great, luminous, constant, central fact, which is the embodiment of the Kingly right of Christ's Vicar on earth, namely : the civil or temporal Princedom and Patrimony of St. Peter, also called the temporal Power of the Pope.

"Thou Art the King of Israel."

I will now, dear brethren, proceed to consider how far the Kingly right of Jesus Christ is acknowledged and becomes a fact of history, how it is hailed by friends, or disavowed, charged against Him, and derided by enemies. Needless to inquire how witnesses friendly or hostile come to the knowledge of the Kingly right of Jesus Christ. Whether through acquiring the knowledge of His Divinity they naturally infer his supreme human right, or whether they learn it from prophecy, or pick it up from the tradition of their race or from Christ's own testimony.

No sooner had Nathanael believed His Divine Nature than he saluted Him also as King : " Rabbi, thou art the Son of God, thou art the King of Israel." Again, as he approached Jerusalem after raising Lazarus, the multitude came forth to meet Him, saluting Him and saying : " Blessed be the King, who cometh in the name of the Lord," and " Blessed be the Kingdom of our father David that cometh." And the prophet, who in the distance of time saw His poverty as He rode into Jerusalem, failed not to mention His rank : " Fear not, daughter of Sion ; behold thy King cometh sitting on an ass's colt."

Jesus of Nazareth the King of the Jews.

I shall possibly be met by the objection founded on the words of the Divine Prisoner : " My Kingdom is not of this world." But on careful inspection it will be found that these words of the Divine Prisoner in the Hall of Pilate harmonize completely with the claims of the Divine Teacher and Vindicator of right at Capharnaum, and with the essential characteristics of the everlasting order of Priesthood.

Let us approach the subject with loving reverence, dear brethren, lifting the eyes of Faith upon the Divine Captive, imploring Him to cast upon us, as upon the Apostle, one look, which may make us hate sin for ever. The Governor has been called outside to the Jews, who would not enter the Hall. In answer to his inquiry the Jews say : " If He were not a malefactor, we would not have delivered Him up to thee." On returning to the Hall, Pilate, according to St. John, simply inquires : "Art thou the King of the Jews ? " And Jesus, putting the Governor to the test, by giving him a chance of stating his own opinion, says : " Sayest thou this of thyself, or have others told it thee of Me ? " " Am I a Jew ? " is the scornful reply of the representative of the usurping power and the indignant outburst of a guilty conscience in self-defence, which told that Christ's question was a thrust home. And now again : " Thy own nation and the chief priests have delivered thee up to me, what hast thou done ? " Jesus answered : " My Kingdom is not of this world. If My Kingdom were of this world, My servants would certainly strive that I should not be delivered to the Jews : but now My Kingdom is not hence." Pilate therefore said to Him : " Art thou King then ? " Jesus answered : " Thou sayest that I am King. For this was I born, and for this came I into the world, that I should give testimony unto the truth." Let us now examine this confession of the Divine Prisoner. Before clearly stating that He is King, although He has implied as much, by referring the case to Pilate's conscience, Christ declares : " My Kingdom is not of this world." Observe, He says not : " My Kingdom is not in this world," but, " of this world." An indirect reply to the previous question concerning His Kingship and a direct one to the statement of Pilate that His nation had delivered Him up. " My Kingdom is not of this world," which obviously means : " My Kingly right is not of this world." I waive My right and choose not to enforce it by appeal to My servants and to violence, as is the custom of the Princes of this world. My people will not have Me to reign over them. The suffrage of the nation is not in My favour. My right is built up neither on the force nor on the suffrage of this world. Mine is a Heavenly Sanctioned right. My earthly Kingship is subordinate to My Divine rule, therefore I would reign over a willing people; "but now My Kingdom is not hence." Pilate therefore said to Him : "Art thou a King then?" And here comes the straight reply of Christ : " Thou sayest that I am King." As a lover of subjection, Our Lord would again have preferred to conceal His right, but as "having been born and having come into this world that He should give testimony unto the truth," He could not withhold it from the conditionally sanctioned authority claiming to hear it. Pilate need not have inquired again: "What is the truth?" Had he been willing he might have discovered it in every word uttered before his Court by the King of the Jews.

But the whole history of the Passion, dear brethren, gives loud testimony of the Kingly character of the Saviour of mankind. Had Christ, as man, and inhabitant of the land given to Abraham, His father, been a subject only among His fellow citizens, if the thing were conceivable, had He clearly disclaimed all earthly title, so that no Jew might suspect Him of possessing any power or freedom below the God-Head with His Father, what charge, I ask you, could the Jews have brought against Him to interest the Political and usurping Power, and to screen, if it had been possible, their Heaven-opposing malice stirred to its depths by a higher claim, for which alone they had twice condemned Him in the Council of the Nation? What would have been the meaning or import of the mock King, saluted, sceptred, and crowned? The Jews were Regicides as well as Deicides, although Regicides because Deicides.

The Saviour was both adored and persecuted at His birth as being the King of the Jews by men who knew Him by no other title, and the title was written over the instrument of His torture. Vain were the efforts of the Chief Priests to destroy its significance. Not: " He said, I am King of the Jews," but " Jesus of Nazareth, the King of the Jews," remained written in the languages of the world.

The unfortunate Governor's sin was that of weakness. No one to my knowledge has been more severe with him. Who reads the Passion goes cordially with him in his persistent efforts to declare the innocence of the Just man. His attitude and his words to the Jews give striking proof that they had not, in the accusations they brought against Him, put their real grievance in the foreground. The Governor was not impressed with the charge of active rivalship with Cæsar, nor with the accusing nation's loyalty to his Imperial Master. And he seemed to make it his business to punish the Deicides for their duplicity. "Behold your King," said he, and again as they insisted: "Shall I crucify your King?" And when the deed was being done, when no doubt Pilate still better realized his sin, he further punished the nation by annulling, as far as in him lay, his own act, and the political charge brought against the Saviour. The inscription written by himself in the three languages was no indictment, but an opposite declaration. And he stood by it: "What I have written, I have written."

Christ the Last Bearer of the Sceptre of Juda.

But such Kingly right should not only be borne out by the facts of acknowledgment. It should agree also with all the conditions of civil and national local right. Let us examine how Christ could civilly and politically come by this earthly power and freedom. We have seen that God is the author of society and therefore of all legitimate rights whether bestowed by or inherited in the nation. He is only the Permitter of usurpation. The Kingly right of Christ was not a usurped right, nor was it bestowed by the nation, which rejected Him, therefore it must have been an inherited right. It must have been the right of the Jewish rulers and of the Jewish nation. And such inherited right of the Son of David and of the Son of Juda was clearly attested by the National prophecy. "The sceptre shall not be taken away from Juda nor a ruler from his thigh till He come." This does not mean that the sceptre should depart before Christ could inherit it, nor that violence or subjugation could snatch away a God-given right. The great national prophecy evidently alludes to the termination of the old order of things, when both the Law and the priesthood should be translated. The sceptre then was safely carried down to Christ. The tribe of Juda had alone endured for that purpose, returning after the Captivity with a small remnant of Benjamin and Levi, the latter to be at its service for the ministry of the temple. Not only the ancestral line of Christ, the guarding of which was the main purpose of the national organization, but the ruling power of the organized tribe, endured, whoever may have been in right the holders of the sceptre, and remained vested in the leading Jewish families. True, the power of the priests seemed paramount within the nation after the Captivity, but, as already abundantly shown, the Priestly authority was at most only co-ordinate with the power of the sceptre, for " which is greater, he that sitteth at table, or he that serveth ? Is not he that sitteth at table ? And again it should not be forgotten when comparing the relative importance of the two tribes of Juda and Levi, that the former did really hand down with the sceptre the elements of which the sacred body of the Redeemer was formed, whereas the latter which foreshadowed the spiritual functions of His Holy soul had nothing to hand down but a shadow. Thus not before Christ transferred elsewhere both the Priesthood and the Sovereign rule was the sceptre taken away from Juda. What though His sceptre were a reed or His crown one of thorns ? His enemies, by seeking to destroy His title, only published it to the world. Jesus the Son of David was therefore the last bearer of the sceptre of Juda.

Translation of the Law and the Priesthood.

We have seen, dear brethren, that the Kingly right of Christ did not remain a mere principle, that it was borne out by the facts of the acknowledgment of friends and could not be smothered by the hatred, disavowal, or derision of enemies. We then proceeded to examine how Christ's claim to Kingly rank harmonized with local right. We have now to consider how the translation of right from the old Law to the New is embodied in the facts of history. Let us go back for a moment to the National prophecy. The Holy Patriarch's words are : " The sceptre shall not be taken away." You will observe that the word "taken away" or "depart" from Juda, does not mean " die out " or " be destroyed " or "cease altogether"; the idea conveyed by these expressions is one of transference, not of destruction or cessation. And the prophetical blessing agrees with the historical statement of one equally inspired. What Jacob expresses by the words "taken away," St. Paul expresses by the word "translation." The two expressions, I take it, were moulded by two aspects of the identical truth. Jesus Christ of the tribe of Juda, "of which no one gave attendance at the altar," without renouncing or forfeiting the power symbolized by the sceptre, gathered to Himself the spiritual power of the priesthood by becoming Himself Pontiff, and transmitted to Peter His undivided Sacerdotal and Kingly Power. " For the priesthood being translated, it is necessary that a translation also be made of the Law."

But there is not only translation of power to men of a New order, there is also translation of the New order to a New territory. St. Peter goes to Rome. Here is an historical fact which embodies more than the mere translation of the Law and the Priesthood. We shall see that St. Peter went forth with no empty title, but with a territorial right. For the Priestly and Kingly authority is transferred from Juda and Jerusalem to the centre of the Gentile world. The works of God are complete and break not down in the middle.*

God said to Abraham : " To thy seed will I give this land;" the Roman power subjugated that land, violated the right of the sceptre, and sentenced to death the King

---

* "Do not think that I am come to destroy the law or the Prophets. I am not come to destroy, but to fulfil."

of the Jews. What more could they have done to forfeit sovereignty at the head of the empire? The eloquence of facts is too great to leave any doubt about the existence of right. We think of God's ways and exclaim : a fair and providential exchange! Who enlightened the Roman sage, or what tradition did he come across to know that some would come from Judea, who should succeed to the mastery at the head-quarters of Imperial Power?

Thus after being associated with Christ, Peter comes under the New order, which as Divinely sworn shall last for ever. The fisherman moves forth from Salem to take possession of the great empire-city, which his order will transform into a city of Peace. As priest of the Most High God, he will there offer the bread and wine of the sacrifice of the New Testament. You may not trace his right or dignity to his race as the Jewish Pontiff's of old. For he is "without father or mother or genealogy" in his succession to the Pontificate and his successors after him." " The Lord hath sworn and He will not repent. Thou art a Priest for ever according to the order of Melchisedech." He carries with him from Sion the Priesthood, the Law, and sceptre, and settles them at the head-quarters of the enemies of the Jewish nation. " The Lord will send forth the sceptre of thy power out of Sion : rule thou in the midst of thy enemies."

If hypothesis were not out of place it might be interesting to consider how events would have shaped if the Jewish nation had not been scattered. Theologians have gone so far as to suppose Christ redeeming the world without passing through Death. I will suppose that a Jewish faction had alone been guilty of Deicide, that no punishment had fallen on the nation as such, that the Jews had remained in their land, that no foreign power had usurped local rights. What would have been the consequence? The Law and the Priesthood would have passed out of the former hands to the successors of the Prince of the Apostles; so far we are certain. But then no reason appears for the dereliction of the land given to the people of God from the beginning. The Chief Apostle's See must have been the throne of David. The whole Jewish Constitution would have been merged into the paternal Government of the Pontiff-King. The Pontificate would have been open to any tribe. The Patrimony of St. Peter would have been the Holy Land. Christians would have been called after Salem and not after Rome. The hypothesis indeed seems necessary to explain the expectations of the nation and the promises which gave rise to them.

The people evidently believed before and after Christ's resurrection that the Theocracy was not abandoned, that God would sooner or later vindicate His right to the Government of one state for the good of the world. We have gathered as much from the shouts of the multitude hailing their King : " Blessed be the Kingdom of our Father David that cometh." A temporal Government under the immediate control of Christ was the natural and legitimate expectation of the early Church instructed in all things spiritual and preparing for the baptism of the Holy Ghost : " Lord," said the assembled Apostles, " wilt Thou at this time restore again the Kingdom to Israel ? " Christ denied not that the restoration would take place, but He indicated neither the time nor the manner.

Although the Pontificate of the New order is not inherited by tribal right, but is open to all nations, the fact of the Jewish race constituting the mother Church would have brought many sons of David through spiritual right to the succession of the everlasting throne of their Father. It depended only on their fidelity. Such expectations were not incompatible with the instructions Christ had given. In the following words of the 131st Psalm we have, with the absolute promise that Christ the Son of David should succeed to his throne, a conditional promise concerning his children and concerning Sion for all time. " The Lord hath sworn truth to David, and He will not make it void ; of the fruit of thy womb I will set upon thy throne. If thy children will keep My covenant, and these My testimonies, which I shall teach them; their children also for evermore shall sit upon thy throne. For the Lord hath chosen Sion: He hath chosen it for His dwelling. This is My rest for ever and ever: here will I dwell, for I have chosen it."

But the children of David did not keep the covenant. Christ's brethren sold Him and resolved His death. The Jews forfeited their right to constitute the mother and mistress Christian Church. The Gentiles were allowed to scatter the nation and raze the Holy City, but in return were called upon to yield Rome and its Sovereignty for the Pontiff-King of the Christian Church. Salem was and Rome is the Holy City. We are not children of Peace, but of the Sword.

Limitation of Territorial Right.

But here some critic might put me to the test by the following objection: You have spoken of the temporal freedom in Christ and in His Vicar as a result of the supreme earthly independence of the Son of Man. What have you to say of the positive relations of the same earthly supremacy? In other words, does not Christ as man inherit the plenitude of temporal power on earth? To this I reply that Christ only laid claim to temporal rule in the country which belonged to Him by ancestral right, and which became through foreign usurpation the foundation of the temporal patrimony of His Vicar in the land of the usurper. No doubt to Christ is given all power in Heaven and on earth. But having given to earthly Kings their temporal rights, He does not withdraw as man what He has given as God. His territorial right was therefore limited, and so is that of His Vicar.

As for the universal arbitration of the Pontiff, which is quite a distinct question, there have been signs that such an event is possible, and nothing more desirable can be conceived for the peace of mankind.

The Papacy, the World, and the Revolution.

The Papacy as it presents itself to the world is the greatest human fact. The genius of man unassisted by Faith, in presence of this fact, has dictated lines which rise almost to the beauty of Biblical poetry and prophetic language. Statesmen of various creeds, familiar with the Government of nations, have surveyed the fact without reference to right and have said: that is well done, that is a necessity; a universal Church spread among the nations cannot be subject to any one of them, therefore its Chief authority must be free.

We also, dear brethren, conclude to the necessity of the Pope's freedom from his universal rule, but we rest that spiritual rule on a Divine institution. I have introduced this argument when treating of Christ's King-ship as a social necessity. It is the familiar theme of eloquent preachers and able Catholic writers. My business has been to endeavour to show you that besides this inferential proof of the necessity of the Pope's temporal power there is contained in Holy Scripture a positive declaration and a Divine vindication of the Pontiff's Kingly character and Princely freedom.

You will conclude then that the constant and luminous central fact of Church history, the temporal Sovereignty enjoyed by the successors of Peter, is not merely the outcome of the good will of Christian nations, nor a provisional state to be succeeded by some more enlightened agreement with rulers of the nineteenth century, but that it is indeed the use, exercise, and actuation of a Divinely bestowed right and power, which Christ also vindicates from age to age.

Christ waived His own rights as King so far as was compatible with His office of Divine teacher and Founder of the Church, but it was to secure the peaceable exercise of the same rights in His representative on earth. He would not have miraculously vindicated and upheld the Princely right of His Vicar unless He had intended such right to be exercised for the freedom of His church in the midst of a strife-loving world.

I alluded in the beginning of this lecture to the present state of the Pontiff. He is in the hands of the worst enemy that has appeared since the world was ruled by the heathen. It is the spirit of national apostasy or the revolution. Men have cast off the yoke of religion and personal authority from their new society. They are driven by the fever of a godless nationalism, wherein they imagine to secure worldly greatness. The evil reaches its climax in the secret hatred of revealed Religion, and of the Pontiff its Chief exponent and Divine foundation. This hatred is embodied and energizing in dark societies, which drive men unconsciously against the Church and against the Pontiff. It is the rebellion of men who hate God, and would prefer any rule rather than His. It is a repetition of history. " We have no King but Cæsar," says the revolted nation. We will own no authority but that which is secular, we will salute no symbol but that of independence.

And thus the Italian revolution, like the Apostasy elsewhere, has been steadily doing the work of the evil one. Short of personal violence to the Pope, which would not be safe for the nation, the revolution has undone the work of God, the civil Princedom, respected in all Christian ages.

Not a remnant is left to Leo of the patrimony of St. Peter. He enjoys the independence of his palace as any important subject might in a civilized country. But, if I mistake not, his Sovereignty is in nowise acknowledged, but in every way violated and insulted. Violated and insulted by foreign swords at his very gates, violated and insulted by the intrusion of foreign courts of justice, violated and insulted by a foreign coin and a foreign stamp, violated and insulted by the perilous prospect of being shut out from communication with the rest of the world should the usurper engage in hostilities with other earthly powers : in one word, violated and insulted by the sacrilegious occupation of a deluded Prince. Your duty is prayer. The duty of constitutional agitation is going on elsewhere. But we may rest assured as regards the event.

The sceptre of Juda was led into Captivity of old, dear brethren, but it returned to its appointed realm. So will the Pontiff's everlasting right be hailed again in the restored Patrimony of St. Peter. Amen.

THE TEMPORAL INHERITANCE OF THE ROMAN CHURCH.

"Semini tuo dabo terram hanc."—GENESIS.

IF there be Scripture evidence relating to the rightful independence of the Holy See, no one will deny that the present day is the opportune time for sifting it. And if the teaching of the Church hitherto on the subject removes it from the domain of ordinary human institutions, nothing is more consistent than to go for information respecting it to that source which records the whole plan of God's dealing with His Church.

With these thoughts I wrote as follows to the *Tablet* on February 22nd, 1890 :—

"I crave your permission to write a few words on the subject of the temporal power of the Pope. After the repeated appeals from the present Pope and his predecessor to the Catholic world on this subject during so many years, it requires no apology to take up the pen to supply, if possible, fresh motives for Catholics to stand together in defence of his temporal rights. The late Encyclical, declaring that 'all are bound to communicate their faith to others, either to the instruction of other Christians, or to their strengthening, or to repel the audacity of those outside the fold,' indicates what kind of warfare on behalf of the Church is expected of the faithful, and that victory will be awarded to faith and to the powerful convictions that spring therefrom. To settle and strengthen our convictions in regard to the sanctity of the Pontiff's rights seems, then, to be of paramount importance if we are 'to repel the audacity of those outside the fold.' But convictions must spring from clearly conceived notions. Can it be said that the inferential proof of the necessity of the temporal power, as a basis of right, is a clearly conceived notion whereon

4

to found solid convictions? Pius IX. is reported to have said (I have good authority for saying so), 'that it could not be defined that under all circumstances the possession of the temporal power was necessary for the exercise of the spiritual.' If temporal power is not necessary under all circumstances, how is the Pontiff's right to be securely founded upon *the necessity* of the temporal power? Hence vagueness in the minds of many, and want of moral power from want of conviction. Yet we are appealed to, not merely to pray that God may hasten His never-failing protection, but distinctly to bear witness to the Pontiff's temporal rights. They have been claimed as such by Pius IX. and his successor. And the Bishops assembled from all parts of the world and of the United Kingdom in 1862 re-echoed the Pontiff's claim with no uncertain sound :—

"'Vox enim Tua,' they declared, 'quasi tuba Sacerdotalis, toti orbi clangens proclamavit, quod "singulari prorsus divinæ Providentiæ consilio factum sit, ut Romanus Pontifex, quem Christus totius ecclesiæ suæ caput centrumque constituit, civilem assequeretur principatum;" ab omnibus igitur nobis esse pro certissimo tenendum non fortuito hoc regimen temporale Sanctæ Sedi accessisse, sed ex speciali divina dispositione illi esse tributum. . . .'

"The Pontiff's temporal right has a foundation, but that foundation is not the necessity of the temporal power. To put the matter plainly, the Pontiff's temporal power is either the gift of men or the gift of God; there is no alternative. If the Pontiff's territorial right be the gift of kings or emperors, sanctioned and approved, no doubt —nay more, even brought about—by the kind providence of God for the better spiritual government of the Church, who shall convince Catholics of the intrinsic and inalienable right of the Pontiff to temporal rule? Who shall persuade Catholics that men, who often repent of their gift, may not take back in one century what they have bestowed in another? We have nothing to do in such case but to pray, as in duty bound, that it may please God to change the hearts of rulers and people, so that, far from interfering with the spiritual government of the Church, they may duly honour it by the surrender of the temporal power over Rome, which alone seems to be its proper guarantee. In such case, no intrinsic or essential right of the Church is violated; no appeal, therefore, can be made to the Catholic faith and conscience of the universe to vindicate by the power of moral suffrage a right which has never rested on aught but the gift of man. Other princes entrusted with temporal rule have been deprived by the will of the people—why not the Pontiff?

"Very different will be the effect on Catholics if they come to acquire the explicit knowledge that the temporal power is no human institution, governed by a general providence of God, which rules all things for the good of men, but an institution of God's own governed by a peculiar dispensation of Divine Providence. They will feel that the right we contend for rests on a solid basis, that their faith is appealed to, that the usurpation of the States of the Church is truly a sacrilege of the first magnitude. Catholic patriots will discover that their national aspirations must yield to a God-given right. The world itself will give way to the appeal of conscience and of faith, as it has ever done before. For 'this is the victory which overcometh the world, our faith.'

" In a thesis (' The Civil Principality,' by the Rev. C. F. P. Collingridge. Burns and Oates) lately published, it is shown that Christ vindicated for Himself and for the Roman Pontiffs, in the person of Peter, temporal independence and therefore temporal power, and consequently that the temporal power of the Pope is not a human, but a divine institution. With the privilege of the insertion of another letter, I hope to show, in reply to a venerable and not unkind critic, and quite apart from the argument of the thesis, the 'title, translation, and extent of the Pontiff's territorial right.'

"P.S.—The thesis, under the heading 'Divine Vindication of Independence,' takes it for granted that the tribute was payable to the Temple. Those who hold that it was collected for Cæsar or his representative, will see that the same reasoning applies in this case, with this difference, that Christ vindicated His own and His Apostles' independence in respect to a foreign usurper, instead of vindicating it among His own subjects, who failed to recognise His lawful exemption."

In the next issue of the same Catholic paper appeared the following letters. The first, which is, on the whole, favourable, is signed by "Catholic Legitimist." It is as follows :—

"Will you permit me to offer a few words in criticism on Father Collingridge's interesting letter in your issue of February 22nd ? Father Collingridge would appear to insist that the Pope's one claim to the temporal power consists in its being the direct gift of God. This most certainly it is, but it should not be forgotten that above and beyond this *immediate* divine sanction, the Pope, considered merely as a temporal sovereign, partakes also of the *mediately* divine sanction conferred by Almighty God on every other legitimate prince or government. We cannot expect Protestants to believe that the temporal power is of directly divine institution ; but we can expect them to believe, with Holy Scripture, that all authority is from above, and that there is thus scriptural warranty for the civil princedom of the Pope equally with, say, the Imperial authority of the reigning family in Austria.

"Father Collingridge would seem to say that if man gave the temporal power, man also could take it away. Does he not for the moment overlook the fact that, as the Church has taught over and over again, *all* authority is of divine sanction ? Can any nation, of its own will merely, depose its sovereign ? What says the Syllabus, to go back no further ? Its 63rd Proposition formally condemns the following error : ' *Legitimis Principibus obedientiæ detractare immo et rebellare licet.*' It therefore follows that, even leaving out of the question the directly divine origin of the temporal sovereignty, the Italians had no more right to rebel against the Pope than the French had to expel Charles X.

"Father Collingridge's argument is, of course, the one that will appeal strongly to most Catholics ; but it is well to lose sight of no single fact that can in any way add to the just and obedient claims of the Pope to the States of the Church, and especially when the fact is such as should logically weigh with any Protestant statesman believing in the truth of Holy Scripture."

The second, which contains an unfavourable criticism, is signed " P. K. Q.," and reads thus :—

" Referring to the letter of the Rev. C. F. P. Collingridge, the following quotation from Cardinal Newman's sermon, 'The Pope and the Revolution,' preached on Rosary Sunday, 1866, at Birmingham, may be interesting. ' Now observe . . . no Catholic maintains that the rule of the Pope as a king, in Rome and its provinces, which men are now hoping to take from him, is, strictly speaking, what is called a theocracy, that is, a divine government. This government, indeed, in spiritual matters, in the Catholic Church throughout the world, might be called a theocracy, because he is the Vicar of Christ and has the assistance of the Holy Ghost ; but not such is his kingly rule in his own dominions. . . .' "

Under the heading " Theocracy of the New Law," the following reply appeared in a subsequent number :—

" Sir,—With your permission I will reply to two correspondents, whose criticism I carefully read in your issue of March 1st. The first, signing ' Catholic Legitimist,' criticises a sentence of mine in reference to the temporal power, as though implying that I overlooked the fact that all authority is of divine sanction. The sentence was : ' Who shall persuade Catholics that men, who often repent of their gifts, may not take back in one century what they have bestowed in another ? ' Had I added the words : ' without violating a God-given right,' which the context warrants, there would have been

"What I wished to insist upon, and again take occasion now to do, is simply that human governments are so far under human control that they are liable to modifications, subject to the laws which govern civil society. Republics have been transformed into monarchies, and *vice versa;* whether with the consent of the whole nation, or in violation of some right or rights, is not always distinctly ascertainable. If the Pope's temporal power is subject to such laws, who shall persuade Catholics that what human agency hath established human agency may not disestablish? Without any violation even of human right, a legitimate monarch might, with the consent of the nation, abdicate his throne with a view of transforming the monarchy into a republic, because human monarchy is not above human control. If the Pope is only an ordinary temporal monarch, who shall persuade Catholics that he may not, if he choose, abdicate in like manner? The teaching of the Church, which I would wish to bring more prominently forward, is that the Pope cannot abdicate his temporal right either to human rulers or people, because it is not subject to human laws. Other governments may change hands, or be modified in form, or disappear altogether; his never. The reason is, to use again the language of the Church, because his civil principality was obtained '*singulari Divinæ Providentiæ consilio,*' and was granted to him '*ex speciali Divina dispositione.*' In other words, his temporal right did not accrue to him from human agency, nor was it acquired by the Pontiff at any time, like the monarchical right of the Christian kingdoms of Europe planted by the Church and consecrated by her unction, but is inherent to his office, which is Christ's own institution.

"Far be it from me, a minister of Christ, to utter a syllable which might detract from the loyalty due to the old Christian monarchies of Europe. Not only does the monarchical form of government best signify to man the monarchy of God, and the term subject most nobly interpret the relation of the creature, but the Christian kingdoms of Europe grew out of the Church and are her legitimate offspring, and therefore the rebellion against this order of things is so far a rebellion against Christ. Even the authority of pagan rulers is sanctioned by God, as we know from the Apostle ; how much more that of Christian monarchs ! But let us not jeopardise the interests of the Papacy by comparing with it even a Christian monarchy. Let us remove all cause of confusion from the minds of Catholics. Those will best consult the interests of Christian monarchy who best consult the interests of the Roman Church, which is the Mother and Mistress of Christian kingdoms and of their respective Churches. I will now take leave of my courteous critic, remarking that what I have supposed him to require, namely, a differentiation between human monarchy and the unique monarchy of the Pope, is precisely what another critic denies. For in what does the temporal power of the Papacy differ from the civil governments of the world except in the very elements which constitute it a theocracy.

"In a theocracy, God rules personally through man chosen by Himself, and is Himself the legislator. The Pope, unless you hold his temporal right to be adventitious, is chosen as temporal ruler by God, because he is already divinely chosen as priest and Pontiff. He is chosen as priest by a divine vocation, which is the personal and immediate action of God. He is constituted spiritual ruler by the positive and divine legislation of Christ. For neither in the old Israel, nor in the new, 'doth any man take honour to himself, but he that is called by God, as Aaron was.' Two divine elections from two distinct families were necessary, it is true, under the ancient theocracy, because Israel was constituted under dual tribal rights. Under the theocracy of the God-incarnate, the Pontiff-king needs only the one election, as being heir of the united authority of Christ. Christ is legislator and responsible even in respect to the limited temporal rule. For having chosen the Pontiff both as spiritual and temporal ruler, He is responsible for his temporal administration, the whole spirit of which is in subservience to the interests of the Universal Church. ' P. K. Q.' delivers his own opinion, no doubt, under the ægis of a great name. I will yield to none in admiration for the great Cardinal, whose example and authority I have always quoted. But on a question still undefined by the Church, his Eminence's utterance is only the opinion of a theologian. And that opinion was uttered a quarter of a century ago, when the lesson of events had yet to be learned, and the protests of the Vicar of Christ were only beginning, and theologians had not considered all the bearings of the question. Rather would it be prudent to hearken to a quite recent declaration of the Pope's representative to the American Church, on occasion of the Catholic Centenary. Archbishop Satolli, speaking of the Holy Father, said: ' He doubts not that the Catholics of America . . . will labour to that end—that the Pope will once more reacquire that independence and liberty which by divine institution appertain to him as Sovereign Head of all the Church and representative of the person and authority of Christ. . . .' If the Pope's independence and liberty appertain to him by divine institution, Christ makes Himself responsible for their exercise. Hence Christ retains and rules over a temporal inheritance among the kingdoms of the earth, whilst his spiritual government extends to all nations. The name coined by Josephus as truly applies, therefore, to the new law as it did to the old."

The following letter on " The Temporal Inheritance of the Roman Church " closes the correspondence :—

" In a previous letter, taking my stand on the teaching of the Church, I indicated that the foundation of the Pontiff's territorial right is neither the necessity of the temporal power, nor any fortuitous growth of circumstances, nor the accidental gift of emperors or kings ; but that the Roman Pontiff holds his temporal right from a special dispensation or ruling of Divine Providence. From the teaching of the Church I will now pass to the inspired word, and reverently seek to elicit its testimony on the subject. It will be found that the Pontiff's temporal right has its root and foundation and title in the remote past, that it was translated from the old law to the new, and, in reply to criticism, that even its extent is ascertainable. I pledge myself to the following proposition which will supply collateral evidence to my thesis : *'God's unrepented gift of land to the ancestors of Christ is the Roman Pontiff's title to temporal power, and an equivalent for the land God gave to the seed of Abraham is the inheritance of the Mother and Mistress Christian Church.'*

" 1. Oh! but the land of Israel was only given until the coming of Christ, will perhaps be the first objection, although too unguarded to credit any serious person with. An ample reply will be found in the question : why ? and the invitation to prove it ; for the promise of land was never otherwise characterised but as 'an everlasting possession.'

" 2. The land of Israel, it may be urged, being subjugated and made a Roman province, and its people scattered, God's gift was undone by violence and usurpation. In reply, it may be pointed out that the conquest and usurpation of the land of Israel were no argument for the cancelling of God's gift when the Assyrians and Greeks conquered the country. Had the Jews remained faithful, many roads towards Jerusalem were opened to them after they had been scattered by the Romans, just as one road was open to them from Babylon after the Captivity.

" 3. The land of Israel, it may be further urged, was necessary for the people of God as a nation to prepare the way for the coming of Christ. This being accomplished, the gift of God was no longer necessary and was cancelled. In reply to this objection it may be pointed out that territorial rights, with political independence, was no more necessary for the worship of God in Israel than in the Mother and Mistress Christian Church. The children of Jacob could have worshipped Jehovah with sacrificial rites as a province of some peaceful empire, which, unlike the government of the Pharaohs and that of most earthly kings, would never have obstructed the work of God. It is, at all events, conceivable in the abstract. You will say : ' It is practically inconceivable ;' when you are met with the rejoinder : 'It is also practically inconceivable that the Mother and Mistress Christian Church will not be obstructed in the work of God without political independence and a territorial right.' Therefore this argument for cancelling God's gift at the extinction of the Church of the Synagogue collapses.

"4. In any case someone may insist the infidelity of the Jews caused the land of Israel to be forfeited. In reply to this objection let it be borne in mind that Christ and the faithful remnant, which then constituted the Mother and Mistress Christian Church, were more important than the carnal majority. Why, then, should they be deprived for the sins of others ? Unless it be proved that the Mistress Christian Church would not thenceforth require territorial independence, there is no reason yet why we should suppose that God repented of His gift.

"And what is more to the point, the land of Israel was never promised to the carnal Israelites, who were constantly being weeded out, but to the true children of Abraham. 'For all are not Israelites that are of Israel ; neither are all they that are the seed of Abraham children ; but in Isaac shall thy seed be called. That is to say, not they that are the children of the flesh are the children of God, but they that are the children of the promise are accounted for the seed.' The promise, then, 'to thy seed will I give this land,' extends to the children of the promise who are accounted for the seed. It would be difficult, nay, impossible, to realise that the

Christian world has not inherited an equivalent territorial advantage for the Mother and Mistress Christian Church to make the promise good. The promise, inclusive of land, was made before the law, and reaches beyond it, not being circumscribed by it. Or, to use the Apostle's expression : ' The law, which was made after 430 years, doth not disannul, to make the promise of no effect ; for if the inheritance be of the law, it is no more of promise, but God gave it to Abraham by promise.' And although the Mistress Christian Church is principal heiress of the Synagogue, all Christians may and should lay claim to a share in her territorial independence. ' If you be Christ's, then are you the seed of Abraham, *heirs according to the promise.*' Some mind may suggest the scruple: ' You are applying to a temporal inheritance words which refer to Christ and His spiritual kingdom.' The plain answer to which is : ' No distinction is made by the Apostle, and the inheritance of territorial right not being struck out of the New Covenant, comes in for the same guarantee of lasting vitality. But a more severe retort would not be uncalled for, for the divorce between the spiritual and temporal inheritance would constitute Christians no longer ' *heirs according to the promise.*'

" No doubt Christ is both principal inheritance and principal heir. But just because Christ is principal heir, is the promise of land chiefly addressed to Him, to be transmitted by Him to His principal joint-heir in the Christian Church : ' To thy seed will I give this land ; ' ' He saith not : and to his seeds, as of many : but as of one, and to thy seed, which is Christ.'

" The principal heir to the land of Israel was, therefore, Christ ; but here the argument must stop, for we could hardly dwell upon the principal temporal heir without getting into the main contention of the thesis and into the thoughts of Palm Sunday ; without calling for the sceptre of Juda and the throne of David, and shouting what the stones would have cried out had there not been an intelligent crowd to perform the loyal duty.

" 5. A difficulty may still be felt by some minds : if the territorial right bestowed upon the Church of the Synagogue be equivalently handed over to the Christian Mistress Church, one should expect to meet with some scriptural intimation or record of so important a transaction. And there is none. Well, some minds might possibly expect from Christ an authentically drawn up document or voucher witnessing to the sale of the Vineyard of Israel and to the divorce of the Church of the Synagogue, and indicating what equivalent he had taken in exchange. They need not go away quite disconsolate. The voucher may be found at the beginning of the fiftieth chapter of Isaias. The language is that of Christ : ' What is this bill of the divorce of your mother, with which I have put her away ; or who is my creditor, to whom I sold you ? Behold you are sold for your iniquities, and for your wicked deeds have I put your mother away. Because I came, and there was not a man.'

"The reflective mind will no doubt discern the meaning of ' the divorce of your mother ' in the sentence. It cannot apply to the Old Covenant, which would have given place to the New in any case. It cannot apply to the law. For the law was either essential and permanent, which Christ came not to destroy, or it was typical and ceremonial and only required fulfilling. The same must be said of the priesthood and the sceptre typically constituted under dual tribal right, which would have been translated to the united authority of Christ, even though iniquity had not abounded. The divorce, then, had nothing in common with the translation of the law and the priesthood. What remained to divorce ? Just the earthly and human side of the Church of the Synagogue : the Vineyard of Israel, with its majority of faithless people, its territory, its seat of spiritual rule on Mount Moriah, and of political rule on Mount Zion. The Jews had been constituted by the gift of God a Church with territorial independence. Christ divorces them, so that they may not even become a secularised nation. But He divorces in order to espouse, and henceforth divorce shall be no more. Having translated to the centre of the Gentile world the law and the priesthood, which are of divine origin, He espouses a new Church with equal territorial dowry, with equal political independence, and with a faithful people to be, in exchange for Israel, the Mother and Mistress Christian Church.

" But the transaction is enshrined in a double metaphor. Besides being a divorce of the Jewish Church, it is also a sale. And he who sells gets an equivalent. But to whom did Christ sell Israel? To whom was due the God-forsaken nation? or, as it is better put : ' Who is my creditor?' It required only registering the question. He redeemed them from the Egyptian to make them heirs of the promised land. He never sold them to the Assyrian or Greek. But the Roman was his creditor. For Rome was predestined to be the heiress of the Synagogue; and the Roman power was only allowed to root up the Church of the old alliance in exchange for the loss of Rome. Rome became the new promised land of the Mistress Christian Church and the patrimony of her first Pontiff. Peter, a son of Abraham, in the spirit and in the flesh, Peter, a principal joint-heir of the promise, was the first Pontiff-king of the New Covenant under the order of Melchisedech.

" 6. Where remains the forlorn hope ? I hold that Christ divorced and sold the inhabitants, but not the territory, therefore he obtained no territorial equivalent for the Christian Church. The condensed reply to which may be quoted from 2 Machabees v.: ' But God did not choose the people for the place's sake, but the place for the people's sake. And therefore the place also itself was made partaker of the evils of the people ; but afterwards shall communicate in the good things, and, as it was forsaken in the wrath of Almighty God, shall be exalted again with great glory, when the great Lord shall be reconciled.'

"My proposition, then, holds good. Should any person, however, deem my position not impregnable, he is welcome to effect an entrance by the weak point and turn me out. No one, of course, will suppose ,for a moment that any new demarcations are being advocated. The thesis points to the central and constant fact of the temporal power of the Pope as the embodiment of a God-given right. The States of the Church, as they have been in times of peace, are the normal equivalent. For God's providence hath interpreted the right of the Pontiff.

"In speaking of demarcations, however, a landmark may be saluted before we leave the subject of the land of the Vicar of Christ. It is the house of Christ : the Santa Casa. It also had its translation, if we believe a well authenticated miracle. Thou wast not sold, O holy house ; but translated to the new promised land.

"Will Catholics throughout the world rise in their moral strength to vindicate the Pontiff's right? No doubt, if they become distinctly cognisant of it. This question, then, is too important to be overlooked ; and should be studied with that love and attention which the interests at stake do certainly command."

THE TRANSLATION OF THE THEOCRACY,

WITH ITS SPIRITUAL AND TEMPORAL INHERITANCE, FROM JERUSALEM TO ROME.

"Therefore I say to you, that the Kingdom of God shall be taken from you, and shall be given to a nation yielding the fruits thereof."—ST. MATTHEW xxi. 43.

SOME months ago a pilgrimage left our English shores for a land once holy, and for Jerusalem, its capital. And what was the general impression of the pilgrims? It may be summed up in the words of the Bishop who was the spiritual leader of the pilgrimage : " They saw the contours of the country, and knew it was the same, though now it looked like a land under a curse, and they only here and there saw the hand of man bring forth what might be produced." Such was the impression of the pilgrims. I may inquire, how could it be otherwise? The first martyr of Christ in that land was heard to say, "that Jesus of Nazareth shall destroy this place" (Acts vi. 14). A sale and a divorce under the Divine hand had occurred, in which it was decreed that the place itself should be made partaker. I have quoted elsewhere the testimony of Holy Scripture in reference to this unique event. In the fiftieth chapter of Isaias we read the following language of Christ : " What is this bill of the divorce of your mother, with which I have put her away; or who is my creditor, to whom I sold you?" And in the second Book of Machabees, chapter v.: " But God did not choose the people for the place's sake, but the place for the people's sake. And therefore the place also itself was made partaker of the evils of the people; but afterwards shall communicate in the good things, and, as it was forsaken in the wrath of Almighty God, shall be exalted again with great glory, when the great Lord shall be reconciled."

No wonder, then, if the once holy land looks God-forsaken! Here is a principle : the land is destined to be partaker of the fate of the people. This principle applies, therefore, as much to the times of Caiphas and Pilate, or to the times of Vespasian and Titus, as to the times of Antiochus, as much to the times of a temporary punishment as to the times of a perma-nent casting off. Therefore, another people being taken up for the Divine government instead of the Jews, another city is chosen instead of Jerusalem.

To-day, in continuation of a theme which has been before my mind for some years, I have undertaken to unfold the Scripture evidence relating to the *Translation of the Theocracy, or Divine Government, with its Inherit-ance, both Temporal and Spiritual, from Jerusalem to Rome.*

Before entering on the subject, I may be allowed to anticipate a possible objection. I may be asked : " Why don't you quote the testimony of theologians and of the Fathers as well as that of Holy Writ ?"

I have only one excuse to plead, that such would be a great undertaking for which I have not sufficient leisure time. So far as I have read and remember their testimony in respect of the Pope's temporal independ-ence, my interpretation is either authorised or not con-demned by them. But when appealing to the testimony of theologians in favour of the temporal power of the High Priest of the New Law and of the political independence of Rome, the Jerusalem of the New Covenant, it should be borne in mind that they were never confronted with anything like the present opposition to the Pope's indepen-dence. For the present opposition is not merely the out-come of violence, or bad behaviour, on the part of Catholic rulers as in the past. It is now a matter of deep specula-tion before the whole world. It is a question taken up and discussed by doctrinaires and decided against the Church.

" My kingdom is not of this world," has been hypocriti-
cally quoted by the worst enemies of the Spiritual Power;
as though Christ meant anything more by this declaration,
than that His temporal power was not based on the gift
of men, nor on the accident of human suffrage, nor on
the conquest of arms, but a divine gift and a divine
inheritance. We cannot, therefore, expect that theologians, not foreseeing the denial of a great truth, should
have sought to defend it. We must not be surprised
even if they passed over Scripture evidence, which is
altogether in harmony with the Pontiff's temporal sovereignty, or still more a direct proof of it. Their interpretation of many passages quoted in this and the
previous theses is so far favourable that they see the
bearing of the text, or declare it to be mysterious, or
partially admit its conclusion, or, not admitting it, fail
to give a satisfactory explanation. The royal dignity of
Christ, for instance, so frequently and emphatically declared in Holy Scripture, is admitted by theologians and
traced as a hereditary right. Yet many hesitate to say
that He really possessed the dignity or exercised the
right. Again, when commenting on the association of
Peter with Christ in the exemption from tribute, some
put it down to the poverty of the Divine Master; whilst
others, with more reason, admit its significance, declaring
the privilege to be granted to Peter alone, because he
alone was heir to the plenitude of authority which Christ
left to his Church. When commenting on the words of
Christ and the Apostles recorded by St. Luke (xxii. 36,
38) : " 'And he that hath not, let him sell his coat, and
buy a sword ;'" and " ' Lord, behold here are two swords.'
And He said to them: ' It is enough'"—some hold that the
passage is mysterious, others explain it of the spiritual
and temporal swords, which both belong to the Church.
Yet if Christ were truly King, with an inalienable right
to be defended by his servants, what more natural than
this public exhibition of right before yielding it in
sacrifice. And if, as proved elsewhere, Peter was as-

sociated with Christ in both temporal and spiritual supremacy, what more natural than the reply of the Divine Master in reference to the two typical swords : " It is enough " ?

Take again the passage in the Acts of the Apostles, (i. 6) : " ' Lord, wilt Thou at this time restore again the kingdom to Israel ? ' But He said to them : ' It is not for you to know the times or moments which the Father hath put in His own power.' "

Here is a passage fully bearing on the kingly character of the Vicar and heir of Christ, and on the political independence of Rome, the Jerusalem of the New Covenant. The times or moments were known to the Father, and fixed by His own power. By a merciful dispensation, the eyes of the Apostles were closed on the future. Only after a lapse of three centuries of bloody persecution should the restoration come, and then not at Jerusalem, but at Rome.

The passage, however, is interpreted by some as though no temporal kingdom should belong to the Church. The question of both Apostles and disciples is ascribed to a want of spiritual-mindedness on their part. The unwillingness of Christ to uplift the veil which screened the future to a wish not to offend their carnal nature and susceptibilities.

But as Christ, in necessarily alluding to " the times and moments which the Father had put in His own power," far from excluding, evidently grants and includes in his reply the fact of the restoration of the kingdom to Israel, the commentator is driven to adduce the spiritual restoration of the Jews, who are to be united to the kingdom of the Church at the end of the world. This is an instance of a theologian wrestling with the obvious meaning of a text, for want of having learned, as we have, the necessity of the " Civil Principality " and the law of invariable restoration by Divine Providence of the temporal kingdom to the Roman Church, which holds the place of Israel.

Take another instance, namely, the interpretation put upon the words of the Archangel to the Virgin Mary : " The Lord God shall give unto Him the throne of David his father, and He shall reign in the house of Jacob for ever." Here, again, from not distinguishing between the spiritual kingdom of the Church throughout the world and the political independence of the Pontiff in Rome, commentators have been driven to convert the throne of David into a spiritual one. But the chair of Moses was the spiritual throne. If it had been intended by God that Christ should inherit for the Church only a spiritual throne, the succession to the chair of Moses should have been pledged : " The Lord God shall give unto him the chair of Moses, and He shall reign in the house of Jacob for ever." But no, it is the throne of David, his father, a distinctly temporal and royal throne, which is pledged to the Church. Therefore we must perforce conclude, that behind His Vicar on that throne, both temporal and spiritual, " Christ shall reign in the house of Jacob for ever."

Without further preamble I hasten now to quote the text on which I trust to engage your kind and religious attention. It is the parable of the vineyard proposed by Isaias, completed by Christ, and recorded by St. Matthew, St. Mark, and St. Luke. The following is from St. Matthew xxi. 33: " 'There was a man, a householder, who planted a vineyard, and made a hedge round about it, and dug in it a press, and built a tower, and let it out to husbandmen : and went into a strange country. And when the time of the fruits drew nigh, he sent his servants to the husbandmen, that they might receive the fruits thereof. And the husbandmen laying hands on his servants, beat one, and killed another, and stoned another. Again he sent other servants, more than the former : and they did to them in like manner. And last of all he sent to them his son, saying: " They will reverence my son." But the husbandmen, seeing the son, said among themselves : "This is the heir ; come, let us

kill him, and we shall have his inheritance." And taking
him, they cast him forth out of the vineyard, and killed
him. When, therefore, the lord of the vineyard shall
come, what will he do to those husbandmen ?' They say
to Him : ' He will bring those evil men to an evil end;
and he will let out his vineyard to other husbandmen,
that shall render him the fruit in due season.' Jesus saith
to them : 'Have you never read in the Scriptures : "The
stone which the builders rejected, the same is become
the head of the corner ? By the Lord this has been
done, and it is wonderful in our eyes." Therefore I
say to you, that the kingdom of God shall be taken from
you, and shall be given to a nation yielding the fruits
thereof. And whosoever shall fall on this stone, shall
be broken: but on whomsoever it shall fall, it shall grind
him to powder.' "

My commentary on this parable may be summed up
in the following argument :—

1. The parable in St. Matthew, chapter xxi., represents the theocracy with its spiritual and temporal
inheritance.

2. But the kingdom of God, which Christ foretold
should be taken from the Jews, and should be given
to a nation yielding the fruits thereof, is identical with
the theocracy and inheritance depicted in the parable.

3. Therefore the theocracy, with its full inheritance,
spiritual and temporal, was, in fulfilment of Divine prophecy, taken from the Jews and given to a nation yielding the fruits thereof.

4. The nation which eventually inherited the theocracy, or kingdom of God, yielding the fruits thereof, can
only be the nation which is privileged to possess the
heir of Him Whom they killed.

5. Now according to Catholic teaching that nation
is Rome, etc.

6. Therefore Rome is the nation which eventually
inherited the theocracy. Therefore the theocracy, with
its temporal inheritance, was translated from Jerusalem
to Rome.

1. The parable in St. Matthew, chapter XXI.,
   represents the theocracy with its spiritual
   and temporal inheritance.

Isaias had applied the parable to Israel; Christ
applies it also to the rulers of the nation, to the authorities of the Church, of the Synagogue, and to Himself.
The ownership of God and the Divine government,
together with the spiritual and temporal elements of
human government, are vividly pourtrayed in the parable
and we find them side by side in the history of Israel.
"The vineyard of the Lord of Hosts is the house of
Israel," says Isaias. The hedge made round about it is
understood by some to represent the protection afforded
by the law, by others to represent the Divine protection. The press dug in it represents the Temple with its
altars. The tower, according to some, is the royal
dignity, which I may interpret as the temporal power.
The husbandmen are the chief citizens and those entrusted with power in this Church-nation. The servants
sent to the husbandmen to receive the fruits of the
vineyard are the prophets and the precursor. The son
sent at last represents Christ, Whom the Jews know to
be the heir, and consequently resolve to kill, that they
may secure the inheritance.

In one word, the parable is intended to give an
outline of the Jewish people and Jewish constitution.
Not only was the law divinely given, and the territory
divinely chosen, and the succession of priests and kings
divinely appointed, but the people also was divinely set
apart from the beginning to be a Church and a nation.
For as the householder planted the vineyard, so did God
from the beginning establish Israel. Moses was commanded to say : "You have seen what I have done to
the Egyptians, how I have carried you upon the wings
of eagles, and have taken you to Myself. If, therefore,
you will hear My voice, and keep My covenant, you shall
be *My peculiar possession* above all people : for all the

earth is Mine. And you shall be to Me *a priestly kingdom*, and a holy nation " (Exodus xix. 4-6).

Other nations were settled in their territory before the law-giver defined the sphere of religion or the limits of the spiritual power. The Israelites were set free and made a nation by God and religion. In other nations the secular power was predominant. In Israel the Church itself was the nation. Neither the spiritual power of the Jewish pontiffs nor the temporal power of the Jewish kings was subordinate. The spiritual and temporal powers had the same divine origin. They were supreme within their own respective spheres and co-ordinate. And whether king reigned or priest governed God held the sovereign sway. Hence Israel was unlike any other nation, a Church with political independence, or a Church-nation and a theocracy.

Now in thus planting Israel from the beginning, God had one only thing in view : to prepare the way for the Incarnation of His Divine Son, Who in the parable is represented as the heir.

It will be seen, therefore, that a temporal inheritance, as well as a spiritual one, was a preparation for the Incarnation of the Son of God. It is obvious also from the parable that the Jews sought to frustrate the Divine plan, by killing the heir and annihilating the theocracy, at the very time of its predestined perfection. " This is the heir, come, let us kill him, and we shall have the inheritance." By these words of the parable, which Christ puts into the mouth of his enemies, He manifestly implies that they understood Him to be the heir. It might be interesting to examine the evidence which forced them to the conclusion that He was the heir. It will suffice, however, to consider in what sense they understood Him to be the heir. At the first glance we may safely judge that they knew Him to be a temporal as well as a spiritual heir. For the spiritual inheritance they had no care, except inasmuch as it might serve their carnal ends. They had corrupted their traditions and

were seeking to establish themselves as a godless nation.
Hence the temporal inheritance was the sole object of
their jealous care, to preserve which they did not hesitate to do away with Him Whom the law and the
prophets indicated as the heir of the Church-nation.
The parable implies manifestly that the Jews understood
that whatever authority existed in the nation was His.
The vineyard was His. His was the protecting hedge,
and the press dug in the vineyard. His was the tower,
and to Him and to His Father belonged the servants
that, in the long past, they had beaten or stoned or
killed. They understood Him therefore to be the heir
to the chair of Moses and to the throne of David, to
be the heir of the kings, and of the priests, and of the
prophets, and of Moses himself. Nay more, He had
proved Himself in their presence to be the heir of God
His Father. God, having ever shared with man the
government of Israel, the inheritance was divine as well
as human, and He was the God-man. It was temporal
and spiritual, and they learned at last that he was born
King of the Jews, and priest according to the order of
Melchisedech.

In how many minds there remained crass ignorance,
after the three years of Christ's public ministry, and in
how many minds there was affected ignorance, the last
day alone will reveal. One certain conclusion must be
drawn from the parable, namely, that the leading portion
of the nation knew Christ to be the heir of the theocracy, and of its spiritual and temporal inheritance.
They knew it before the recitation of the parable.
They had questioned His authority in Israel, and He
informs them in reply that they were fully aware of His
title and claims. He informs them that He also was
aware of their murderous design.

The parable in St. Matthew, chapter xxi., is therefore a vivid representation of the theocracy, with its
spiritual and temporal inheritance, at the time when the
Heir appeared who could and did lay claim to its full
inheritance, human and divine.

2. But the kingdom of God, which Christ foretold should be taken from the Jews, and should be given to a nation yielding the fruits thereof, is identical with the theocracy and inheritance depicted in the parable.

By putting the case of the Jews in the form of a parable Christ had elicited their opinion that justice required an eviction and a change of hands. " They say to Him : ' He will bring those evil men to an evil end ; and will let out his vineyard to other husbandmen, that shall render him the fruit in due season.' " He now confirms their opinion, and shows them that they are themselves concerned, first by an appeal to Scripture : "The stone which the builders rejected, the same is become the head of the corner ;" and, secondly, by His own prophetic declaration : "Therefore I say to you, that the kingdom of God shall be taken from you, and shall be given to a nation yielding the fruits thereof." This record of the decreed translation of the kingdom of God to another nation is only to be found in St. Matthew. Elsewhere is recorded the judgment of the chief priests and ancients of the people in the case proposed in the parable, together with their discovery that it applied to them. Here Christ leaves the parable to come to what the parable means. Here He ceases to speak of the vineyard and inheritance to make a declaration in agreement with the Jews concerning that which the vineyard and inheritance signify, namely, the kingdom of God. Here He drops the figure of a first and second set of husbandmen to speak of the Jews themselves and of another nation destined to yield the fruits of the kingdom of God.

He reasons thus with the Jews: "You agree that the lord of the vineyard will let it out to other husbandmen that shall render him the fruit in due season. That vineyard is the inheritance that belonged to you. By your own showing, it should be taken from you. Therefore, the kingdom of God shall be taken from you. You shall be deprived of God's ownership and government so as to cease to be His *peculiar possession.* You shall be deprived of the Divine protection. You shall be deprived of the spiritual inheritance of God's service and of the temporal inheritance which made you a nation. And that which shall be taken from you shall be given to a nation yielding the proper fruits."

It is clear, therefore, that, in speaking of the kingdom of God in this place, Christ means the inheritance of Israel pourtrayed in the parable. And as God had His share in that inheritance as well as priest, king, and people, it is likewise clear that the kingdom of God is here meant for the theocracy with its spiritual and temporal inheritance.

3. THEREFORE THE THEOCRACY, WITH ITS FULL INHERITANCE, SPIRITUAL AND TEMPORAL, WAS, IN FULFILMENT OF DIVINE PROPHECY, TAKEN FROM THE JEWS AND GIVEN TO A NATION YIELDING THE FRUITS THEREOF.

If the two foregoing propositions are true, this last one follows of necessity. It is not, therefore, here necessary to set about proving it. It may be noted, however, that the kingdom of God represented in the parable, being a temporal as well as a spiritual kingdom, is not meant merely for the spiritual kingdom of the Universal Church, nor for the inheritance of the Faith among the Gentiles—I use the word merely because the theocracy of the God Incarnate is both a limited temporal kingdom and a universal spiritual one. The kingdom of God is none the less spiritual, and relates none the less to souls, and to Heaven hereafter, because the Incarnate God retains the temporal inheritance which was prepared for Him of old.

This conclusion receives a powerful confirmation from the words made use of by Christ. In speaking of the translation of the inheritance of Israel He might have said: "The kingdom of God shall be given to others," whereas He says : "shall be given to a nation yielding the fruits thereof." These words leave no doubt about the succession. It is one nation succeeding to the privileges of another nation that we have to go in search for.

Had Christ, on the other hand, said: "The kingdom of God shall be taken from you and given to the nations," we might have been puzzled at the alternative of the Jews retaining the monopoly of true religion in the world had they remained faithful, or at the other alternative of the Gentiles only receiving the Faith on account of the transgression of Israel ; but still we should have understood a spiritual inheritance. For a spiritual inheritance can extend throughout the world, whereas the temporal inheritance is limited in extent and must be confined to one people.

We should in such case have speculated in vain on the fate of the temporal inheritance of Israel. Perhaps forgetting, as some have done, that the Jews can never re-establish themselves on the old footing of the Mosaic law for want of genealogies, we might have concluded that the land of Israel, through pious remembrance called the Holy Land, still belonged to the Jews, who are destined to flourish there again before the end comes.

But we have not to speculate on the cancelling of God's temporal gift to Israel, nor on the breakdown of the kingdom of God. "The kingdom of God shall be taken from you, and shall be given to a nation yielding the fruits thereof." That is, shall be given to the Church which is fitted to be, instead of Israel, the Mistress Christian Church.

Reason and common sense bear out this interpretation. You must believe " the kingdom of God given to a nation yielding the fruits thereof " to be the theocracy with its temporal inheritance ; or you must believe that the Jews were destined, if they had been faithful, to retain a monopoly of the true Faith.

Had Christ in His mercy been able to gather the Jews, as the hen doth gather her chickens under her wings, what, then, would have happened? Surely, such repentance of the Jewish people would not have been fatal to the Gentiles! Yet in such an hypothesis the kingdom of God would not have been given to another nation. Therefore, the kingdom of God is not here identical with the inheritance of the Faith. .

If you insist that it is, you must, perforce, conclude that such Faith would have remained with the repentant Jews, and would not have been given to another nation ; and consequently that the conversion of the Jews to Christ would have been fatal to the Gentiles, which is absurd.

Therefore, it is once more proved that the theocracy, with its full inheritance, spiritual and temporal, was in fulfilment of Divine prophecy taken from the Jews and given to a nation yielding the fruits thereof.

4. The nation which eventually inherited the theocracy, or kingdom of God, yielding the fruits thereof, can only be the nation which is privileged to possess the heir of Him Whom they killed.

In order to discover the nation which hath succeeded to Israel by inheriting from Christ the kingdom of God, we must look out, not for a twofold dynasty of priests and kings, as under the old law, but for the heir of Christ, Who translated to Himself both the law and the priesthood, and united in His Person the whole authority of the ancient theocracy. Where that heir is at home, there shall the inheritance be, and there, consequently, the kingdom of God, or the theocracy.

Now in the natural order of things Jerusalem should have been the home of the heir of Christ, because in the normal state the theocracy should have remained in Israel. The Jews were entitled, if they had been willing to be gathered to the forgiving heart of the

Redeemer, to remain His principal inheritance. From Jerusalem the Faith would have continued to spread throughout the world for all time. Christians would have been named after Israel, their centre, and not after Rome. The theocracy established by God through Moses, without leaving its ancient home, would have received, and continued to hold, its predestined perfection in the Incarnation, which combines in one person the twofold authority of Pontiff and King. The order of Aaron and succession to the sceptre of Judah· having reached their appointed goal, would have been merged into the order of Christ typified by Melchisedech.

But the natural order of things was not destined to endure. A violent act removed the theocracy to another centre. It was the cutting down of the natural branches of the olive tree to graft on the wild olive, and make it produce not the wild, but the original fruit. Whereas the wild tree should have been cut down, and should have received the graft from the old cultivated stock. It was the divorce and sale recorded by Isaias, followed by a fresh marriage with equal rights. It was the rejection of the stone by the Jewish builders, which became elsewhere the head of the corner.

And where was the theocracy removed to? Let us look for the heir of Christ. Once more, where he is at home there is the inheritance.

5. Now according to Catholic teaching the nation which is privileged to possess the heir of Him whom they killed is Rome.

We all hold that the Vicar of Christ is the heir to the plenitude of authority which He left to His Church. And that Rome, the Apostolic See, belongs to him. The only difficulty which besets some minds is the temporal inheritance of the old theocracy. Considering that the theocracy, as we have seen from Christ's words showing the application of the parable, was given to another nation, and that such other nation can only be Rome, it follows that Rome hath inherited the temporal inheritance of the theocracy. For the whole theocracy was handed over, and not merely a part of it. Christ, however, makes the light of the parable twice vivid by coupling with it another illustration, namely, that of the corner-stone rejected by the Jewish builders.

If the stone, which was the God Incarnate, heir of the theocracy, had not been rejected by the builders, it would have remained planted in Jerusalem. Peter and his successors, who are associated by inheritance in the firmness of that corner-stone, on which the Christian Church is built, would have remained in Jerusalem. Who, then, will venture to say that if the theocracy had thus remained in Israel, the temporal inheritance would have been forfeited? Who is prepared to assert that the Jewish Church would have been placed in a less favourable position for becoming the Mistress Christian Church? Or that political independence would not have been as much her birthright after as before the Incarnation? Or does the translation of the spiritual power of the theocracy to Rome involve the loss of the temporal inheritance? If the temporal inheritance had legitimately been conserved to a Mistress Christian Church in Jerusalem, why not to the heiress of the Church of Jerusalem? If the spiritual inheritance could be translated to Rome, why not the temporal inheritance?

In any case, no other nation claims, like Rome, to possess the heir of Him Whom they killed, neither do Catholics look elsewhere for the direct succession to Christ.

6. THEREFORE ROME IS THE NATION WHICH EVENTUALLY INHERITED THE THEOCRACY, OR KINGDOM OF GOD, YIELDING THE FRUITS THEREOF.

Schismatics in the East and in the West, to whom Rome is not the Jerusalem of the New Covenant, have fallen off the very foundation of religion, which is the unbroken succession of God's central and personal gov-

ernment in the world. A government which begins with
the patriarchs and Abraham, "heir of the world" (Romans
iv.), and extends to the reigning Roman Pontiff. Therefore, finally, the theocracy being handed over to another
nation, and no other nation being privileged to possess
the heir of Christ but Rome, it follows that *the theocracy,*
with its temporal inheritance, was translated from Jeru-
salem to Rome.

THE NON-DESTRUCTION OF THE LAW OF ISRAEL.

We have seen in the foregoing thesis that the
theocracy, the only everlasting kingdom on the earth
according to the prophets, did not come to an end with
the casting off of the Jewish people and of their ancient
home in Israel. It has been shown that the Divine
government, together with the priestly and kingly human
rule, were translated to Christ and to the new order
introduced by Him, and that the transference of such
Divine and human government to another centre, Rome,
was according to the Divine plan.

But government, whether human or divine, pre-
supposes a legislation. We might conclude, therefore,
without going further afield, that the law of Israel did
not come to naught any more than the authority and
legal powers established by it ; and, consequently, that
what is termed the new law and the law of grace
is only the fulfilment of the old by the heir of the
theocracy.

It may be interesting, however, to attempt a short
analysis of the Scripture evidence relating to the non-
destruction of the law of Moses. We read in St.
Matthew, ever the most faithful evangelist of the sacred
humanity and royal dignity of Christ (chapter v.
17, *et seq.*) : " Do not think that I am come to destroy
the law, or the prophets. I am not come to destroy,
but to fulfil. For amen I say unto you, till Heaven
and earth pass, one jot, or one tittle shall not pass of the
law, till all be fulfilled. He, therefore, that shall break

one of these least commandments, and shall so teach men, shall be called the least in the kingdom of Heaven," etc.

Here it should be observed that the law of Moses enjoined obedience, not only to the moral precepts, but to the authorities, divine and human, spiritual and temporal, constituted by the law. Therefore the words above quoted apply not only to the removal of certain dispensations, and to the perfect observance of the moral law, but to the recognition of the constituted authorities. Hence it was a public duty to acknowledge the Lord of Hosts as protector of Israel. It was a duty to pay tithes and acknowledge the authority of Levites and priests, a duty to acknowledge the authority of the succession of kings appointed by God, and it was the sin of rebellion or schism to break away from such authority. It will be seen, therefore, that if the law was not destroyed, but fulfilled, by Christ, so it fared with the theocracy.

It may be objected that Christ, in the passage just quoted, is speaking of the natural law and not of the law of Moses. If this were so, as indeed some commentators declare, it would be vain to seek a confirmation of the thesis from the words of Christ: "I am not come to destroy, but to fulfil."

But a little reflection will enable us to see that the declaration of Christ refers to the Mosaic law and not to the natural law. In the first place, Christ in the same breath makes an identical declaration in respect to the prophets. He would not have put the natural law in juxtaposition with the prophets, but the positive Divine law given through Moses, which, together with the prophets, were the interpretation of God's will and special designs in respect to His chosen people. Secondly, the supposition that Christ meant " I am not come to destroy the natural law," is absurd. The natural law, according to St. Thomas, is a participation of the eternal law by the rational creature. Christ could not be suspected, by friend or foe, of any intention of destroying it. Those who did not believe Him to be the Son of God, could at least infer the absence of such intention from His holy life and doctrine. Those who believed Him to be God, believed Him therefore to be the author of the natural law. And to say that "He came to fulfil the natural law" is also absurd, for the natural law had no reference to His coming and could not be fulfilled in that sense ; whereas the Mosaic law and the prophets were to be fulfilled by His coming. In the third place, the Jews to whom Christ spoke were not anxious about the natural law, which applies to all nations and to all men, but about their own law. It was quite natural, then, to seek to remove their apprehensions. The fulfilling of the law of Moses by Christ might seem in many respects a destroying. Christ declares that He came only to fulfil. Many dispensations had been granted under the old law, which though imperfect in respect to the law of Christ, was perfect for the time and people, as being God's own interpretation of the natural law. The withdrawal by Christ of such dispensations was not a destroying, but a fulfilling of the ancient law. The Jews had not been taught forgiveness of enemies, but mere justice and strict retribution. They knew not the perfection of indissoluble marriage, nor of monogamy, nor of celibacy. The removal of the relative imperfections of the law was not a destruction of the law. Not only the repeal of certain dispensations, but the fulfilling of all types and figures might appear to the Jews fatal to the law. Therefore Christ had to prepare the faithful Israelites for the cessation of the ceremonial law, with its typical sacrifices, and to warn them that in supplying the reality, He destroyed not the law, but merely that which was preliminary in the law.

Therefore, when declaring that He came not to destroy the law and the prophets, but to fulfil, Christ meant not the natural law, but the law of Moses. Therefore the law of Moses is fulfilled, and still endures in the law of Christ. Therefore the non-destruction by Christ of the law of Moses leaves intact that which was permanently established by such law, namely, the theocracy and its spiritual and temporal power. The theocracy, the most remarkable provision of the law of Moses, was not in itself of a preliminary or typical character; therefore it was not destroyed at the coming of the heir. Yet the form given to it by Moses was typical and indicative of imperfection. The delegated authority of the theocracy was divided between priest and king, and, as shown elsewhere, such separation of the spiritual and temporal powers in the government of the Church-nation could only be a type of the imperfection of the theocracy before the Son of God assumed a body and soul in the mystery of the Incarnation. It should be borne in mind that the human government of the theocracy has ever stood alone. It is like no other government that history describes. The two powers in Israel were co-ordinate and supreme. Before the Incarnation it was lawful for kings to hold spiritual authority and to be the high priests of the nation. But not in Israel. Since the Incarnation the very reverse is the law. Only in the theocracy of Rome are the spiritual and temporal powers combined. No other Christian king may hold spiritual power. The reason is that before the Incarnation the nations were not called together, but since the Incarnation the peoples of the world are assembled into one Church. They could not be assembled if they had more than one spiritual ruler; and that spiritual ruler is the heir of the delegated authority of the theocracy.

NOTE FOR ELEVENTH PAGE.

After the words "Never was a high priest saluted or recognised as king," I have, for the sake of accuracy, added the words "by the nation" in the French edition.

That the two dignities were to be kept apart, and reserved to the priestly and kingly families respectively, may be shown both from Holy Scripture and from Josephus :—

1. We gather from the author of the first book of Machabees (chapter xiv.) that the Asmoneans were elected by the Jews, to be, not their kings, but their princes and high priests until the coming of Christ. "The Jews and their priests had consented that he (Simon) should be their prince and high priest for ever, till there should arise a faithful prophet . . ." (verse 41). "And it pleased all the people to establish Simon, and to do according to these words" (verse 46).

2. That the royal dignity belonged exclusively to the descendants of David, Josephus bears the following testimony. When he describes how the high priest introduces Jehoash, whom the Queen Athaliah, a precursor of Herod, had sought to destroy with the whole house of David, he quotes the following words, addressed by Jehoiada to the priests and Levites and heads of tribes assembled for the purpose and sworn to observe secrecy and lend assistance : "This is your king, of that house which you know God hath foretold should reign over you for all time to come" (Book IX. chapter vii.)

3. That such royal dignity did not belong to the Asmoneans may be deduced also from the testimony of Josephus, who records how the diadem was usurped by Aristobulus : "When their father Hyrcanus was dead, the eldest son, Aristobulus, intending to change the government *into a kingdom*, for so he resolved to do, first of all put a diadem on his head, "four hundred eighty and one years and three months after the people had been delivered from the Babylonish slavery" (Book

XIII. chapter xi.) The historian then proceeds to detail the barbarous cruelty of the self-made king to his mother and brethren.

4. That the nation was conscious that the priestly race were not entitled to kingly rule, Josephus bears testimony later on in Book XIV. chapter iii. After the tyrannical reign of Alexander, and the more peaceful reign of Alexandra, Aristobulus and Hyrcanus, her sons, quarrel over the succession, and present themselves before Pompey to settle the dispute. The historian says : " He (Pompey) came from Pella to Damascus ; and there it was that he heard the causes of the Jews, and of their governors Hyrcanus and Aristobulus, who were at difference with one another, as *also of the nation against them both*, which did not desire to be under *kingly government*, because the form of government which they received from their forefathers was that of subjection to the priests of that God whom they worshipped ; and (they complained) that though these two *were of the posterity of the priests*, yet did they *seek to change the government* of their nation to another form in order to enslave them."

DECLARATION OF THE BISHOPS.

READ BY CARDINAL MATTEI, DEAN OF THE SACRED COLLEGE.

Beatissime Pater,

Ex quo Apostoli Jesu Christi sacro Pentecostes die Petro Ecclesia Capiti in oratione adhærentes, Spiritum Sanctum acceperunt, et divino ejus impulsu acti, cunctarum fere nationem viris in Urbe sancta congregatis, unicuique sua lingua potentiam Dei mirabilem annunciarunt, nunquam, ut credimus, ad hanc usque diem tot eorumdem hæredes, iisdem recurrentibus solemniis, venerandum Petri Successorem, orantem circumsteterunt, decernentem audierunt, regentem roborarunt. Quemadmodum vero Apostolis media inter nascentis Ecclesiæ pericula nil jucundius accidere potuit, quam divino Spiritu recens afflato assistere primo Christi in terris Vicario; ita nec nobis præsentes inter Ecclesiæ sanctæ angustias, antiquius sanctiusve aliud esse potuit, quam quidquid inest venerationis pietatisque erga Sanctitatem Tuam pectoribus nostris, ad pedes Beatitudinis Tuæ deponere, simul et unanimiter declarare, quanta prosequamur admiratione præclaras, quibus Supremus Pontifex Noster eminet virtutes, quantoque animo iis quæ Petrus alter docuit, vel quæ tam firmiter stata rataque esse voluit, adhæreamus.

Corda nostra novus inflammat ardor, vividior fidei lux mentem illuminat, sanctior animam corripit amor. Linguas nostras flammis illius sacri ignis vibrantes sentimus quæ Mariæ, cui assidebant Apostoli, mitissimum cor ardentiori pro hominum salute desiderio incendebant, ipsos vero Apostolos ad magnalia Dei prædicanda impellebant.

Plurimas igitur agentes Beatitudini Tuæ gratias, quod nos ad Pontificium solium difficillimis hisce temporibus accurrere, Te afflictum solari, nostrosque Tibi, cleri item ac populi nostræ curæ commissorum animi sensus aperire permiseris, Tibi uno ore unaque mente acclamamus, omnia fausta, cuncta bona adprecantes. Vive diu, Sancte Pater, valeque ad Catholicam regendam Ecclesiam. Perge, ut facis, eam tuo robore tueri, tua prudentia dirigere, tuis exornare virtutibus. Præi nobis, ut bonus Pastor, exemplo, oves et agnos cœlesti pabulo pasce, aquis Sapientiæ cœlestis refice. Nam Tu sanæ doctrinæ nobis Magister, Tu unitatis centrum, Tu populi lumen indeficiens a divina Sapientia præparatum. Tu petra es, et ipsius Ecclesia fundamentum, contra quod inferorum portæ nunquam prævalebunt. Te loquente, Petrum audimus, Te decernente, Christo obtemperamus. Te miramur inter tantas molestias totque procellas fronte serena et imperturbato animo sacri muneris partibus fungentem, invictum et erectum.

Dum tamen justissima in his gloriandi nobis suppetunt argumenta, non possumus quin simul oculos ad tristia convertamus. Undequaque enim menti nostræ se sistunt immania eorum facinora, qui pulcherrimam Italiæ terram, cujus Tu, Beatissime Pater, columen es et decus, misere vastarunt ipsumque tuum et Sanctæ Sedis principatum, ex quo præclara quæque in civilem societatem veluti ex suo fonte dimanarunt, labefactare, ac funditus evertere connituntur. Nam neque perennia sæculorum jura, neque diuturna regiminis pacifica possessio, neque tandem fœdera totius Europæ auctoritate sancita et confirmata impedire potuerunt, quominus omnia susdeque verterentur, spretis legibus omnibus, quibus hactenus suffulta stabant imperia.

Sed ut ad nostra propius accedamus, Te, Beatissime Pater, iis provinciis, quarum ope, et dignitate Sanctæ Sedis, et totius Ecclesiæ administrationem æquissime providebatur, nefario usurpatorum hominum scelere, qui non habent *nisi velamen malitiæ libertatem*, spoliatum cernimus. Quorum iniquæ violentiæ cum Sanctitas Tua invictissimo animo obstiterit, plurimas et gratias, Catholicorum omnium nomine, censemus rependendas.

Civilem enim Sanctæ Sedis principatum ceu quiddam necessarium ac providente Deo manifeste institutum agnoscimus; nec declarare dubitamus, in præsenti rerum humanarum statu, ipsum hunc principatum civilem pro bono ac libero Ecclesiæ animarumve regimine omnino requiri. Oportebat sane totius Ecclesiæ Caput Romanum Pontificem nulli principi esse subjectum, imo nullius hospitem; sed in proprio dominio ac regno sedentem suimet juris esse, et in nobili, tranquilla, et almo libertate Catholicam Fidem tueri, ac propugnare, totamve regere ac gubernare christianam rempublicam.

Quis autem inficiari possit in hoc rerum humanorum, opinionum, institutionumque conflictu necessarium esse ut servetur extrema in Europa medius, tres inter veteris mundi continentes, quidam veluti sacer locus, et sedes augustissima, unde populis principibusque vicissim oriatur vox quædam magna potensque, vox nempe justitiæ et veritatis, nulli favens præ cæteris, nullius obsequens arbitrio, quam nec terrendo compescere, nec ullis artibus quisquam possit circumvenire?

Qui porro vel hac vice fieri potuisset, ut Ecclesiæ Antistites securi hoc ex toto orbe accurrerent cum Sanctitate Tua de rebus gravissimis acturi, si ex tot et tam diversis regionibus gentibusque confluentes, Principem aliquem invenissent his oris dominantem, qui vel Principes ipsorum in suspicione haberet, vel illis, suspectus ipse, adversaretur? Sua sunt etenim et christiano, et civi officia; haud quidem repugnantia inter se, sed diversa tamen; quæ adimpleri ab Episcopis quomodo possent, nisi perstaret Romæ civilis principatus, qualis est Pontificum, juris alieni omnino immunis, et centrum quodammodo universalis concordiæ, nihil ambitionis humanæ spirans, nihil pro terrena dominatione moliens?

Ad liberum ergo Pontificum Regem venimus liberi, Ecclesiæ rebus utpote Pastores, et patriæ utpote cives bene et æque consulentes, neque Pastorum, neque civium officia posthabentes.

Quæ cum ita sint, quisnam Principatum illum tam veterem, tanta auctoritate, at tanta necessitatis vi conditum, audeat impugnare? Cui, si vel jus illud humanum, in quo posita est principum securitas populorumque libertas attendatur, quænam alia potestas possit comparari? Quæ tam venerabilis et sancta? Quæ sive pristinis, sive recentioribus sæculis monarchia vel respublica juribus tam augustis, tam antiquis, tam inviolabilibus possit gloriari? Quæ omnia si semel in hac Sancta Sede despecta atque proculcata fuerint, quisnam vel princeps de regno, vel respublica de territorio possint esse securi? Ergo, Sanctissime Pater, pro religione quidem, sed et pro justitia, juribusque, quæ sunt inter gentes rerum humanarum fundamenta, contendis atque decertas.

Sed de hac tam gravi causa vix nos decet amplius verba proferre, qui Te de ipsa non tam disserentem quam docentem sæpe sæpius audivimus. Vox etenim Tua, quasi tuba sacerdotalis, toti orbi clangens proclamavit, quod "singulari prorsus divinæ Providentiæ consilio factum sit, ut Romanus Pontifex, quem Christus totius Ecclesiæ suæ Caput centrumque constituit, civilem assequeretur principatum;"* ab omnibus igitur nobis esse pro certissimo tenendum non fortuito hoc regimen temporale Sanctæ Sedi accessisse, sed ex speciali divina dispositione illi esse tributum, longave annorum serie, unanimi omnium regnorum et imperiorum consensu, ac pæne miraculo corroboratum et conservatum.

Alto pariter et solemni eloquio declarasti "Te civilem Romanæ Ecclesiæ Principatum ejusque temporales possessiones ac jura, quæ ad universum Catholicum orbem pertinent, integra et inviolata constanter tueri et servare velle; immo Sanctæ Sedis Principatus Beatique Petri patrimonii tutelam ad omnes Catholicos pertinere; Teque paratum esse animam potius ponere quam hanc Dei, Ecclesiæ, ac justitiæ causam ullo modo deserere."† Quibus præclaris verbis nos acclamantes ac plaudentes respondemus, nos Tecum et ad carcerem et ad mortem ire paratos esse; Teque humiliter rogamus, ut in hac constantia ac firmissimo proposito maneas immobilis, angelis et hominibus invicti animi et summæ virtutis spectaculum factus. Id etiam a Te postulat Christi Ecclesia, pro cujus feliciori regimine Romanis Pontificibus civilis principatus providentissime fuit attributus, quæque adeo sensit ejusdem tutelam ad ipsam pertinere, ut, Sede olim Apostolica vacante, gravissimis in angustiis, temporales Romanæ Ecclesiæ possessiones omnes Constantiensis Concilii Patres, uti ex publicis patet documentis, in unum administrarent; id postulant Christi fideles per omnes terrarum orbis regiones dispersi, qui libere ad Te venire, libereque conscientiæ suæ consulere gestiunt; id denique ipsa civilis deposcit societas, quæ ex tui regiminis subversione sua ipsa nutare sentit fundamenta.

Sed quid plura? Tu tandem aliquando scelestos homines et honorum ecclesiasticorum direptores justo judicio damnans omnia quæ

* Lit. Ap. xxxi mar., 1860, pp. 3, 5. Allocutio, xx jun. 1859, p. 6. Encycl. xix jun., 1860, p. 4. Allocutio, xvii dec., 1860.
† Epist. Encycl., xix jan., 1860.

patraverant "irrita et nulla" proclamasti ;* actus omnes ab iis inten-
tatos "illegitimos omnino et sacrilegos" esse decrevisti ;† ipsosque
talium facinorum reos pœnis et censuris ecclesiasticis obnoxios jure ac
merito declarasti.‡

Hos tam graves Tui oris sermones, tamve præclara gesta nostrum
est reverenter excipere, iisque plenum assensum renovare. Sicuti enim
corpus capiti, cui jungitur membrorum compagine unaque vita, in
omnibus condolet, ita nos Tecum consentire necesse est. Tibi in omni
tua hac acerbissima afflictione, sic conjungimur, ut quæ tibi pati con-
tingat, eadem et nos, amoris consensu, patiamur. Deum interea sup-
plices invocamus, ut tam iniquæ rerum perturbationi finem ponat,
Ecclesiamque Filii sui sponsam, tam misere expoliatam ac oppressam
pristino decori ac libertati restituat.

Sed mirum nobis non est tam acriter, et infense Sedis Apostolicæ
jura impeti et impugnari. Jam enim a pluribus annis, eo devenit non-
nullorum hominum insania, ut non amplius singulas Ecclesia doctrinas
rejicere, vel in dubium revocare conentur ; sed totam penitus veritatem
christianam, christianamque rempublicam funditus evertere sibi pro-
ponant. Hinc impiissima tentamina vanæ scientiæ, falsæque eruditionis
contra Sacrarum Litterarum doctrinas, ipsarumque inspirationem ; hinc
malesana sollicitudo juventutem Ecclesiæ matris tutelæ substractam
quibusvis sæculi erroribus, vel seclusa sæpius omni religiosa institutione,
imbuendi ; hinc novæ eæque perniciosissimæ de sociali, politico æque
ac religioso rerum ordine theoriæ, quæ impune quaquaversus spargun-
tur ; hinc multis familiare, in his præsertim oris, Ecclesiæ auctoritatem
spernere, jura sibi vindicare, præcepta proculcare, ministros vilipendere,
cultum deridere, ipsos de religione errores, imo ecclesiasticos quoque
viros in perditionis viam misere abeuntes laudare ac in honore habere.
Venerabiles Antistites ac Dei Sacerdotes exauctorantur, exulare coguntur, aut in carceres detruduntur ; quinimo ante tribunalia civilia, pro
constantia in sacro ministerio obeundo, contumeliose pertrahuntur.
Gemunt Christi Sponsæ suis expulsæ tectis, inediæ fere consumptæ, vel
cito consumendæ ; viri religiosi ad sæculum inviti remeare coguntur ;
sacro 'Ecclesiæ patrimonio violentæ manus injiciuntur ; pessimorum
librorum, ephemeridum, et imaginum colluvie, fidei, moribus, veritati,
ipsi verecundiæ continuum asperrimumque bellum infertur.

Sed qui talia moliuntur optime norunt in Sancta Sede, velut in arce
inexpugnabili, robur ac vires omnis veritatis ac justitiæ inesse, quibus
retundantur hostium impetus ; ibi esse speculam, ex qua vigiles Summi
Custodis oculi paratas insidias a longe conspiciunt, suis annuntiandas
commilitonibus. Hinc odium implacabile, hinc insanabilis livor, hinc
continuum scelestissimorum hominum studium, ut Sanctam Romanam
Ecclesiam ejusque Sedem deprimant, ac si fieri unquam posset, prorsus
exscindant.

---

* Allocutio, xxvi sept., 1859.
† Allocutio, xx jun. 1859.
‡ Litteræ Apostolicæ, xxvi martii, 1860.

Quis, Beatissime Pater, talia conspiciens, vel etiam recensita audiens sibi temperet a lacrymis ? Justo igitur dolore correpti oculos ac manus ad coelos levamus, divinum illum Spiritum toto mentis affectu implorantes, ut qui hac die olim nascentem Ecclesiam sub Petri regimine sanctificavit et roboravit, eam nunc, Te pastore, Te duce, tuetur, ampliet, ac glorificet. Testis sit votorum quæ nuncupamus, Maria per Te Immaculatæ titulo hoc ipso in loco solemniter aucta ; testes hi sacri cineres quos veneramur Sanctorum Romanæ Ecclesiæ Patronorum Petri et Pauli ; testes venerandæ exuviæ tot Pontificum, Martyrum, ac Confessorum, quæ hanc ipsam, quam premimus terram, sanctam reddunt ; testes tandem præcipue nobis adstent Sancti isti, qui Coelitum Ordini hac ipsa die supremo Tuo judicio adscripti, hodie Ecclesiæ tutelam novo titulo sunt suscepturi, primasque Omnipotenti Deo preces pro Tua quoque incolumitate suis de altaribus oblaturi.

Adstantibus igitur istis omnibus, nos Episcopi, ne illud impietas vel ignorare simulet, vel audeat denegare, errores quos Tu damnasti, damnamus, doctrinas novas et peregrinas, quæ in damnum Ecclesiæ Jesu Christi passim propagantur, detestamur et rejicimus ; sacrilegia, rapinas, immunitatis ecclesiasticæ violationes, aliaque nefanda in Ecclesiam, Petrique Sedem commissa reprobamus, et condemnamus.

Hanc vero protestationem, quam publicis Ecclesiæ tabulis adscribi petimus, Fratrum etiam nostrorum qui absunt nomine, tuto proferimus ; sive eorum qui, tot inter angustias, vi detenti domi hodie silent ac plorant, sive qui gravibus negotiis, aut adversa valetudine impediti, nobiscum hodie adesse nequiverunt. Jungimus insuper nobis fidelem nostrum Clerum ac populum, qui eodem ac nos in Te amore, eadem pia reverentia animati, suum in Te studium, qua precibus sine intermissione fusis, qua opibus in Obolo S. Petri mira, ut plurimum, largitate oblatis lucentissime comprobarunt, probe scientes sacrificiis suis id quoque curari, ut dum necessitatibus Supremi Pastoris consulitur, simul et ejusdem libertati servandæ prospiciatur.

Utinam ad communem hanc totius Orbis christiani, imo omnis socialis ordinis causam in tuto locandam universi populi conspirarent ! Utinam intelligerent erudirenturque Reges et sæculi potestates, causam Pontificis omnium principum regnorumque esse causam, et quo tendant nefarii adversariorum ejus conatus, ac tandem *novissima providerent !*

Utinam resipiscerent infelices illi aliquot ecclesiastici et religiosi viri qui vocationis suæ immemores debitam Ecclesiæ Præsulibus obedientiam denegantes, atque ipsum quoque Ecclesiæ magisterium temere usurpantes, in viam perditionis abierunt !

Hoc a Domino Tecum flentes, Beatissime Pater, enixe atque ex corde exoramus dum ad Tuos sacros pedes provoluti, a Te robur coeleste expetimus, quod Apostolica ac Paterna Benedictio tua valet impertire. Sit hæc copiosa et ex intimis penetralibus Cordis Tui largiter effluens, ut non tantum nos, sed absentes quoque dilectissimos Fratres itemque Fideles nobis commissos irriget ac perfundat. Sit talis quæ nostros et totius Orbis dolores leniat et demulceat, infirmitatem sublevet, operam ac laborem fæcundet, feliciora demum Ecclesiæ Sanctæ Dei tempora acceleret.

Marius, card. MATTEI, évêque d'Ostie et de Velletri.
Constantinus, card. PATRIZI, évêque de Porto et de Sainte-Rufine.
Aloisius, card. AMAT, évêque de Preneste.
Antonius Maria, card. CAGIANO DE AZEVEDO, évêque de Tusculum.
Hieronymus, card. D'ANDREA, évêque de Sabine.
Ludovicus, card. ALTIERI, évêque d'Albano.
Engelbertus, card. STERSEX, archevêque de Malines
Ludovicus-Jacobus-Mauritius, card. de BONALD, archevêque de Lyon.
Fredericus-Joannes-Joseph, card. SCHWARZENBERG, archevêque de Prague.
Dominicus, card. CARAFA DE TRAETTO, archevêque de Benevent.
Xystus, card. RIARO SPORZA, archevêque de Naples.
Jacobus-Maria-Ant.-Cæsar, card. MATHIEU, archevêque de Besançon.
Thomas, card. GOUSSET, archevêque de Rheims.
Nicolaus, card. WISEMAN, archevêque de Westminster.
Franciscus-Augustus, card. DONNET, archevêque de Bordeaux.
Joannes, card. SCYTOWSKI, archevêque de Strigonie (Gran).
Franciscus-Nicolaus-Maddalena, card. MORLOT, archevêque de Paris.
Joseph-Maria, card. MILESI, abbé commend. et ordinaire des Trois-Fontaines.
Michael, card. GARCIA CUESTA, archevêque de Compostelle.
Cajetanus, card. BEDINI, évêque de Viterbe et Toscanella.
Ferdinandus, card. DE LA PUENTE, archevêque de Burgos.
Melchiades FERLIST, patriarche de Constantinople.
Catillus BELGRADO, patriarche d'Antioche.
Joseph TREVISANATO, patriarche de Venise.
Thomas IGLESIAS Y BARCONES, patriarche des Indes occidentales (Espagne).
Antonius HASSOUN, primat de Constantinople, du rite arménien.
Aloisius-Maria CARDELLI, archevêque d'Acrida (en Macédoine *in partibus*).
Stephanus MISSIR, archevêque d'Hiéranopolis, du rite grec (Irenopol, *in partibus*).
Laurentius TRIOCHE, archevêque de Babylone, du rite latin.
Tobias AUN, archevêque de Béryte des Maronites (Beyrouth).
Emmanuel MARONGUI NUREA, archevêque de Cagliari.
Joannes-Joseph-Maria DE JERPHANION archevêque d'Alby.
Joannes-Franc. COMETTI, archevêque de Nicomédie.
Melionus DE JOLLY, archevêque de Sens.
Leo DE PRZYLUSKI, archevêque de Gnesen et Posen.
Alexander AZINARI DE SANMARZANO, archevêque d'Ephèse.
Edoardus HURMUZ, archevêque de Sirac, du rite arménien.
Raphael D'AMROSIO, archevêque de Dyrrachium (Durazzo).
Joseph-Maria DEBELAY, archevêque d'Avignon.
Paulus CULLEN, archevêque de Dublin.
Thomas-Ludovicus CONNOLLY, archevêque d'Halifax.
Joannes-Baptista PURCELL, archevêque de Cincinnati.
Joannes HUGHES, archevêque de New-York.
Renatus-Franciscus REGNIER, archevêque de Cambrai.
Maximilianus DE TARNOCZY, archevêque de Salzbourg.
Antonius LIGI BUSSI, archevêque d'Iconium.

Aloisius CLEMENTI, archevêque de Damas.

Silvester GUEVARA, archevêque de Venezuela.

Joannes ZWYSEN, archevêque d'Utrecht.

Fredericus DE FURSTENBERG, archevêque d'Olmutz.

Paulus BRUNONI, archevêque de Taron (*in partibus*), vicaire apostolique, patriarche pour les Latins à Constantinople.

Athanasius SABUCH, archevêque de Tyr, Melchite.

Andreas BIZZARRI, archevêque de Philippes (*in partibus*).

Franciscus-Xav. APUZZO, archevêque de Sorrente.

Andreas GOLLMAYR, archev. de Goritz et de Gradisca.

Vincentius TIZZANI, archevêque de Nisibe.

Petrus VILLANOVA CASTELLACCI, archevêque de Pétra.

Vincentius SPACCAPIETRA, archevêque de Smyrne.

Michael ALEXANDRIORUM, archevêque de Jérusalem, rite arménien.

Marianus RICCIARDI, archevêque de Reggio (en Calabre).

Salvator NOBILE VITELLESCHI, archevêque de Séleucie.

Alexander FRANCHI, archevêque de Thessalonique (Salonique).

Gregorius SCHERR, archevêque de Munich et Frisingue.

Georgius-Claudius-Ludovicus-Pius CHALANDON, archevêque d'Aix.

Joseph-Dominicus COSTA Y BORRAS, archevêque de Tarragone.

Ludovicus DE LA LASTRA Y CUESTA, archevêque de Valladolid.

Gustavus D'HOHENLOHE, archevêque d'Edesse.

Cajetanus PACE FORNO, archevêque de Rhodes, évêque de Malte.

Philippus GALLO, archevêque de Patras.

Petrus GIANELLI, archevêque de Sardes.

Emmanuel-Gargia GIL, archevêque de Saragosse.

Goffredus BROSSAIS SAINT-MARC, archevêque de Rennes.

Julianus-Florianus DESPREZ, archevêque de Toulouse.

Spiridion MADDALENA, archevêque de Corcyre (Corfou).

Marianus BARRIO Y FERNANDEZ, archevêque de Valence (en Espagne).

Franciscus-Augustus DELAMARRE, archevêque d'Auch.

Carolus DE LA TOUR-D'AUVERGNE, archevêque de Bourges.

MELETIOS, archevêque de Drama, rite grec.

Petrus-Dominicus MAUPAS, archevêque de Zara.

Ignatius GIUSTINIANI, évêque de Scio.

Raphael-Sanctes CASANELLI, évêque d'Ajaccio.

Ludovicus-Carolus FÉRON, évêque de Clermont.

Guillelmus SILLANI, ancien évêque de Terracine.

Nicolaus-Joseph DÉHESSELLE, évêque de Namur.

Ignatius BOURGET, évêque de Marianopolis (Saut-Sainte-Marie).

Jacobus GILDIS, évêque de Lymira (vicaire apostolique à Edimbourg).

Fredericus-Gabriel DE MARGUERYE, évêque d'Autun.

Joseph MONTIERI, évêque de Ponte-Corvo.

Ludovicus DELEBECQUE, évêque de Gand.

Ludovicus BESI, évêque de Canope.

Georgius-Antonius STAHL, évêque de Wurzbourg.

Thomas-Joseph BROWN, évêque de Newport.

Carolus GIGLI, évêque de Tivoli.

Franciscus-Maria VIBERT, évêque de Maurienne.

Joannes Amatus DE VESINS, évêque d'Agen.

Joannes TOPICH, évêque de Philippopoli.

Nicolaus CRISPIGNI, évêque de Mandela (Poggio Mirteto).

Andreas RŒSS, évêque de Strasbourg.

Nicolaus WEISS, évêque de Spire.

Joseph-Armandus GIGNOUX, évêque de Beauvais, Noyon et Senlis.
Joannes-Baptista-Leonardus BERTEAUD, évêque de Tulle.
Joannes-Jacobus-David BARDOU, évêque de Cahors.
Guillelmus ARNOLDI, évêque de Trèves.
Joannes-Franciscus WEHLAND, évêque de la Nouvelle-Orléans.
Paulus-Georgius DUPONT DES LOGES, évêque de Metz.
Joannes-Bernardus FITZ-PATRICK, évêque de Boston.
Joannes MAC-CLOSKEY, évêque d'Albany.
Petrus SEVERINI, évêque de Sappa, en Albanie.
Joannes-Martinus HENNY, évêque de Milwaukie.
Joannes-Baptista ROSANI, évêque d'Ærythrée.
Joannes DONEY, évêque de Montauban.
Petrus-Joseph DE PREUX, évêque de Sion.
Gaspard BAROWKI, évêque de Zytomir.
Carolus MAC-NALLY, évêque de Clogher.
Bernardus-Maria TIRABASSI, évêque de Ferentine.
Urbanus BOGDANOVICH, évêque de Europo *(in partibus)*.
Jacobus-Maria-Joseph BAILLES, ancien évêque de Luçon.
Joannes-Baptista PELLEI, évêque d'Acquapendente.
Stephanus MARILLEY, évêque de Lausanne et Genève.
Theodorus-Augustinus FORCADE, évêque de Nevers.
Ludovicus-Antonius-August. PAVY, évêque d'Alger.
Antonius-Martinus SLOMSCHEK, évêque de Lavant.
Guillelmus-Bernardus ULLATHORNE, évêque de Birmingham.
Aloisius RICCI, évêque de Segni.
Joseph-August.-Victor DE MORLHON, évêque du Puy.
Joannes TIMON, évêque de Buffalo.
Amadeus RAPPE, évêque de Cleveland
Guillelmus KEANE, évêque de Cloyne. .
Joseph-Maria-Benedictus SERRA, évêque de Daulo.
Paulus DODMASSEI, évêque d'Alexia (Alessio, en Albanie).
Angelus PARSI, évêque de Nicopoli.
Joannes-Georgius MULLER, évêque de Munster.
Camilius BISLETI, évêque de Corneto et de Civita-Vecchia.
Joannes-Thomas MULLOCK, évêque de Saint-Jean de Terre-Neuve.
Dominicus CANUBIO Y ALBERTO, évêque de Segorbe.
Joannes-Antonius BALMA, évêque de Ptolémaide (Sainte-Jean d'Acre), *in partibus.*
Aloisius KOBES, évêque de Metone, *in partibus*, vicaire apostolique d e la Guinée.
Julianus-Maria MEIRIEU, évêque de Digne.
Joannes-Anton.-Maria FOULQUIER, évêque de Mende.
Franciscus KELLY, évêque de Titopoli.
Antonius-Felix DUPANLOUP, évêque d'Orléans.
Joannes-Antonius BAUDRI, évêque d'Aréthuse, *in partibus*, suffragant de l'archeveque de Cologne.
Joannes RANOLDER, évêque de Vestprim (Hongrie).
Petrus-Simon-Ludov. DE DREUX-BREZE, évêque de Moulins.
Joseph ARACHIAL, évêque de Trébizonde, rite arménien.
Franciscus PETAGNA, évêque de Castellamare.
Guillelmus DE KETTELER, évêque de Mayence.
Antonius-Carolus COUSSEAU, évêque d'Angoulême.
Clemens MUNGUIA, évêque de Mechoacan.
Carolus-Franciscus BAILLARGEON, évêque de Thoa, *in partibus.*

Guillelmus TURNER, évêque de Salford
Mathias-Augustinus MENCACCI, évêque de Civita-Castellana.
Joannes-Petrus MABILE, évêque de Versailles.
Thomas GRANT, évêque de Southwark.
Caietanus BRINCIOTTI, évêque de Bagnorea.
Joannes-Bapt.-Paulus Maria LYONNET, évêque de Valence (en France).
Ignatius FEIRGELLE, évêque de Saint-Hippolyte (Saint-Pœlten).
Ludovicus RAYNALD, évêque de Transylvanie.
Joannes-Jacobus-Antonius GUERRIN, évêque de Langres.
Ludovicus-Eugénius REGNAULT, évêque de Chartres.
Joseph LAVOCQUE, évêque de Saint-Hyacinthe.
Joseph CARDONI, évêque de Carista.
Gesualdus VITALI, évêque d'Agathopolis, *in partibus*, suffragant de Velletri.
Laurentius BLANCHERI, évêque de Legione, *in partibus*.
Aloisius FILIPPI, évêque d'Aquila.
Joseph-Maria GINOULHIAC, évêque de Grenoble.
Franciscus-Joseph RUDIGER, évêque de Linz.
Joseph CAIHAL Y ESTRADE, évêque d'Urgel.
Joannes KILDUFF, évêque d'Ardagh.
Joannes LOUGHLIN, évêque de Brooklyn.
Joannes-Franciscus a Paula VEREA, évêque de Linarès (Mexique).
Jacobus ROOSEVELL-BAYLEY, évêque de Newark.
Petrus ESPINOSA, évêque de Guadalaxara.
Aloisius CIURCIA, évêque de Scodra (Scutari).
Ottocarus DE ATTEMS, évêque de Seckau.
Nicolaus BEDINI, évêque de Terracine.
Ludovicus-Maria-Joseph CAVEROT, évêque de Saint-Dié.
Hieronymus FERNANDEZ, évêque de Palenica.
David MORIARTY, évêque de Kerry.
Benedictus RICABONA, évêque de Trente.
Olympus-Philip GERDET, évêque de Perpignan.
Aloisius JONA, évêque de Montefiascone.
Petrus BARAJAS, évêque de Saint-Louis du Potosi.
David BACON, évêque de Portland.
Franciscus-Alexander ROULLET DE LA BOUILLERIE, évêque de Carcassonne.
Joannes-Joseph VITEZICA, évêque de Veglietz.
Cajetanus RODILOSSI, évêque d'Alatri.
Nicalaus-Renatus SERGENT, évêque de Quimper.
Pelagius-Antonius LAVASTIDA, évêque de Tlascala.
Guillelmus VAUGHAN, évêque de Plymouth.
Laurentius SIGNANA, évêque de Sutri et Népi.
Nicolaus PACE, évêque d'Améla.
Claudius-Henricus PLANTIER, evêque de Nimes.
Jacobus DUGGAN, évêque de Chicago.
Clemens SMITH, évêque de Dubuque.
Andreas CASASOLA, évêque de Concordia (Etats vénitiens).
Antonius-Joseph JORDANT, évêque de Fréjus et Toulon.
Laurentius GILLOOLY, évêque d'Elphin.
Daniel MAC-GETTIGAN, évêque de Raphoe.
Joannes DOLTON, évêque de Port-Grace (Harbour-Grace, Terre-Neuve).
Joannes FARRELL, évêque d'Hamilton.
Stephanus SEMERIA, évêque d'Olympe *in partibus*, vicaire apostolique
    de Jafnapatam.
Carolus-Nicolaus DIDIOT, évêque de Bayeux.

Conradus MARTIN, évêque de Paderborn.
Joannes-Honoratus BARA, évêque de Châlons.
Joseph WIBER, évêque de Halia, *in partibus*, suffragant de l'archevêché de Strigonie (Gran).
Laurentius BERGERETTI, évêque de Santorin.
Michael MARSZWLKI, évêque de Wladislav.
Vincentius GASSER, évêque de Brixen (Bressano).
Franciscus MARINELLI, évêque de Porphyre.
Fortunatus MAURIZI, évêque de Veroli.
Fredericus-Jacobus WOOD, évêque de Philadelphie.
Joannes MAC-EVILEY, évêque de Galway.
Thomas FURLONG, évêque de Fernes.
Guilelmus-Joseph CLIFFORD, évêque de Clifton.
Petrus-Hendricus GERAUD DE LANGALERIE, évêque de Belley.
Ludovicus DELCUSY évêque de Viviers.
Joannes SIMOR, évêque de Giavarino.
Joannes-Bapt. SCANDEDLA, évêque d'Antinoé, vicaire apostolique de Gibraltar.
Paulus MELCHERS, évêque d'Osnabruck.
Petrus-Antonius DE POMPIGNAC, évêque de Saint-Flour.
Anastasius-Rodrigus YUNTO, évêque de Salamanque.
Joannes Ignatius MORENO, évêque d'Oviedo.
Antonius DOMINGUEZ Y VALDECAGNAS, évêque de Cadix.
Michael O'HEA, évêque de Ross.
Bernardus GONDE Y GORRAL, évêque de Plasencia.
Franciscus a Paula BENAVIDES, évêque de Siguenza.
Fernandinus BLANCO, évêque d'Avila.
Joannes-Joseph CASTANER Y RIVAS, évêque de Vich.
Cosmas MARRODAN Y RUBIO, évêque de Tarragone.
Mathæus JAUME Y GARUN, évêque de Minorque.
Petrus-Lucas ASSENSIO évêque de Jaca.
Joseph-Maria PAPARDO, évêque de Sinope.
Clemens PAGLIARI, évêque d'Anagni.
Franciscus MAC-FARLAND, évêque d'Hartford.
Franciscus LACROIX, évêque de Bayonne.
Ignatius SENESTRY, évêque de Ratisbonne.
Joannes-Sebast. DEVOUCOUX évêque d'Evreux.
Edoardus HORAN, évêque de Kingston.
Franciscus-Kerril AMHERST, évêque de Northampton.
Paschalus VUIHIC, évêque d'Antiphelle, vicaire apostolique en Egypte.
Andreas ROSALES Y MUNOZ, évêque de Jaen.
Michael PAYA Y RICO, évêque de Cuença.
Petrus CUBERO Y LOPEZ DE PADILLA, évêque d'Orihuela.
Joannes-Antonius-Augustus BELAVAL, évêque de Pamiers.
Valentinus WIERY, évêque de Gurk.
Antonius HALAGI, évêque d'Artuin, rite arménien.
Joannes-Joseph LYNK, évêque de Torouto.
Joseph-Lopez CRESPO, évêque de Santander.
Ludovicus-Maria-Oliverius EDIVENT, évêque d'Aire.
Petrus-Jeremias-Michael-Angelus CELESIA, évêque de Patti.
Alexander-Paulus SPOGDIA, évêque de Ripatransone.
Joannes MONETTI, évêque de Cervia.
Petrus MAC-INTYRE, évêque de Charleston.
Michael DOMENEC, évêque de Pittsburg.

Alexander BONNAZ, évêque de Csanad et Temeswar
Darius BUCCIARELLI, évêque de Pulati (Turquie).
Gerardus-Petrus WILMER, évêque d'Harlem.
Georgius BUTLER, évêque de Sidonie, *in partibus.*
Patricius-Franciscus CRUISE, évêque de Marseille.
Joseph-Maria COVARUBIAS, évêque d'Antequera.
Robertus CORNTHWAITE, évêque de Beverley.
Aloisius DI CANOSA, évêque de Vérone.
Laurentius STUDACH, évêque d'Orthosie, vicaire apostolique de Suède et Norvège.
Joseph BERARDI, archevêque élu de Nicée.

Burns and Oates, Ld., Printers, London, W.

THE "CIVIL PRINCIPALITY" UNDER CRITICISM.

" *The Romans will come and take away our place and nation."—*S. JOHN xi. 48.

THE TEMPORAL SOVEREIGNTY OF CHRIST AND THE ASSOCIATION THEREIN OF THE CHIEF APOSTLE.

SUCH has been the influence of men like him who signed himself Febronius, and of the writers of the Gallican school that even at the present day our ideas are confused in reference to the sanctity of the Pontiff's rights. Among the many Scripture evidences showing the Civil Principality of the Popes to be an inheritance of the Incarnation, none was more clear than the declaration of Christ under the circumstances in which He spoke : "My kingdom is not of this world." With equal truth may the present Pontiff, heir to the full authority of Christ, repeat the self-same declaration. But in neither case does it derogate in the least from the reality of the temporal kingdom of Christ and of the Roman Church, heiress of the synagogue and of the kingdom of Israel and Mother and Mistress of the Christian Churches and kingdoms of the world. You cannot take up an old French book on Canon Law, but you meet with this solemn text, twisted from the natural meaning, to insinuate that the Popes have no temporal power direct or indirect among the nations of the world. And at the present day, to suit the convenience of those who would upset the spiritual sovereignty of the Pontiff, it is applied indeed in reference to the Civil Principality, but in the hope of destroying it for ever.

Let me remind my readers that one of the charges brought against the King of the Jews was that He said :

"I am the King of the Jews," whereas he was not. Let me remind them that Pilate would not admit this charge, but gave it against the Jews, making them regicides. We have therefore no alternative but to follow the doctrine of the carnal Jews, who declared Christ to be no temporal King or to be guided by the inspiration of Pilate, who upheld that prophetic title. For my part I subscribe myself a disciple of Pilate and of the Apostles who inquired : "When wilt thou restore the kingdom to Israel?" and bowing to the inscription on the Cross and acknowledging that temporal sovereignty belongs essentially to His Sacred Humanity, I exclaim with more than ordinary loyalty : "Hail, King of the Jews!" And may the time come, when in imitation of the dedication of the Holy House, I may see inscribed on some new church those pregnant words : "To Jesus of Nazareth, the King of the Jews."

In the beginning of this year (1891) I was invited by one of the Bishops to submit my doctrine to a Roman theologian. I did so. The theologian I selected is a celebrated Canonist.* He kindly forwarded one of his works and wrote a letter giving his views on the subject from the "public ecclesiastical law." He wound up by saying : "Mihi videtur substantia tuæ demonstrationis cum his convenire, si spiritum potius quam litteram attendamus." He also said : "Non est facile invenire doctorem, qui privata auctoritate suscipere vellet examen operis tui. Insuper ejus judicium, eo quod privatum, minoris esset utilitatis." I was then referred to some Fathers of the Society of Jesus in England, and the result was an unfavourable criticism. The first part of my reply to that criticism was published in the *Tablet* of the 11th and 18th April, 1891, under the heading, "The Foundation of the Civil Principality and the Witness of Sacred Writ." It is as follows :—

Sir,—Last year you were good enough to give insertion to correspondence bearing upon the above subject. Having been

* Mgr. Cavagnis.

favoured in February last with some points of adverse criticism,* I think you will allow that it is useful that they should see the light of day together with such reply as I am able to give.

The criticism, although one, represents the minds of three theologians. My opponents, unlike the ancient Curiatii, are not to be separated in the conflict. It may be I will devote them to the same doom as those noble and worthy men. The most remarkable point of attack relating to St. Matthew, xvii. 25, is

* 1.—The Author of this work undertakes to prove not only a truth of Divine Revelation, but an organic and essential institution in the Divine conception of the Church.

2.—The proofs are drawn, not from Catholic tradition or existing faith, nor from the Fathers or the Schools, or from authentic definitions or decisions, but immediately from what the Author speaks of as the "obvious sense" of Sacred Scripture, unsupported by any theological reasoning. This is simply to decide a matter of revelation by private judgment.

3.—Ignorance of this revelation from the time of the Apostles to the present day is taken for granted. Therefore all theological reasons are not only omitted, but excluded.

4.—The interpretations of Scripture offered are, moreover, opposed to the common teaching of the Fathers and of the Schools. The conditional covenant made with the Israelitish nation, with its temporal endowments, has been absolutely made void, and the absolute covenant made with Abraham and David has been translated, not to another geographical centre, such as Rome, but to the heavenly Jerusalem, the City of God, the spiritual kingdom of Christ, the rule of which embraces all nations. This is the common teaching, founded on the Catholic interpretation of the Scriptures.

5.—The Author's interpretation of Scripture, in addition to being wholly unwarranted is throughout infected with logical inconsequence and paralogisms. One example will suffice. It does not follow that "in the custom of things" exemption from taxes includes exemption from political control, or even, should it include the latter, that such exemption includes independent political authority over others. The words of Our Lord referred to in this argument (Matthew, xvii. 24) shows the fitness of Peter having an independent kingdom, but they cannot prove his divine right to it as a Divine gift.

6.—The Author argues from the inalienability of the "Patrimony of Peter to its Divine institution." He forgets that this is equally true of the "Patrimony of the Church," which is certainly of human gift. A rule of law says that what has been dedicated (by man's gift) to Divine service can never after be turned to profane uses. Inalienability, therefore, does not prove Divine gift.

7.—The Church has never gone beyond saying that temporal power is necessary (in certain circumstances) to the Church, and that it exists by Divine ordinance and provision. These words have a definite theological and canonical signification, and are contradistinguished from "Divine right" and from "immediate Divine institution." The words of the Holy See must be accepted in their plain meaning, and it should be remembered that they carefully avoid such expressions and such teaching as that used by the Author of this brochure.

in the following words : " It does not follow that, ' in the custom of things,' exemption from taxes includes exemption from political control, or even, should it include the latter, that such exemption includes independent political authority over others. The words of our Lord referred to in this argument (Matth. xvii. 24) show the fitness of Peter having an independent kingdom, but they cannot prove his Divine right to it as a Divine gift."

The first sentence of this criticism may be safely admitted but exemption from political control and independent political authority over others do include exemption from taxes. Hence the declaration and vindication of the right of exemption from taxes may or may not include exemption from political control and independent political authority over others. And in St. Matthew, xvii., we have to deal with a declaration and vindication of exemption from taxes. In other words, if a subject vindicates his right of exemption from taxes, he vindicates it as a subject, without claiming exemption from political control, etc. He vindicates his right on the ground of privilege, in view of services rendered, not therefore as an inherent right, but as suitable under certain circumstances and dependent on the will of the sovereign. For whosoever rightly claims exemption from taxes claims it in the measure of his right. But if a sovereign nave occasion to vindicate his right of exemption from taxes, he vindicates it unconditionally. The question then is : Does the vindication of exemption from taxes miraculously wrought by Christ, as recorded by St. Matthew, include exemption from political control and independent political authority over others ? Was such vindication a sovereign act ?

My first answer to this question is as follows : When a vindication of the right of exemption from taxes necessarily implies the exercise of sovereign power in the temporal order, then such a vindication includes both exemption from political power and independent political authority over others. Now such is the vindication recorded in St. Matthew, xvii. The law of Moses exempted only the Jewish Pontiffs from tithes and taxes. No Jewish subject could therefore claim exemption from taxes due to the Temple. If Christ had been a Jewish subject during His public ministry He could not have vindicated His human exemption by miraculously paying the tax as God. We must, therefore, conclude that He was not Jewish subject. If not subject, it was either, first, because He held the temporal power inherited from His royal ancestry, or, secondly, because He held some spiritual title to exemption. If the former, then in vindicating His sovereign title, He exercised sovereign power in the temporal order, etc. If He were not King in succession to David, but held and vindicated some spiritual title to exemption from taxes, then it follows that one "sprung out of Juda," "of which no one gave attendance at the altar," "in which tribe Moses spoke nothing concerning priests," actually declared and vindicated an exemption which was a tribal and family right not His own. We cannot admit in Christ a violation of the still existent law of Moses. Wherefore we must conclude that in the vindication recorded in St. Matthew, xvii., is included not merely a translation of the Aaronic privilege to one of the Royal tribe, but in very truth a translation of the legislative power of Moses to Christ—"translato enim sacerdotio, necesse est ut et legis translatio fiat." The determining of the respective tribal rights of Levi and Juda required the exercise of political as well as spiritual power on the part of Moses. And the abolishing by Christ of such tribal rights implied the exercise of political as well as spiritual power. The old law was only abrogated by Christ at His death, but before that abrogation Christ had succeeded to the legislative power of Moses, and gave proof of it by vindicating a right of exemption from taxes, which implied a translation of all the power of the law and the priesthood to Himself.

So in whatever way we choose to understand the vindication of exemption in Christ, we cannot refuse Him therein the exercise of sovereign power in the temporal order. Hence the vindication miraculously wrought by Christ of His exemption as man and of His chief Apostle's exemption from taxes, not being the act of a subject, but a sovereign act, such vindication includes both "exemption from political control" and "independent political authority over others."

In your last issue conceding the point that exemption from taxes does not include political supremacy, I set myself to consider the question: "Does the vindication of exemption from taxes by Christ," recorded by St. Matthew (ch. xvii.), include "exemption from political control" and "independent political authority over others?" And, seeing that under the Mosaic Law such vindication necessarily involved political supremacy, I answered the question affirmatively. The same question may be answered in another way, as follows: When a declaration and vindication of exemption from taxes is undertaken by one, who is otherwise known to possess supreme power in the spiritual and temporal orders, such declaration and vindication of exemption relate not to any inferior title, but to the supreme human title of him who vindicates such exemption, and hence such vindication includes, not only " exemption from political control," but " independent political authority over others." And such is the declaration and vindication recorded by St. Matthew. This argument, like the previous one, was condensed elsewhere, when it was shown that Christ's political authority was a social necessity, since to abolish or fulfil the Mosaic Law, which was vested in both spiritual and temporal powers, both spiritual and temporal powers were pre-required. The vindication of exemption by one holding such powers was a sovereign act, in which the Chief Apostle was materially and formally associated.

My opponents speak of the " custom of things." It was one thing under the old Law, and is quite another under the new, as we have seen. In the same way the circumstances under which Christ exercised His public ministry must not be confounded with the circumstances of the Christian Church. The Christian Church can exercise the functions of her divine ministry among the nations of the world without their consent, because the temporal power of the nations is subordinate to the divine right of the Church. In Israel, where the temporal power was co-extensive with the Church and co-equal in divine right, no spiritual power could be exercised that was not in agreement with the whole Law. Any attempt on the part of a Jewish subject to effect a change in the Law of Moses, even in spiritual things, would have been a violation of the Law, not merely in its spiritual enactments, but in its integrity. To lay the foundations of a new society by selecting fresh depositaries of power, to preach a higher doctrine, to institute a new sacrifice and new rites, would have been in a Jewish subject a violation of the Law, and most justly would the lawyers have inquired, " By what authority dost thou these things, and who hath given thee this authority?" (Matthew, xxi.). The reason why this question was out of place is that Christ was not a Jewish subject, but the heir of the whole authority of Moses. The work of His public ministry, although apparently so spiritual, required political supremacy. For Christ during three years was laying the foundation for the translation of the Priesthood to the new order, and we know that the translation of the Priesthood involved the translation of the Law. The authority that Christ held and exercised was, in one word, the authority of the heir of the theocracy.

It would be a very poor objection to say that because Christ had not recourse to violence, or did not command the armed men of the nation, or was not recognised by those who did, that therefore He could not hold or exercise political supremacy. The work that Christ as man began and consummated required equal legislative power with that of Moses, and therefore equal political supremacy ; for it was the taking over of the whole power delegated to Moses in order to translate to a new order of men the Law and the Priesthood. The vindication of exemption from taxes being undertaken by one holding and exercising full supremacy over the Law and Priesthood of the Church-nation could not be otherwise than a sovereign act, in which the Chief Apostle representing the Roman Pontiff was materially and formally associated. Such vindication includes therefore " exemption from political control " and " independent political authority over others." It will be seen that the reasoning in both arguments applies whether the coin of the tribute were *profanum* or *sacrum*.

The Pontifical Acts of Pius IX.

AND

The Declaration of the Bishops in 1862.

The ground is now shifted, and in the following points of criticism the same opponents address themselves to my interpretation of the Pontifical Acts of Pius IX. and of the Declaration of the Bishops in 1862.

They say : " The Church has never gone beyond saying that temporal power is necessary (in certain circumstances) to the Church, and that it exists by Divine ordinance and provision." These words have a definite theological and canonical signification and are contradistinguished from " Divine Right " and from " immediate Divine institution."

My opponents will pardon me if I assert that " the Church *has* gone beyond saying that it (temporal power) exists by Divine ordinance and provision." The language both of the Pope and of the Bishops in reply characterises not merely the existence of the Civil Principality, but its origin. And the character impressed is not one of every-day Divine ordinance or provision. The Pope teaches that " the Roman Pontiff obtained the

Civil Principality by a singular counsel of Divine Providence." The Bishops declare that "we are all, therefore, bound to hold as most certain that such temporal rule was not added to the Holy See by the effect of hazard, but was granted to it by a special Divine dispensation." I am ashamed to have occasion to quote these words again. Surely they differ widely in meaning from mere existence by Divine ordinance and provision. The Premiership of New South Wales exists by Divine ordinance and provision, and so does the Mayoralty of Colchester and the Princedom of Monaco. But no " singular counsel of Divine providence" nor "special Divine dispensation" ever presided over their origin or destiny.

My opponents say: "The author argues from the inalienability of the 'patrimony of Peter to its Divine institution.' He forgets that this is equally true of the ' Patrimony of the Church,' which is certainly of human gift. A rule of law says that what has been dedicated (by man's gift) to Divine service, can never after be turned to profane uses. Inalienability, therefore, does not prove Divine gift."

Here is a comparison established by my critics between the Patrimony of St. Peter and the Patrimony of the Church. I will let it pass, as though it were correct, for the sake of argument. It would still remain that the Civil Principality is the only patrimony belonging to the Church which is contradistinguished from others by such language of the Ecclesia docens.

The Church lands and Church property of St. Sophia of Constantinople, or of York Minster, or of Notre Dame de Paris were not granted nor obtained by "a singular counsel of Divine Providence" or "a special Divine dispensation." There inalienability, therefore, cannot raise them to the dignity of the Civil Principality nor bring the latter down to their human level.

I may further remark that of the Civil Principality I used the expression, "absolutely inalienable," by which I meant even by dispensation of the Church or by forfeiture through the extinction of the Faith within the nation. It cannot be said that ordinary Church property is absolutely inalienable, otherwise St. Charles and a host of others could not have made over to the poor the Church plate and sacred vessels ; nor could the churches and cathedrals of a whole nation like England have become forfeited through the extinction of the Faith. That they are so forfeited is clear from the " Declaration of the Bishops, the Vicars Apostolic in Great Britain." In Section IX., " On the Claim of British Catholics to the Property of the Church Establishment in England," we read as follows :— " British Catholics are charged with entertaining a pretended right to the property of the Established Church in England. We consider such a charge to be totally without foundation. We declare that we entertain no pretention to such claim. We regard all the revenues and temporalities of the Church Establishment as the property of those on whom they are settled by the laws of the land. We disclaim any right, title, or pretention with regard to the same."

The inalienability of the Civil Principality is intimately connected with the infallibility of the Pope, which guarantees the Roman Church against a national extinction of the Faith. But this, by the way.

The comparison, however, is inexact. The Patrimony of St. Peter is not a mere " Dominium " like any other patrimony of the Church. It is also a " jurisdictio " and a " jurisdictio suprema."

And it is of such jurisdiction or temporal sovereignty that the late Pope and the Bishops gathered around him in 1862 spoke in such exceptional terms. The contradistinction established by the teaching of the Church on that occasion is not merely between the Patrimony of St. Peter and any other patrimony of the Church, but between the Civil Principality of the Vicar of Christ and other kingdoms, which are of this world. Of no temporal kingdom, except that of Israel and that of the Papacy, can it be said that its rulers "obtained it by a singular counsel of Divine Providence." Nor can it be said of any other nation, except Israel and the States of the Roman Church, that "we are all, therefore, bound to hold as most certain that such temporal rule was not added to it by the effect of hazard, but was granted to it by a special Divine dispensation."

It is true that I argued, as a separate proposition, from the absolute inalienability of the Patrimony of St. Peter to its Divine institution. If you hold that unlike other kingdoms, governed by natural laws, the Civil Principality cannot be absorbed into a larger kingdom ; if you maintain that from a monarchy it cannot be merged into a republic ; if you insist that temporal sovereignty is no adventitious right of the Roman Pontiffs : that unlike other Princes, it is beyond their power to abdicate : that their dynasty as temporal rulers must, and is entitled to go on, whereas all other forms of government are changing, or liable to change—can I, in my sober senses, still believe that the Civil Principality is subject only to the natural laws which govern the kingdoms of this world ? On the other hand, who will deny that Catholics do believe in the absolute inalienability of the Civil Principality ?

My reasoning may be summed up as follows :— Absolute inalienability characterises no kingdom of this world—that is, deriving its origin from natural laws ; but absolute inalienability characterises the Civil Principality ; therefore the Civil Principality is a kingdom not merely of this world—that is, a kingdom deriving its origin not from natural laws, but from Divine institution.

Here a most important although delicate distinction has to be kept in view. I do not say that the Divine institution of the Civil Principality is sufficient to establish it in this world. The co-operation of human Law is essential to that end. Hence my meaning when referring to the circumstances under which Christ uttered those words : " My kingdom is not of this world," which the present Pontiff might utter with equal truth. Let the human Law once more harmonise with the Divine, and the Pope could say no longer : "*Now* my kingdom is not from hence."

The Civil Principality, therefore, is a kingdom not of this world (1) primarily and originally, in the sense that it is the Divine gift of territorial sovereignty bestowed upon the Sacred Humanity of Christ and promised to His ancestors, the Patriarchs. (2) It is a kingdom not of this world accidentally, for want of the co-operation of the human Law ; and (3) it is a kingdom of this world secondarily and ordinarily, because " the singular counsel of Divine Providence " which hath presided over it from the beginning will not allow a Divine inheritance to be long disputed by the will of man.

But we are not left to infer a Divine origin and destiny for the Civil Principality from a practical belief in its absolute inalienability. The teaching of the late Pope, together with the declaration of the Bishops, proclaims a higher than human or natural origin for the Patrimony of St. Peter, and therefore a supernatural or Divine origin, which is the foundation of its absolute in-alienability. The words quoted by my opponents may be contradistinguished from Divine right, etc., not those of the late Pope and of the declaration of the Bishops in 1862.

Before proceeding further with the discussion of the Pontifical Acts of Pius IX. and of the " Declaration of the Bishops," it occurs to me here to meet a severe point of criticism from my opponents. Of my recourse to the Holy Scriptures, which they declare to be un-supported by any kind of authority, they say : " This is simply to decide a matter of revelation by private judgment."

Now the facts of the case are otherwise than they suppose. For years before reading anything concerning the temporal power of the Pope in Holy Scripture, I had in my mind the words of the late Pope and the " Declaration of the Bishops." Whether or no I interpret those authentic documents rightly, is not to the point. What is certain is that a definite meaning, which I had not seen before, became attached, in my mind, to certain passages of Holy Writ in consequence of my reading of such documents. And that meaning became too strong to withhold. Provided then I have not misunderstood the teaching of the late Pope and of the " Declaration of the Bishops " in 1862, I claim that my reading of Holy Scripture is a true development of Christian doctrine. In any case, I have not sought to decide a matter of revelation by private judgment.

It is urged against me that " my proofs are drawn, not from Catholic tradition or existing Faith ; " and under another head of criticism, that ignorance of this revelation (concerning the Civil Principality) from the time of the Apostles to the present day is taken for granted.

Now that which is taken for granted is not ignorance, but implicit Faith : an implicit Faith which underlies the greatest fact of history. I mean the constant, luminous and central fact of the territorial independence of the Popes. If my three opponents explain that fact without recourse to the implicit Faith of the ecclesia docens and the ecclesia docta, I will consent to go over to Alba. The mere human or political power of the Papacy cannot account for it. It is founded on the obedience of faith. It may be objected, no doubt, that it was the faith of Princes and people in the Divine right of the Popes to absolute independence of all civil jurisdiction, which, under the Divine protection, secured and maintained their territorial independence. Very good, but that faith in the Divine right of the Papacy could not, humanly speaking, be acted upon, without the recognition of the Civil Principality. Territorial independence became the embodiment of the faith of the Church in the Divine independence of the Supreme Pastor. Now what is this, but practical faith in the Civil Principality as of Divine appointment? And is not practical faith at least an implicit faith? And let it not be supposed that such practical faith was a mere theological deduction without a specific object. According to the teaching of the Church during the late Pontificate, the origin and existence of the Civil Principality must be ascribed to "a singular counsel of Divine Providence" and to "a special Divine dispensation." But such "singular counsel of Divine Providence" and "special Divine dispensation" is not a modern event. The Civil Principality was thus characterised from the beginning. Therefore from the beginning the Civil Principality was a point of Catholic doctrine, which was duly acknowledged by the implicit faith of Christians, which also explains its preternatural vitality.

I come now to another objection: " The interpretations of Scripture offered are opposed to the common teaching of the Fathers and of the Schools." It would have been interesting, had I intended writing a book, to attempt the analysis in detail of the teaching of the Fathers bearing upon the subject of the Civil Principality. But my critics have abstained altogether from quoting any Scripture to show my opposition to the Fathers. They have quoted my interpretation of St. Matthew (ch. xvii.) as a sample of logical inconsequence. I don't think they have been fortunate in that. I have proved that the vindication of independence by Christ was a sovereign act, wherein St. Peter had an equal share. I had previously made clear that Christ, who, as man, could only be subject or Prince within His own country, unless we detract somewhat from His Sacred Humanity, had a ministry to exercise, which was incompatible with the position of a subject. The mere fact of His being Supreme Legislator in a Church, which was also a nation, would entitle Him to political supremacy, let alone His succession to David. The passage in St. Matthew, giving, as it does, the clearest evidence of the association of St. Peter in the twofold sovereignty of Christ over the Church and kingdom of Israel is fundamental, and my reading of it directly traceable to the teaching of the Church in the Pontifical Acts of Pius IX. and in the " Declaration of the Bishops " in 1862. My opponents, no doubt, felt that if this position could be got at, others would more easily give way.

To the general charge that my interpretations are in opposition to the Fathers I will oppose the following considerations :—

1. Of theologians distinctly holding that the temporal sovereignty of the Popes is not of Divine right a certain number is to be met with in modern times. But they cannot be said to constitute a chain of theological testimony and still less a venerable tradition.

2. A chain of powerful evidence will be found reaching through the ages that by Divine institution the Christian Church is a spiritual kingdom. This unanimous testimony of the Fathers is in refutation of the corrupted tradition of the carnal Jews, who misinterpreting their prophets expected an universal empire of the Messias, of which Jerusalem should have been the political centre.

Now here it is important to make a distinction between two kingdoms described in Holy Scripture as of Divine institution. One is universal, and the other is circumscribed. The former is spiritual, and the latter is both spiritual and temporal. And to both kingdoms is pledged an everlasting destiny. The corruption of their tradition by the Jews did not consist in their belief in a temporal kingdom of the Messias, but in mistaking the character of the Messias and assigning Him a temporal instead of a spiritual empire. A proof of this lies in the fact that one of their deadly errors consisted in rejecting Christ as their legitimate King, and charging it against Him, that whereas He was not King, He pretended to that title. The Apostles, on the other hand, who had given occasion to this accusation by saluting or acclaiming their Divine Lord as " King of Israel " and restorer of the " kingdom of David " (St. Mark, xi. 10), were anxious concerning the temporal kingdom, when the moment of His final departure had arrived. " Lord," said they, " wilt Thou at this time restore again the kingdom to Israel ? " This was a legitimate inquiry, unless we go so far as to rank the Apostles at this moment with their carnally-minded contemporaries and suspect them of aspiring to a carnal empire of Christ.

This distinction being made between the spiritual empire throughout the world pledged to the Messias and the ancestral kingdom of Israel equally promised to Him, let us go back to the Fathers. It cannot be denied that, when setting themselves to refute the Jewish pretentions to a political empire of Christ, their language goes far in rejecting the Scripture evidence of a perpetual temporal kingdom assigned to the Church, which succeeds to Israel. The Scripture evidence of the everlasting destiny promised to the kingdom of David and of its inheritance by the Messias was a strong foundation for the Jewish contention. That evidence had to be rebutted in the sense attributed to it by the Jewish doctors. But it would be unfair to the Fathers not to bear in mind the special object they had in view. It was not to deny a temporal kingdom to the Mistress Christian Church, but to show forth the spiritual character of Christ's universal kingdom. To apply their language to the Civil Principality, which was never in question until this nineteenth century, would prove much more than that it is not of Divine institution. It would be an argument for its unfitness.

Whilst treating of the doctrine of the Pontifical Acts of Pius IX. and of the " Declaration of the Bishops " in 1862, it may not be out of place to give a fuller reply to a question put by way of criticism from another quarter : " How much temporal power " or what extent of territorial jurisdiction is required ? It is clear, that if the temporal sovereignty of the Popes be of Divine right, it is a determinable quantity. If the States of the Church are indeterminable by any theological reason, the temporal sovereignty of the Roman Pontiffs cannot be of Divine institution. This was a searching criticism, which I had not foreseen. Yet, if the doctrine which I advance be Catholic doctrine, it should stand this test. Now in addition to this speculative question, there are the facts of history. The Popes have enjoyed the sovereignty of various Patrimonies unequal in extent.

In reply to these difficulties, let me remind my readers that the temporal Princedom of the Roman Pontiffs has depended upon two immediate causes—(1) the claim to temporal sovereignty put forth by the Pontiffs and (2) the implicit faith of Princes and people in that sacred right. But underlying both the Pontifical claims and the assent of the Faithful, there was a specific doctrinal truth : the reality of the Civil Principality as proclaimed by the Pontifical Acts of Pius IX. and the " Declaration of the Bishops " in 1862. If so, that point of doctrine was susceptible of a clearer apprehension as time went on. And side by side with the development of doctrine concerning the Pontiff's temporal sovereignty came a readjusting of territorial boundaries. The doctrinal character impressed on the Civil Principality by the late teaching of the Church besides reaching back to its origin has the effect of consecrating its boundaries before recent spoliations. For such teaching of the Pontiff and of the Bishops has reference to the States of the Church as they have been in modern times. It is reasonable, therefore, to conclude, and that on theological grounds, that the Civil Principality had reached its normal development before recent spoliations, and that its territorial extent had been finally determined.

Now, how does my general doctrine square with this conclusion of a determinate Civil Principality? I had proved before being put to the test of territorial measurement, that the temporal sovereignty of the Roman Pontiffs is an inheritance of the Incarnation and of the ancestral right of Christ. The States of the Church should then be equivalent to the territory of ancient Israel. There was no escape from this conclusion. Is it a mere coincidence? They are so, as nearly as one can make out. Not being willing to trust to my own researches nor having the proper books at hand, I wrote to a learned Jesuit. And the following information is extracted from his letter, dated January 29th, 1891 :—

"As to the comparative extent of the Land of promise and the old Papal States, there is some room for difference of view as to the exact boundaries of the former, so that authorities differ ; but the most recent at hand gives the area as about 12,000 square miles, which, I have reason to believe, means geographical miles.— (The volume on Asia in Stanford's *Compendium of Geography and Travel*, by Keane and Temple, p. 83. London, 1886.)

In the *Gazeteer of the World*, issued about the year 1850, by Fullarton, of Edinburgh, without any editor's name, the area of the Papal States is given as 12,120 square geographical miles.

PRACTICAL SCOPE OF SCRIPTURE INTERPRETATION.

WHILST engaged on the last pages my attention has been called to a recent criticism,* the reply to which will help to show the practical object of this writing. The critic, whilst praising and recommending my work, raises a doubt, which indicates that he has not given sufficient thought to the point he discusses. He says : " Even assuming the correctness of the explanation of the words, ' My kingdom is not of this world,' as meaning ' My right to rule on earth is built up neither on the force nor on the suffrage of the world,' it is hard

---

* Reviewer in the *Month* for August, 1891.

to see why the Pope should claim to exercise a dominion which Our Lord possessed indeed, but 'waived.'" It would be fair to retort : " If Christ waived it and won His empire by spiritual dominion, why should not the Holy Father do the same ? " Now, if I have been understood to say that Christ waived His temporal right before that hour when He waived all rights, I have been misunderstood. Let the Pope then yield all his rights, even life itself, when called upon to imitate His Divine Master, but let not his temporal right be singled out for surrender without protest. That Christ kept His political title in the background was in the proper order, and still less to be wondered at when we remember that it was the best known title of the Saviour to the Hebrew world. As for Christ "winning His empire by spiritual dominion" alone, that is a myth. Christ won His empire by sweet and gentle means, but these are not incompatible with political dominion. We should not give Christ the name of Saviour unless He had exercised the powers of a Saviour. Neither would the prophets have given Him the title of King in succession to David unless He had truly exercised political dominion. A fine excuse, too, my critic would invent for wicked Christian kings. I can imagine their rejoicing at the thought that Christ had been a Divine pattern to subjects, but not to temporal rulers. But this would lead too far. Let me respectfully utter a sigh, and ask my critic to read once more what I have said in reference to " Christ's Kingship a Social Necessity," an argument which I have further pointed under the title, " Christ's Temporal Sovereignty and the Association therein of the Chief Apostle." No one, I should say, will be found to assert that political power may not be exercised or vindicated without recourse to armed men and to bloodshed. Such would be a dangerous doctrine and hardly edifying to Christian States and people. Such recourse, in any case, is not wanting to the Royalty of Christ. If Peter was told : " Put up thy sword into the scabbard," it was *his* sword, according to the Master's expression. And he had armed himself for his Divine Master's defence not without a peremptory command. And if when that sword did execution, the Master repaired the evil done, it was not because He exercised not temporal power in Israel, but because He chose at that hour to surrender all rights.

The writer adds : " The fact is that the argument from experience is of far more force in this matter as an argument than that from Scripture. The Pope must have temporal power, because it is necessary to the free exercise of his spiritual power as universal guide and teacher of all the earth." Yet, as is well known, it could not be defined that the temporal power is necessary. This does not speak much for the argument of necessity taken alone. Neither did many of the clergy of Italy in recent times deem that argument very powerful, when they agitated for the renunciation of the temporal power on the part of the Pontiff and brought on themselves the heaviest ecclesiastical penalties. I have shown elsewhere that the argument drawn from the necessity of the temporal power of the Pope does not supply a Divine foundation to the Civil Principality, and that in the absence of a Divine gift or foundation, Catholics will logically and inevitably struggle with their better instincts and drop to the conclusion that the only alternative is a natural or political foundation, with all its vicissitudes and uncertainties. I am aware that by the late authentic declarations of the Church a theological argument has been evolved for the *necessity* of the Civil Principality as well as for its *licitness*, and that both belong to Catholic doctrine. Nevertheless, as shown in Ecclesiastical law, the former could not be raised to the dignity of a dogma, referring, as it does, to the contingent element of historical circumstances, which is not to be sought for in Revelation.

There is, however, a sense in which the Catholic doctrine of the historical necessity of the temporal power has a strong hold on the minds of Catholics. For although the denial by some modern theologians of the Divine institution of the temporal power has been a stumbling block to many, yet it is logical to infer, on account of the historical necessity of the Civil Principality, that God must have made provision for that which is historically necessary. And this is the implicit faith of ages. God will not allow the temporal power of the Papacy to perish like the republic of Venice, or the kingdom of Poland, or the empire of Constantinople. The statue of the kingdoms of the world may crumble, but the "stone cut out of the mountain of Israel without hands," which is the theocracy of the God Incarnate, and which, according to the law of analogy, must also be a temporal kingdom, "itself shall stand for ever."

But if God must have made provision for that which is historically necessary to the Church, it is again logical to seek such provision in Revelation. And if such provision be found, there follows a true development of Christian doctrine.

I am not describing here the process of thought by which I originally felt authorised to say "the Civil Principality is revealed in Holy Scripture," but pointing to an additional authorisation of the recourse to Holy Scripture. I did not go to Scripture in consequence of my reading and interpretation of the late declarations of the Church on the subject of the Civil Principality. It was the reading of those declarations which fixed my reading of Scripture. And the feature of that authentic teaching which struck me is the Divine character impressed upon the Civil Principality, and its differentiation thereby from other kingdoms.

I conclude from Holy Scripture that the Civil Principality is a definable point of Catholic doctrine. My remote object is to further, however unfitly and unworthily that may have been done, the definition of such a point of doctrine by the Church. Such a definition would remove much vagueness and apparent contradiction, and the comparative indifference of some Catholics would give place to alacrity. Then, indeed, one might look to the moral suffrage of the Catholic world to secure and maintain, by international treaty, that which belongs to it and to the Father of Christendom. No doubt in past times wars and political complications have reseated the Pontiff on his temporal throne. History may repeat itself. But I submit that the restoration of his temporal kingdom to the Pope by moral suasion is " a consummation *more* devoutly to be wished."

In what such a definition should consist time will tell. Its object would certainly not be the historical necessity of the temporal power. But we are warranted in believing that the Church may yet deliver the doctrine that the "Civil Principality" is a sacred inheritance of the Incarnation.

I come now to the immediate object of this under-taking. It is to get the question ventilated. It is to seek the help of theologians. The question is important. If it be possible to put forth clearer notions concerning the sanctity of the Pontiff's rights, we should contribute to that end. For clear notions are the foundation of strong convictions. As I have said already, "This is the victory, which overcometh the world, our faith." It is not right, therefore, to pass this question by. I should be put out of court, or failing that, the doctrine here set forth should be more carefully examined. Allusion has been made by some critic to the greater or lesser usefulness of this doctrine in our Protestant country. Are our Protestant brethren the only brethren we have to consult for? Or rather shall we not most intelligently consult their interests, by seeking to be the first in the field to offer reparation to our common Father, who have been his most rebellious children? There is much more to be written on this subject, and much perhaps to be rewritten. I could plead many an excuse for not wishing to write a volume. Perhaps the plea that I have not enjoyed one half-hour's student's life in any English school or college may suffice. The following words of the Archbishop of Edinburgh may be quoted in conclusion of this paper. They express my strong conviction. Speaking of my work, his Grace wrote : " It appears to me to open up a vein of precious ore that well deserves to be worked out ; even more thoroughly than you have done."

Burns and Oates, Ld., Printers, London.

INTRODUCTORY.

To the Laity.

THE original thesis on "the Civil Principality of the Vicar of Christ," which is the substance of a lecture and other addresses delivered in Australia, and whereof this pamphlet is a further development, was submitted, in September, 1889, to Cardinal Manning, before publication. His Eminence spoke in distinctly encouraging terms; declaring, among other things, that the author had taken a higher view of the subject than he himself, and that the thesis should be published. Wishing to have another authority and witness, I asked the then Bishop of Salford to read my work. His letter, which is inserted in the beginning, points to the very foundation of the whole argument. It may be summed up as follows : Christ, "made under the law," was not really subject to the payment of tribute : therefore Christ, as man, was Sovereign.

But whilst a theological contribution to the literature of the Temporal Power of the Pope must necessarily come under the authority of the Church, it need not, therefore, and does not thereby seek to, screen itself from the criticism of intelligent laymen. Even among those who disclaim " Divine guidance" in matters theological, how many may be found whose natural endowments and high attainments do fit them to be at least fair witnesses of that which claims to be Catholic doctrine. The Protestant reader, who rejects the notion of the Sovereign spiritual power granted to the Prince of the Apostles and inherited by the Roman Pontiffs, may have little sympathy with the claim to Temporal Power inherited from the same source. Yet, granting the former for the sake of argument, he may impartially witness and decide whether the latter be not equally founded. The discussion of " the Temporal Power" from the theological standpoint may be less familiar, and perhaps less interesting to the lay mind ; but the claim here set forth on its behalf, that it is the inherited "kingdom of God" or kingdom of the Incarnation scripturally revealed, should hardly fail to arouse some interest among the learned of our Bible-loving Nation.

C. F. P. C.

THE THEOCRACY AND THE LAW OF NATIONAL CADUCITY.

"Let us cast away their yoke from us. He that dwelleth in Heaven shall laugh at them. . . . But I am appointed King by Him over Sion, His holy mountain, preaching His commandment. The Lord hath said to me: Thou art my son, this day have I begotten thee. Ask of Me, and I will give thee the Gentiles for thy inheritance. . . . Thou shalt rule them with a rod of iron, and shalt break them in pieces like a potter's vessel. And now, O ye kings, understand: receive instruction, you that judge the earth."
—PSALM ii.

ENGLAND AND THE THEOCRACY.

AN argument insisting on the instability of human Governments, and contrasting therewith the permanent character of the Papacy, with its twofold power, might suggest the suspicion that the writer may be wanting in patriotic spirit, since he cannot fail to apply the same law of national caducity to his own country.—But is true patriotism encouraged by blinking an important question or ignoring facts? Rather let us take pains to get at the exact appreciation of the value of home and Empire by ascending to the most commanding standpoint. There was a time when, looking over the map of the world, a child dwelt exultingly on the large share which fell to Britannic power, and mused with interest on the prospects of the Empire in every part of the globe. His patriotism needed not to be sustained by any consideration save that such was the inheritance of England. Many a child has had the same thoughts, I suppose. But is it right always to think as a child? Are there not interests, transcending those of time and space, which determine the growth or decline of empires? He Who "taketh away kingdoms and establisheth them" still preserves England as the centre of a mighty empire, in spite of her partial defection from Christ. How long is that Empire destined to last? We may safely reply: Exactly so long as the Empire answers to God's general plan. And the most important feature of that plan we are familiar with, namely, the Church, or God's kingdom on earth. That kingdom is destined to outlive all kingdoms and empires. No well-wisher of home and of the Empire will fail, then, to take note of the presence of Christ's kingdom. Whatever England does in opposition to that kingdom will come to grief. Whatever the Empire accomplishes in subservience to its interests will hold good. May England hold firmly to the Christian institutions she still retains from olden time, and which are so essential for the creation of new Christian nations over the expanse of the globe. And may her people return to the unity of the Faith, which consists not in adopting Catholic doc-trines and ritual as a pleasant reaction on the gloomy past, but in receiving them, as of old, in the obedience of the Faith from the same hand which planted the kingdom of God in this land. For without the inward and out-ward obedience of the Faith to Christ's Vicar, our people would only throw off the Protestant yoke to be captured by schism.

The return of the English people to honour Christ in His Vicar—an infallible, because divinely appointed, test —will be encouraged by following the traces of St. Peter through the land, who, without travelling personally over this island, has given his name to our principal cathedrals and churches. That return to the common Father of Christendom will be helped by getting at the page of history which discloses the intimate and constant relations of this country with Rome; or, again, by an appeal to the early Fathers, whose testimony conspires to make Rome the Mistress Christian Church of the nations; or, even if we happen to deal with philosophic though believing minds, by an appeal to reason, which demands a centre for the kingdom of God, where all nations may unite, and connects the divine commission, to "teach all nations," with infallible authority to execute that commission.

Yet there is, perhaps, another path to Rome through the Temporal Power; another way of bringing home to our countrymen the spiritual supremacy of the Roman Pontiff, to defend which our martyrs died. That which appears most wanting to our separated brethren is to see that Rome, in spite of all that history unfolds of human weakness as displayed therein, is a true centre of Theocracy, *and the only centre*. The Petrine spiritual privileges should have sufficed, no doubt, for that end. But supposing that the lowest of the privileges of St. Peter and his successors, viz., the Civil Principality, now a distinctly Catholic doctrine, have not been sufficiently traced to Holy Scripture, and in particular to the association of St. Peter in the twofold sovereignty and independence of Christ with respect to Israel, I submit with most dutiful feeling, that we have not yet done all in our power to show our wandering brethren that the Roman Church hath directly succeeded to the Church of Israel; that the divine protection extended of old to the people of God is principally concentrated over the Holy See; that, the original meaning of "the kingdom of God," referring, as it does, to a limited kingdom and to the essential title and terrestrial position of the God-incarnate, all the privileges of the ancient Church, including local autonomy are inherited by the Roman Church; that the Roman Pontiff-Kings, belonging to the order of Christ typified by Melchisedech, are the successors of the Pontiffs and Kings of the old Theocracy; that there has been no break or interruption in the divine government and Theocratic law through the falling away of ancient Israel, and that the translation of the Theocracy to Rome involves the forfeiture of no inheritance, human or divine. Thus, whilst we do full honour to the royalty of Christ, and hence to the sacred humanity, and get at the foundation of the rightful independence of the Roman Pontiffs, we succeed in throwing a fuller light on the close, direct, and complete succession of the Christian Church to the Church of the Synagogue.

THE LAW OF NATIONAL CADUCITY AND THE SOLE EXCEPTION THERETO, FROM CHURCH DOCUMENTS.

ORGANIC life has its periods of health and decline. It is subject, moreover, to obstruction from without and to an untimely end. This is a law of nature. And the phenomena which are observable among creatures of the animal and vegetable kingdoms in the forest or the open plain, in the air or in the depths of the ocean, are observable likewise in the organic life of society under the law of nature.

A temporal kingdom founded on mere human right is subject to decline and fall. History is made up of the record of Civil Governments that have passed away. Those that are chronicled as actually laying claim to continuity with the long past are but a remnant. And if the identity of Civil Governments were tested by the strict continuity of religion, of race, of language, of custom, of political scope, or of anything much beyond the organised supply of the pressing wants of the hour within a temporarily fixed geographical area, scarcely any of them would be acknowledged by the original legislators in each land. The instability of Civil Governments and of human laws, which are their organs, is traceable in great measure to the mutability of men's minds. A common standard of right and of truth is not wanting, but, even when, made manifest by positive revelation, it has failed, through man's perversity, to give a common direction to the human mind and secure stability and peace. Division of the human family, and arbitrary power, with its attendant insecurity, are the result. Might, hardly held in check by the Christian conscience of the world, supplies the place of truth and right—hence no mere human government can be *de jure* everlasting. The weaker tend to more immediate absorption by the greater. And when the fact is accomplished, and time has worn out all traces of bitterness, no one thinks of going back on the past. Such is the law of national caducity : a natural law by virtue of which Civil Governments are prone to decline and fall, accidentally through insecurity from without, but essentially through instability from within.

Without losing sight of these notions, let us now face the Temporal Power of the Pope and the Roman Question Is the Temporal Kingdom of the Papacy founded on mere human right ? Is such an hypothesis compatible with the later theological developments of the question set forth in authentic documents already frequently quoted ?

If the Temporal Kingdom of the Papacy be founded on human right alone, it is like all other Civil Governments, subject to the law of national caducity. Confiscate it, and hold it fast till time has set the seal of legitimacy, if not on your enterprise, at least on your work. That seal has been set on the French Republic. The Republic of Brazil is, no doubt, awaiting it. The German Empire seems to have secured it. And so does Russia and Austria. Who pleads for the kingdom of Poland at the present day ? It is gone, like the Republic of Venice, or the Empire of Constantinople, or the kingdoms of the Heptarchy. And such is, or may be, under the hypothesis, the fate of the Civil Princedom —the conclusion is natural and logical, if we admit the premisses.

Is such a conclusion compatible with the teaching of the Church ? Clearly not. The Civil Sovereignty of the Pope has been authentically pronounced to be a title invulnerable by human agency or lapse of time. It is a doctrinally settled prerogative destined to live as long as the Church. May I, then, at one and the same moment set forth the invulnerable character under all possible circumstances of the Roman Pontiff's civil title, and teach that his Civil Sovereignty is exclusively *jure humano ?* I reply that I may not logically do so. For such teaching would involve contradiction. The following letter to a Catholic paper may help to elucidate my meaning :—

Without trenching upon the ground of actual controversy, I will ask your leave to make some remarks bearing upon it. Although it should, I think, be admitted that a mind which has not gone through the process of theological training for years, is not likely to be equally equipped for treating the *loca theologica*, it need not, therefore, be concluded that such an untrained mind is incapable of giving a sound opinion on the most difficult theological subjects, such as the Temporal Power of the Pope. The Faithful have in all times joyfully signified their assent when the most abstruse points of doctrine have been finally elucidated. Does not this indicate their previous implicit knowledge, which comes of the passive infallibility of the Church-taught?

If, on the other hand, a point of doctrine have not been elucidated up to the requirements of the age—if, for instance, some apparent contradiction hang like a cloud over that point of the horizon which all are endeavouring to explore, can it be a matter of surprise if the most gifted minds should chafe from time to time, suffer misgivings, and give forth at last an uncertain sound? Where does the fault lie in such a case? Surely not with the laity.

From the time of the reduction of the Heptarchy into one kingdom, and before, till the dream of Napoleon III. of the *grandes agglomérations* was realised in Italy, and unfortunately for him in Germany too, the world has learned this great law of nature : that petty kingdoms do not return ; that accomplished facts, when sufficiently established, remain what they are; and that, miracles apart, the universe does not go back on its course. One exception has hitherto held good against this invariable law of nature : the Temporal Princedom of the Papacy. Has not its time come at last? If so, why not meet the inevitable with a good grace and seek, if possible, some manner of compromise?

But no, the Catholic instinct recoils from that which is unholy. The successors of Peter have uttered Catholic doctrine concerning their Temporal Kingdom. The Civil Principality is *relatively necessary* to the Church.

But here comes the real difficulty and the source of perplexity for many a Catholic mind versed or unversed in Church law. Does the Civil Principality, in spite of the authentic Catholic doctrine hitherto promulgated, remain a human thing? Were its conception, birth, and increase the result of mere human activity or natural causation, as in the case of small kingdoms which have faded away? For if so, it is subject to the same natural laws, and may yet disappear for all time. You may adduce the divine right of the Vicar of Christ to absolute independence of all Temporal Sovereignty which all theologians admit; but that divine right is powerless to withdraw the Civil Princedom from the natural conditions of a purely human kingdom *if the Civil Princedom be truly such.*

No doubt, if through some anti-prescriptive law and invarible power of self-recovery the Civil Principality is not subject to the natural conditions and frailty of mundane institutions, it ceases to be a purely human thing.

If not a purely human thing we must give up tracing it to a purely human or natural cause. We must renounce the idea cherished by many modern theologians that the Civil Principality was founded by Pepin or Charlemagne. We may not any better trace its inception to the evacuation of the Holy City by Constantine, nor will it suffice to stop at the first Roman Pontiff. He brought his patrimony to Rome from elsewhere.*

But when I appeal to the theological mind to face this dilemma, I must not be told that the Civil Princedom has ever been subject to the law of caducity; witness, the conquest, persecutions, insurrections, and exiles which have, from time to time, brought to naught the civil rule of the Pontiffs; but that, at the same time, the Civil Princedom is not irretrievably subject to that law, since its invariable restoration by God's Providence is a matter of history. I do not contend that the Civil Princedom is in no sense " of this world," and that it is beyond the reach of violent enterprise; but that it is proof against the permanent consequences of political violence which are fatal to the form or fate of other Civil Governments.

It might be insisted that the Civil Princedom has

---

* This letter was addressed to the *Catholic News* in April, 1892, *à propos* of Mr. Lilly's Birmingham speech on the Temporal Power.

hitherto survived all political disturbances, and is *de jure* entitled to survive them all ; not in virtue of its being an exception to the law of national caducity, but because the Pontifical monarchy is attached to a perpetual dignity : *alligata dignitati perpetuæ*. In this singular case, the Romans and neighbouring peoples having, as a matter of historical fact, voluntarily accepted the Pontifical monarchy, have irrevocably conferred upon it supreme and independent authority, and cannot, therefore, rationally withdraw their consent. In reply to this stricture it must be observed that since legitimate monarchies may lapse—not through lack of legitimate right, but through the fatal result of prescription—the Pontifical monarchy must fall back exclusively on its perpetual dignity, so far as ecclesiastical law is concerned, to retrieve its transcendent right. But what is this, if not an admission, that the Civil Princedom is not founded on human right alone ? The more we study the Pontifical claims to Civil Sovereignty the more do we become impressed with the wide difference between that which is claimed for the head of the Catholic Church and that which is claimed for the Civil Governments of the world. Political wisdom has never attempted anything beyond organising a nation and securing it, as long as possible, from decay and ruin. No human legislator has ever claimed that the Civil Government which he has helped to establish was essential to the world at large or intrinsically entitled to endure for ever. Ambition, no doubt, and sometimes fanaticism, have led men to the conquest and temporary consolidation of empires ; but they depended for success, not on the evidence of a transcendent right, but on the arbitrament of the sword. No Civil Government in Christian or heathen lands has ever put forth a self-sufficient claim for the sake of humanity to outlive conquest and prescription and all the vicissitudes of time. No mere civil ruler could be conscious of such a claim, because such a claim transcends the natural law. To become convinced that such is the claim of the Roman Church, we need only penetrate below the surface of modern authentic documents. The following letter may help to throw some light on the subject :—

The impression left on Catholic minds, after reading Mr. Lilly's rejoinder to Signor Crispi in this month's *New Review*, will no doubt be that the ex-Premier of Italy has been unfairly dealt with; that "the turbidness of thought" ascribed to him in reference to the Pontifical claims applies less to his ideas concerning the nature of those claims than to the difficult task he has set himself of contesting them; and that his objections thereto might have been met by more pertinent argument. Signor Crispi charges the Pope with being a theocrat. Mr. Lilly disproves it by setting the Pope's Civil Sovereignty on a level with other sovereignties. But the Civil Princedom proclaims in unmistakable accents : " We live not on the square with such as these." And the difficulty instinctively felt by Signor Crispi returns as threatening as ever.

Mr. Lilly sets forth the origin of Civil Sovereignty: "What is the origin of Civil Authority or Sovereignty?" Catholic philosophy answers, with St. Paul, that its origin is divine. " There is no power but of God." But in what sense is it divine ? In this : that it is natural. . . . The State, whatever its form (and there is no immutably best form), is not a mere arbitrary device of man, but issues from the nature of things. It is essential to human life, and therefore it is of divine institution. . . . In this sense, and in no other, is Civil Sovereignty of divine origin."

With these words, and with all that Mr. Lilly says concerning the origin of Civil Sovereignty, I am bound to agree. But does the definition (Mr. Lilly offers no other) strictly apply to the Civil Princedom of the Popes ? It would be of no small comfort to Signor Crispi if it did. Certain theological considerations, which no Catholic can afford to lose sight of, and to which I will strictly confine myself here, would lead us at least to doubt it. One of these may be expressed in Mr. Lilly's own words : " The Pope's Civil Princedom . . . is as essential as ever for the peaceful and complete discharge of his œcumenical office." Here the doctrine of the relative necessity of the Civil Princedom is alluded to. This doctrine having been authentically delivered by the Church, is a Catholic and permanent doctrine binding the consciences of the Faithful for all time. Now let us not merely glance at the letter, but seek to get at the inner spirit and full meaning of this point of doctrine.

" Drink deep, or taste not the Pierian spring." Though it may not appear on the surface, this one point of doctrine involves the most complete differentiation in favour of the Civil Princedom among the Civil Governments of the world. It is a living, indestructible, and ever-energising principle, which laughs at conquest, annihilates the power of prescription, and neutralises the virtue of accomplished facts. No time, no circumstances, so long as human events continue to unfold themselves as in the past and this world pursues its course, can affect this doctrine. Catholics throughout the world and throughout all time will shape their conduct in accordance with its meaning. The Papacy, not without divine assistance, will ever seek to embody it in its normal and corresponding fact. Without it, Signor Crispi or other statesmen might hope that the flux of time would help the work of consolidating United Italy, just as larger kingdoms, like England, have been permanently established by the absorption of smaller ones. With it, such must be to every Catholic mind a vain and cruel expectation. The Papacy can never cease to claim a Civil Princedom, and consequently that which according to the dictates of the natural law is requisite for a Civil Princedom, namely, a capital and its adjacent territory. The Church may alienate any other ecclesiastical property, when it either ceases to be necessary to the Church or yields to a higher necessity ; for instance, the wants of the poor. But the Civil Princedom, or territorial embodiment of the Pope's Temporal Sovereignty, is absolutely inalienable either by the Pope or the Church assembled. Such are the inferences to be drawn from the first point of Catholic doctrine.

What, then, is this smallest of kingdoms, which claims exemption from the law of caducity, to which all others are subject? Have other kingdoms defied the law of prescription or legislated to counteract for all time the perishable nature of human institutions? Has any other nation been fenced round by all the power of a law appealing to the faith of millions of men, and avowedly framed to make it outlive the vicissitudes of time? We know of nothing similar in the annals of Christendom. My nation has a claim over me which I am bound by the natural law to acknowledge. But where is the Civil Government, which has proclaimed the necessity of its existence so long as the Church lasts—that is, for all time—and sought to enforce such a claim by an appeal to the conscience of mankind? Men have a truer sense of the proportion of their affairs, and do not claim that which the natural law has never yielded, and is powerless to secure.

Such a claim, sound in its foundation, universal in its appeal, and indestructible in its nature, is the law of the Civil Princedom. If, then, the exceptional law which governs it shapes the Civil Princedom to be everlasting, like the Papacy, may it not possibly have had the same origin as the Papacy? Will it be considered stange if Catholics, disagreeing so far with Mr. Lilly, venture to suspect that since a higher law than the natural is destined to sustain the Civil Princedom for all time, so a higher than the natural law may have presided over its origin?

The previous argument drawn from the necessity of the Civil Princedom does not of itself, I admit, prove a positively divine origin thereto, yet it points to it as most probable. For it shows that the Civil Princedom is not subject to what I have termed the law of caducity in the political world, and, so far, is raised above the natural law and is governed by a higher law taking its rise in the Roman Theocracy. Another condition is required to set the Civil Princedom so completely apart from the law of caducity in human affairs as to warrant the belief that it is included in the divine government and derives its origin therefrom. For the law of caducity being both spiritual and temporal, the Civil Princedom must be both spiritually and temporally inalienable. That it enjoys the latter prerogative has been decided by Church legislation ; that it enjoys the former is a matter of Catholic belief ; the Roman Church can never be infected with heresy. Local churches are liable to perish through the extinction of the Faith just as nations disappear through the loss of their autonomy. Local sees are liable to become vacant through the dispersion or perversion of the flock. And the spiritual alienation of a kingdom from the Church by the national extinction of the Faith is followed by its temporal alienation, as the substance is followed by the shadow. The Holy See and the Roman Church are an exception to the rule. For in that see is the heir to the promises. The Pope will ever retain his spiritual sovereignty in the Roman Church, because as Bishop of Rome he is the successor of St. Peter and cannot be without a local flock. He will retain his Temporal Sovereignty, because the legislation, which has decreed it, transcends the natural law and is neither intended nor likely to be nugatory. Here, then, we have a Church-nation completely raised above the level of spiritual and temporal governments. As far as legislation goes we cannot conceive the Civil Government of the Papacy to be more absolutely inalienable or more removed from the natural law. And our doubts as to its being "in no other sense of divine origin" than the Civil Governments of the world reach that point of intensity when we logically go over to the opposite doctrine. Thus we are forced to the conclusion that the Civil Princedom is in *some* other sense of divine origin than the Civil Governments of the world, because it cannot be said to be natural and because it could not be raised above all other Civil Governments without a superadded divine sanction. That a hostile Italian states-man, better able to appreciate the Pontifical claims as being in close contact with the Roman Church, and most interested to secure all information, should conclude that the Civil Princedom is an integral feature of the Roman Theocracy is not, therefore, to be wondered at.

I now pass from the argument of superadded divine sanction vouchsafed to the Civil Princedom, to show that such sanction is the object of the emphatic teaching of the Church. I allude principally to the Pontifical Acts of Pius IX. relating to this question.* The teaching of the Pontiff in those Acts is quoted and authentically interpreted by the assembled Bishops of the Catholic world in 1862, in the following words of their declaration : " Sed de hac tam gravi causa vix nos decet amplius verba proferre, qui te de ipsa non tam disserentem quam docentem sæpe sæpius audivimus. Vox enim tua, quasi tuba sacerdotalis, toti orbi clangens proclamavit quod 'singulari prorsus divinæ Providentiæ consilio factum sit, ut Romanus Pontifex, quem Christus totius Ecclesiæ suæ Caput centrumque constituit, civilem assequeretur principatum'; ab omnibus igitur nobis esse pro certissimo tenendum non fortuito hoc regimen temporale Sanctæ Sedi accessisse, sed ex speciali divina dispositione illi esse tributum, longave annorum serie, unanimi omnium regnorum et imperiorum consensu, ac pœne miraculo corroboratum et conservatum."

From which we gather the teaching of the late Pope that "the Roman Pontiff obtained the Civil Principality by a particular design," or as another version renders it, " by a particular decree of Divine Providence." I will content myself with appealing to the unbiased mind of the reader, be he a Catholic or a Protestant, to decide whether any Civil Government that history makes mention of, with the sole exception of the ancient theocracy of Israel, can lay claim to an origin so specially divine. But let us hear the Bishops' interpretation of this deliberate utterance. They declare that "we are all, therefore, bound to hold as most certain that such temporal rule was not added

---

* *Lit. Ap.* xxxi. mar., 1860. *Allocutio* xx. jun., 1859. *Encycl.* xix. jun., 1860. *Allocutio* xvii. dec., 1860.

to the Holy See by the effect of hazard, but was granted to it by a special 'Divine dispensation.'" Now what do the Bishops mean by *non fortuito accessisse ?* There is no such thing as fortuitous causes, although the expression is current in the language. Causes, however, are said to be fortuitous in proportion as their effect is unforeseen or not intended They cease to be fortuitous in proportion as their effect is foreseen and particularly intended or controlled. How does this apply ? The Civil Princedom came into shape and being as the Roman Empire broke up into several kingdoms. There is the effect. Did Divine Providence, which controls all events, particularly intend the birth of the Civil Princedom, then the natural causes which determined it were not fortuitous. The dice, if we may without risk compare human things to divine, were loaded ; it was not an ordinary throw. On the other hand, had there been no particular intention on the part of divine Providence in reference to the Civil Princedom, when bringing it into existence along with other kingdoms, then the natural causes which conspired to its formation would have been comparatively fortuitous. In excluding fortuitous causes, the Bishops confirm the Pope's teaching, that although natural causes brought about the temporal rule of the Holy See, they were mere instruments in the hands of Him, Who had a particular design for securing the independence of the central authority of the Universal Church.

Of Civil Governments in general Mr. Lilly says: " The State. . . . issues from the nature of things. It is essential to human life, and therefore it is of divine institution. . . . In this sense, and in no other, is Civil Sovereignty of divine origin." Manifestly, therefore, this definition is inapplicable to the Civil Sovereignty of the Popes, which issued no doubt from the nature of things, but not as other sovereignties. Their origin, although divine, must be ascribed to causes comparatively fortuitous. The Civil Princedom owes its origin to a particular Divine dispensation, which transcends, if only in virtue of its unique character, any sanction granted to other Civil Governments. Far from being on a natural level with ordinary sovereignties, it therefore owes its origin to a superadded divine sanction.

Again, Mr. Lilly says very correctly, I think, " there is no immutably best form " of the State. But this can hardly apply to the Civil Princedom as it does to States in general. If the Romans, forgetting their glorious traditions of service to the Universal Church, and forming a republic, offered to the Pope a presidency of three or four years, or with a more loyal turn of mind legislated for a Septenate, who does not see that claiming a right vindicated by other people in ancient and modern times they would place themselves in absolute antagonism with the Papacy? Why, then, seek to minimise the truth felt by Signor Crispi? It is no service to a man who fumes because the road is blocked, to inform him that it is available for ordinary purposes. It may prove cruel advice, if, forgetting his truer instincts, he resolves to ride through a shadow and dashes against a rock. Better inform Signor Crispi at once that other monarchs may absolutely consent to see their kingdoms absorbed into greater ones or merged into republics with varying terms of office, because history records the facts of such given or wrested consent ; but that the Holy Father cannot stoop to this law of caducity as being bound by a higher one.

Now in all that I have said, I have set myself to prove one thing only : that we may not prudently assume that the Civil Princedom of the Pope is merely *jure divino* in the same sense as other Governments ; and that there are grounds for believing it to be an integral feature of the Roman Theocracy. There remains the argument from Scripture, which I believe to be conclusive, but it is unnecessary for my present purpose. Enough has been said to show that if Signor Crispi's quarrel with the Papacy is attributable only to his wish to secure for Italy what has been legitimately, or at all events successfully, accomplished elsewhere in ancient and modern times, he is entitled to sympathetic usage. For only Italian patriots are confronted with an insuperable difficulty. As for his views on the Roman Theocracy, they might have been more prudently allowed than controverted. It is useless to strain at a word when you have to swallow its meaning.

It is Mr. Lilly's contention that "while Catholics unquestionably regard the Pope's government of the Universal Church as a Theocracy, they as unquestionably do not so regard his Civil Princedom." " Where there is no parity of principle," says De Quincey, " there is no basis for comparison." We are bound as Catholics to regard the Pope's government of the Universal Church as a Theocracy. That is a dogma. We are as free as the air, whether so to regard or not his Civil Princedom. Here the dogma is conspicuous by its absence.*

* The above correspondence, dated June 20th, 1892, appeared in the *Tablet.*

THE THEOLOGICAL DETERMINATION OF THE CIVIL PRINCEDOM.

THE POPE is entitled to a Temporal Kingdom. We are agreed that such is a point of Catholic doctrine ; but venture not on the delimitation of its boundaries, for such precision might result in too great a call on our loyalty. If such be without unfair suspicion the mental attitude of the reader, let him ask himself whether a Civil Sovereignty can be exercised over an unassigned territory ? He will not be slow in perceiving that a negative is the only reply. For a Civil Sovereignty incapable of territorial delimitation would be either *nil* (that is, a contradiction in terms) or the absorption of all the Civil Governments of the globe. We cannot help, therefore, admitting that there exists an assignable territory to the Civil Sovereignty of the Roman Pontiff. Moreover, that territory constituting a kingdom, and not a private property, must have its metropolis or capital with lesser towns and provinces in local subordination. This is an elementary notion which nature suggests. Has such a territory been assigned to the Roman Church, and if so, by what agency ? It is not necessary here to dwell again on the constant historical fact of the Temporal Power, nor to show that its existence and survival are due to the implicit faith of people and rulers, and, more fundamentally still, to its nonfortuitous origin ; nor to point out that as there is in the Church a gradual unfolding of doctrine, so there should be a corresponding adjustment of the Pontiff's territorial right : the important point to consider here is that the Civil Princedom has been theologically determined. The numerous Pontifical Acts, which during the last half-century have authoritatively appealed to the faith and practical conduct of Catholics in reference to the Civil Princedom, do not apply to an unknown territory. The Civil Principality of the Roman Pontiff, a well-known quantity, is the object which those authentic documents have in view. The Church, in other words, lifts her voice to claim a determinate right ; and whatever may be otherwise the issue of her teaching, it concerns not an unknown or squeezable quantity, but a geographically determined territory. In his development of the theological argument from the above-mentioned authentic documents, Cavagnis says : " In reference to the legitimacy of the dominion over this or that town, the judgment of the Church is authoritative and imposes an obligation of acquiescence. As to the legitimacy of Rome in particular, the judgment of the Church bears on a point of such gravity that error could not be allowed by Divine Providence."*

Judging from a recent discussion, there is a tendency in some minds to imagine that the Civil Princedom, considered, as a concrete term, or perhaps rather, to mean the territory only as distinguished from the abstract right, is a shifting quantity, to be bartered away from time to time under the pretext of a Concordat. A correspondent of a Catholic paper having asked to be enlightened on some points bearing on the Temporal Power of the Pope, received the following reply ·---

A correspondent having asked for answers to certain questions on this subject, we think that they may be usefully given in this column.

1. " Is not the Temporal Power necessary for the full and free exercise of the Pope's spiritual authority ? "

Yes. In an Encyclical, dated June 18th, 1859, Pope Pius IX. spoke as follows : " We publicly declare that Civil Principality is necessary to this Holy See, in order that without any impediment it may be able to exercise its sacred power for the benefit of religion."

2. " If yea, and being invested by every lawful title with sovereign dominion and independence, can the Head of the Church, under any circumstances, surrender his right thereto ? "

* Quoad legittimitatem in specie dominii hujus vel illius urbis, judicium ecclesiæ esse auctoritativum ideoque obligationem imponere sese eidem accommodandi ; imo et quoad legittimitatem complexivam et specificam urbis Romœ, hoc judicium est in re tam gravi, ut error a divina Providentia permitti non posset.

With much diffidence we submit that the following answers must be given to this difficult question. Under no circumstancer can the Pontiff surrender his right to some Temporal Power ; but it is in his power, as supreme administrator of the goods of the Church, if he sees fit, to cease to claim the civil dominion over this or that particular territory. It is useful to refer to the case of a Concordat, which seems analogous. By a treaty of this sort, the Pontiff, for reasons recognised by himself as good, agrees to acquiesce in certain arrangements as to the nomination of Bishops and the like, in derogation of the common law of the Church.

3. " Is not the right inalienable and not to be barred by any length of deprivation or persecution ? "

The right is inalienable, except with the concurrence of the Pontiff; and no length of unjust exclusion can deprive him of it. It is, therefore, the duty of every one concerned to do his part to restore him to that which has been unjustly taken from him.*

Imagining that a column was open for the full discussion of so practical a question as that of "the Temporal Power," and being most anxious to secure the help of an able and conscientious writer, I wrote as follows to the editor :—

Sir,—On the 12th of last month some interesting questions were put to you, concerning the Temporal Power of the Pope, to which you replied. It seems to me a pity that the inquiry then begun should have been allowed to drop, for your replies are of such a nature as to invite more questioning. May I be allowed some further interrogations on so important a subject?

1. You say : " Under no circumstances can the Pontiff sur-render his right to *some Temporal Power.*" I will ask, as a first question : Does the law which binds the Roman Pontiff in this respect bind any other earthly ruler, whether Bishop or King ? If not, must we not conclude that *some Temporal Power* of the Papacy is governed by a higher than the natural law which governs other kingdoms? And if that conclusion be rigorous, can any higher law than the natural law be conceived, as governing *some Temporal Power* of the Papacy, except that of the Divine Government? In other words, is not *some Temporal Power* of the Papacy of right divine?

2. You say : "But it is in his (the Pontiff's) power as

° The above reply comes under the several headings of " The Antidote," and " Catholic Controversy," and the " Temporal Power " in the *Catholic News* of May 14th, 189?

supreme administrator of the goods of the Church, if he sees fit,
to cease to claim the civil dominion over this or that particular
territory." And you proceed to allege the analogy of a
Concordat.

Allow me again to inquire whether the Roman Pontiff, who
now retains a portion of the old Papal States, could, if he saw
fit, cease to claim the remainder? In other words, could the
Roman Pontiff was ever fit to cease to claim the Papal States, as
he ceases to claim Avignon or other distant and abandoned
patrimonies?

3. Again, is that which you describe as *some Temporal Power*,
which under no circumstances the Pontiff can surrender, a fixed
quantity, or does it expand or contract with the altered conditions of the political atmosphere? If the former, should it not
be ascertainable as the normal territory of the Papacy? If the
latter, might it not be contracted to the territory covered by
the Vatican Basilica, the Vatican Palace, and the Vatican
Gardens? or even to the spot covered by the Pontifical Throne?

4. If *some Temporal Power* is absolutely inalienable, as you
seem to admit, is the world left in the dark as to what that precisely is? Has the Pontiff no rule by which he may discern
between that which he may cease to claim and that which he
may not?

5. Have not some territories, now forsaken, come into the
possession of the Roman Pontiff by the merest accident or even
by sad misfortune, such as Avignon? May he not surrender
them for ever? And if so, is there any analogy between such
absolute alienation and a Concordat which does not alienate the
Pontiff's right? On the other hand, what can a Concordat have
to do with *some Temporal Power* the right to which the Pontiff
can surrender under no circumstances? Are we not driven,
therefore, to distinguish between the providential principality of
the Vicar of Christ and fortuitous patrimonies?

6. Is not that which you describe as *some Temporal Power*
absolutely inalienable by the Pontiff, the territory which provi-
dentially corresponds with the divine independence and Temporal
Sovereignty of the Popes? And, judging by history and the
natural law, can a Temporal Sovereignty exist without at least
one capital together with its adjacent provinces?

7. Do the authentic documents which have hitherto set
forth the Catholic doctrine relating to the Civil Principality
refer to all the territories the Popes have ever possessed, or only
to the Papal States?

My hope for a fuller discussion of these points by

an able hand was rather abruptly deceived by the following note appended to my letter :—

The answer to these questions must be sought in the authoritative teaching of the Church and not elsewhere. We are not aware that we have any teaching upon the subject that materially goes beyond the declaration which we quoted from Pope Pius IX., that Civil Princedom is necessary to the Holy See. The words do not seem to define anything as to the possibilities that the future may have in store. We only know that God's Providence will be over His Church to the end.

Although one may be thankful that some discussion took place having a useful tendency, it was disappointing not to ascertain whether the writer's views on the analogy of a Concordat had undergone any change.

The Ultimate Guarantee of the Pope's Independence.

A recent Protestant writer* says : " Have not events abundantly proved the worthlessness of territorial independence, when there is not the material strength to maintain it ? . . . The only thing that could make a Parliament thus minded (Revolutionary) leave the restored Papal dominion alone would be the existence of a European treaty ; and if a European treaty is to be the ultimate guarantee of the Pope's independence, it cannot greatly matter whether tne thing guaranteed is the independence or the territory which is to confer the independence."

The writer of these lines might be invited to consider whether there exists in the nature of things a concrete entity or any entity made up of political independence without territorial sovereignty. A European treaty, indeed a treaty more representative still, is very desirable to secure the recognition of the Pope's independence. But the guarantee afforded would be worthless if its object were a mere phantom or a contradiction in terms. He might, secondly, be asked to gauge the

* In the *Spectator*, October 15th, 1892.

ultimate value of a European treaty, either by reference
to history and experience, or by testing the foundation
of international treaties or the stability of the signatory
Powers. All political parties within a given state could
not be bound by such a treaty. Besides, political parties,
like Civil Governments, cannot boast indefinite continuity.
Nous avons changé tout cela is found to be quite
sufficient philosophy to account for the most radical
changes.

Two things from the theological standpoint constitute
the ultimate guarantee of the Pope's independence : (1)
that the necessity of the Civil Princedom is a Catholic
doctrine and appeals to the Faith and practical conduct of
Catholics in Rome and out of Rome, not for a mere span
of years, but for all time ; and (2) that the Faith of
the Roman Church as well as of the Church at large is
secured by Divine promise. Hence the recognition of
the Civil Princedom is a result divinely guaranteed for
all time.

It may be useful here to remark, for the sake of any
reader unacquainted with the language of the Church on
this point, that the word *relative* as applied to the
necessity of the Civil Princedom, is not intended to
refer to any present times or circumstances, so that at
some future time the Civil Princedom might cease to
be necessary. The term is used in contradistinction with
"absolute" necessity. The Civil Princedom is not
absolutely necessary, since the Church existed and
made headway during three centuries of violent persecution and is making headway without the Civil
Princedom at the present day.

But in relation to the normal state of the Church,
which is not that of violent persecution, the Civil
Princedom is necessary. Hence the term "relative
necessity."

Cavagnis says* : "Sed quid important praesentes
circumstantiae ? Praesertim alludunt ad divisionem gen-

* "Inst. juris publici ecclesiastici." Felix Cavagnis, Rome.

tium christianarum in plura regna, ex qua fit ut Papa oportet sit a quolibet independens ut liber sit. Ceterum etsi unicum esset regnum christianum quod orbem saltem civilem universum complecteretur, adhuc saepe saepius summus Pontifex plura pateretur a rege vel imperatore christiano cum eiusdem illicitis deberet sese opponere decretis, ut ostendit historia ipsa romani imperii post datam Ecclesiæ pacem ; si enim sub piis imperatoribus servata est erga Pontificem debita reverentia, tamen sub impiis aut minus piis plures quoque Pontifices in exilium acti vel in carcerem detrusi. Si tamen unicum esset magnum imperium ut tunc temporis, certe et pro Pontifice requireretur validius regnum ut de facto esse posset liber."

THE THEOLOGICAL DETERMINATION OF THE CIVIL PRINCEDOM FROM HOLY SCRIPTURE.

IT has been observed that Civil Sovereignty cannot be exercised over an unassigned territory. No national territory is indeterminate. But neither is sovereignty as an abstract right. Sovereignty, as a general term, is, of course, indeterminate : but a Civil Sovereignty is a fixed quantity, though conceived in the abstract. Although, as we have seen, not only the abstract quantity of the Civil Princedom as a right, but the corresponding territory itself is determined by theological argument, I do not insist, when arguing from Scripture evidence, that the latter is necessarily *de jure divino* an everlasting institution like the former. I do contend that the Civil Principality is a divinely determined sovereign right, which neither the Pope nor the Church assembled could alienate ; and therefore the territory which, at least by human or natural law, legitimately falls to the Pontiff, partakes of the sacredness of his divine right, so far as it extends. And such territory becomes a determinate kingdom or Principality, which cannot be bartered away under any guarantees without a violation of divine right.

Nay, supposing it were not beyond the power of the Pontiff to transfer the Apostolic See to some other kingdom willing to become subject to him, his inalienable temporal right would follow him, and the territory, with which it corresponded, would still be a determinate Civil Princedom proof against the law of national caducity. This is, of course, a mere speculation, intended only to meet the objection that Rome, given sufficient time for the change, might pass from a temperate to a glacial zone or otherwise become uninhabitable. There does not, indeed, seem to be anything in the Divine promises precluding the possibility of a physical calamity overtaking the Civil Princedom. The theological argument of the necessity and legitimacy of the Pontifical States is drawn from authentic documents. These, in their turn, emanate from the Theocracy, against which the gates of hell shall not prevail. We may conclude that the Roman Pontiff will retain his right to the Civil Princedom with Rome as a capital, in spite of evil spirits and evil men. But the Divine promises do not include protection against a physical catastrophe. Rome and its provinces might be destroyed by volcanic eruption, subsidence, cataclysms, or the inroads of the sea. From which it should be concluded that the Apostolic See might be transferred. Authors are not wanting who have speculated on the possibility of the Pope transferring the Apostolic See, should Rome be destroyed by infidels or barbarians. I do not go so far. For then, at least, the site would remain, and with it the possibility of restoration. The territory, still in existence, would not cease to be theologically determined, and that theological determination to come under the Divine guarantee against any human or hellish enterprise: "the gates of hell shall not prevail against it."

Against the contingency of a physical catastrophe the Catholic tradition, which seems to refer to the Roman Church, as to a perpetual local centre for the mother-church of the world, consecrated by the death of the Chief Apostle, is of great weight. This would lead us to infer that Providence will not allow Rome to become physically uninhabitable, as Herculaneum and Pompeii, and such other places as have disappeared by the formation of lakes or the gradual encroaching of the sea. Yet it may be urged, in reply, that the Roman Pontiffs are the successors to St. Peter, not in virtue of their being the Bishops of Rome, but in virtue of the Divine appointment of a succession of Sovereign Pontiffs to the Chief Apostle. The succession to the See of Rome is not the essential title, but rather the legitimate mode of succession to the universal pastorate. The legitimate mode of succession might be altered without prejudice to the essential title. The speculation is allowed only to show that the Sovereign Pontiff's rights are as proof against physical catastrophe as against national caducity.

It may be objected that if the Civil Princedom be an inheritance of the lawful right of Christ to local Civil Sovereignty, its boundaries should have been divinely determined like those of the kingdom,* to which Christ succeeded ; and therefore the territory should be included in the Divine institution as well as the abstract right of Civil Sovereignty.—I deny the parity of the two cases and the conclusion. The delimitation by God of the territory of ancient Israel was necessary to determine the Civil Sovereign right of Christ. That being once done and a determinate right being inherited by St. Peter and the Roman Pontiffs, the determination of the corresponding territory was safely left as the expression and embodiment of a sacred deposit to the Church and the Faithful, who could not fail to respond to what was in truth "a singular decree of Divine Providence." If a Civil Sovereignty was due and divinely decreed to the humanity of Christ, then the most natural revelation of the extent of such Civil Sovereignty was the divine delimitation of its territorial boundaries. Men could not become cognisant of the

* *Vide* Num. xxxiv.

nature and extent of that Sovereign civil right, except by its interpretation in human measurement done by God Himself.

It is nothing to the point that such delimitation coincided with that of the tribal portions. The latter was temporary, because genealogical distinctions were to cease to be the basis of spiritual and temporal rights in the Christian Church. The former was conditional upon the Jewish nation not unfitting itself to remain the centre of the Christian Theocracy. In neither case was the territorial delimitation a permanent institution, like that of the Civil Sovereignty of Christ. The territory of ancient Israel was inadequate to hold all the Israelites, had they remained at home. Yet they were not to add to that territory. The Temporal Theocracy is a fixed quantity. Its final object, therefore, was not to provide a home for all the posterity of Jacob for all time, but to supply political independence to the Divine Government and a Civil Sovereignty for one of the seed of Abraham, whose future ministry was incompatible with permanent subjection to the law. *Et Semini tuo dabo terram hanc.* The authority of the Apostle has been quoted in evidence that this promise was principally addressed to Christ, and that of St. Matthew in proof that the Roman Pontiffs were, in the person of St. Peter, associated in that Civil Sovereignty of Christ.

The territory of Civil Governments is ever decreasing or increasing. Fixity of territorial boundaries, like fixity of Civil Sovereign right, is an attribute, which belongs to no government of this fallen world. It is the finished superstructure of a non-fortuitous foundation, and it answers to the immutable purpose of the Founder.

The fixed territory of the Civil Princedom was elsewhere characterised as "an equal territorial dowry" for the local church espoused by Christ after the divorce of the Synagogue. But if a physical catastrophe destroyed "the place" the Roman flock would be cut adrift ; what, then, it may be asked, would become of the indissoluble marriage between Christ and the Mother Church? I reply, that although such a catastrophe would be the act of God, it would not partake of the character of a divorce. The Papacy and Apostolic Church with the Civil Princedom would be removed to another centre. For, once more, "God did not choose the people for the place's sake, but the place for the people's sake."

I have dwelt at some length on the possibilty of a physical catastrophe overtaking the Apostolic See and the Civil Princedom, not because I believe it to be possible *in se*, but to show that whilst such a catastrophe is not precluded by the Divine promises to the Apostolic Church, it is not calculated to frustrate them. But does it follow, because the possibility of physical ruin is not precluded by the Divine promises, that we have no guarantee against such a contingency. It does not follow by any means. If we have no spoken guarantee from God against a physical destruction of the Roman Church, it is simply that such a promise was not required. Such a Divine promise was required against the avowed and determined enmity of free agents at war with the Church. And such Divine promise is sufficient to show the mind of Christ in reference to the Roman Church. It is not likely that God would let loose upon His Church the blind elements which are docile in His hand, whilst bridling the rebellious course of fallen but intelligent creatures. It is not here a question of any creature prevailing against the Church *in toto*, but merely as to whether the course of nature would be allowed to prevail, or rather whether it could ever be the course of nature to prevail against the Apostolic Church, where the gates of hell must fail to do so. In other words, whether physical catastrophe could succeed where the law of national caducity breaks down.

In the foregoing argument, I have striven to establish this truth : that although the geographical determination of the Civil Princedom may be *de jure humano*, yet because such determination is the mere faithful acknowledgment or vindication of a determinate divine right of Sovereignty, the concrete existence of the Civil Princedom is as much of divine right as the Catholic Church. This is the conclusion from Scripture evidence.

The Conditional Covenant.

In the fundamental thesis of this little work allusion was made* to the hypothesis that the Jewish nation had not been punished as such, but had remained in their land. The hypothesis ultimately rests on the then possible contingency of the nation not incurring the guilt of deicide. The prophecies which foretold Christ's Passion left the Jews absolutely free : free as a nation and individually free. Had it been otherwise, the endeavours of Our Saviour to gain them, His loving and constant desire to gather them, His most pathetic regret at witnessing their obduracy, would have been meaningless and vain. The hypothesis, then, that the Jews had been gathered to Christ is legitimate, and affords a theological basis of reasoning. The inquiry, " What, then, would have happened if the Jews or the leading part of the nation had repented or remained faithful ? " is a legitimate inquiry. And the reply is warranted : " The law and the priesthood, together with the sceptre of Juda, would have passed out of the former hands to the successors of the Prince of the Apostles." This was the unconditional fulfilment of the national prophecy of Jacob ; but no reason appears for the dereliction of the land given to the people of God, and principally to Christ from the beginning. The chief Apostle's see would have been the throne of David. The whole Jewish constitution would have been merged into the paternal government of the Pontiff-King. The succession of the Roman

* Page 29.

Pontiff-Kings to the double line of David and Aaron in the ancient Theocracy rests, therefore, not only on the positive foundation supplied by the association of St. Peter in the twofold sovereignty and independence of Christ, and on the translation of "the kingdom of God" to the Roman Church; it has a rational basis also, although a negative one, in the logical outcome of an unfulfilled but legitimate hypothesis.

As this hypothetical ground may be profitably explored to get a back view of certain Scriptural facts, let us press forward without unnecessary alarm. The hypothesis that the Jews had not sinned as a nation, and that, without forfeiting their temporal inheritance, they had become the Mistress Church and centre of Christian Theocracy, belongs to the terms of the old covenant.

The word covenant signifies a contract or mutual agreement between two or more parties. God had established various convenants with mankind from the beginning of the world. They served to embody the various relations between God and His rational creatures. We are concerned with the covenant by which God immediately prepared the way for the Incarnation. God made that covenant with Abraham and the Patriarchs. It was renewed to the Israelites under Moses and frequently re-echoed by the Prophets. That covenant was absolute. It included all that was essential to prepare the way for Christ. It included, therefore, the national existence of the Jews or Church-nation until the coming of Messias, who was beforehand constituted their King. It included, therefore, the preservation of at least the tribe of Juda and the tribe of Levi, together with the family of Aaron and the family of David. It included the possession of the land of promise, which was essential to the national existence and essential to the Incarnation, since God could not come except as King. Whence the preaching of the " Incarnation," which was undertaken by Christ, was the Gospel of "the kingdom of God," whereas after His death and resurrection, the Apostles dwelt more emphatically on these mysteries.

Although the covenant was absolute with respect to a remnant of the Jewish nation, predestined to possess the land and prepare the way for the exercise of the two-fold sovereignty and independence of Messias within His kingdom, yet was it conditional in respect to the posterity of Jacob taken as a whole. The Israelites, and later on the Jews, were not to enjoy that land in peace except they remained faithful to the law of the covenant. They were liable to be scattered among the Gentiles or to be put to the sword by the enemy invading their land. The prophecy of Jacob may be taken as most emphatically expressive of the absolute covenant so far as it interested the Jewish nation. It was addressed as a blessing to the fathers of the two families of kings and priests essential to the constitution of a Church-nation, destined to be rightfully inherited as "the kingdom of God." The absolute covenant as established with Abraham interests more than the Jewish race. It applies to all the Faithful of Christ, through whom the faithful Abraham is constituted " heir of the world." As mentioned before,* " the promise, inclusive of land, was made before the law, and reaches beyond it.

As expressive of the conditional covenant we may quote from Exodus, chapter xix. : " If, therefore, you will hear My voice, and keep My covenant, you shall be My peculiar possession above all people ; for all the earth is Mine. And you shall be to Me a priestly kingdom and a holy nation." We need only mention here that this covenant had not come to an end during the public ministry of our Blessed Lord. The Jews, had they repented and returned with all their hearts to the God of Israel and to His Son and Heir, standing in their midst, would have experienced His protection as in the days of old. Christ, their natural and legitimate King, Who as God had protected them for fourteen centuries would not now have abandoned them because He had come in the flesh and had justified His title to be King of Israel.

* Page 45.

He would have sacrificed His life in the defence even of their temporal interest, had they only been faithful. He was pledged to it by the terms of the covenant. And the Jews throughout all time would have remained the centre of Christian Theocracy, the "priestly kingdom" and "holy nation," which characteristic privilege the Fathers have since attributed to the Holy Roman Church.

As expressive of the conditional covenant, the twenty-ninth chapter of Deuteronomy is remarkable throughout. The following quotation begins with the twenty-fourth verse : "And all nations shall say : 'Why hath the Lord done thus to this land? What meaneth this exceeding great heat of his wrath?' And they shall answer: 'Because they forsook the covenant of the Lord, which He made with their fathers, when he brought them out of the land of Egypt.'"

Again, in the twenty-third chapter of Josue we read: "Josue (verse 2) called for all Israel . . . and said to them: 'I am old, and far advanced in years. And you see all that the Lord your God hath done to all the nations round about, how He Himself hath fought for you. . . . Only take courage, and be careful to observe all things that are written in the book of the law of Moses; and turn not aside from them neither to the right hand nor to the left. . . . And then the Lord God will take away before your eyes *nations that are great and very strong*, and no man shall be able to resist you. One of you shall chase a thousand men of the enemies: because the Lord your God Himself will fight for you, as He hath promised. . . . When you shall have transgressed the covenant of the Lord your God . . . then shall the indignation of the Lord rise up quickly and speedily against you, and you shall be taken away from this excellent land, which He hath delivered to you.'"

As expressive of the absolute, together with the conditional covenant, the words of the 131st Psalm have already been quoted : " The Lord hath sworn truth to David, and He will not make it void : of the fruit of thy womb I will set upon thy throne. If thy children will keep My covenant, and these My testimonies which I shall teach them : their children also for evermore shall sit upon thy throne. For the Lord hath chosen Sion : He hath chosen it for His dwellling. This is My rest for ever and ever : here will I dwell, for I have chosen it."

In other words, if the Jews had repented or had remained faithful to the covenant, they would have secured the protection of the God of armies, then Incarnate. They would therefore have retained the kingdom of David, now become "the kingdom of God." Christ would have taken away before their eyes *nations that were great and very strong.* Jerusalem would have remained the city of the Great King. The land, which meant sovereign political independence, would have been confirmed to them together with the extraordinary spiritual privileges and exalted position of the Mistress Christian Church.

The law and the covenant, with its conditional terms were not altered at the coming of Christ, for " He was made under the law." We are now, therefore, in a better position to realise the subtlety and insidiousness of that question put to Christ by those who had some acquaintance with the law :—

"Is it Lawful to give Tribute to Cæsar or not?"

Before answering the question, let it be observed that the coin of Cæsar's tribute was a penny, and had nothing in common with the didrachma payable to the Temple. It was of different value, and probably of Cæsar's own coining for the purpose of taxation.

Was it lawful to pay this tribute to Cæsar? In one sense it was lawful and in another sense it was unlawful. The speediest solution of the problem, which had puzzled the doctors of the law, and was the burning question of

the hour, will be found in the precise terms of the conditional covenant, which they had neither forgotten nor
overlooked, but which became a dead letter to the carnal
minded, who failed to distinguish in their midst the Heir
of the Lord of the vineyard of Israel, or who, distinguishing Him, resolved His death.

According to the terms of that covenant God was
the pledged protector of Israel : God Himself fought for
His chosen people, provided they were faithful to His
law. But if through idolatry they forsook Him, or if
through hypocrisy, worldliness, and a godless frame of
mind, they fell away from the whole spirit of the covenant,
as happened in the times before Christ, He gave them
over to their enemies. The punishment being in accordance with the covenant was lawful, and therefore the
payment of tribute to a foreign master, a part of that
punishment, was equally lawful. Had the Jews remained faithful to the covenant, had they repented, the
payment of tribute would have been unlawful, and they
might safely have relied on the power and protection of
the God of armies.

Through their wilful blindness and that of their
immediate ancestors, the Romans had usurped power
over Israel. That power was allowed to Cæsar, according to the terms of the conditional covenant between
God and Israel. It was the duty of the Jews to undergo
their deserved punishment. Hence Christ said : " Render,
therefore, to Cæsar the things that are Cæsar's "—but if
payment of tribute were due to Cæsar as a punishment,
there was something due to God : that was repentance,
and the keeping of the law of the covenant, not merely in
the letter but in the spirit—" and to God the things
that are God's."

Thus Christ avoided offending the Imperial power
of Rome, by admitting its conditional right ; and He
avoided hurting the national susceptibilities of His
countrymen, by implying that the payment of tribute
was connected with the forsaking of the Lord and the
violation of His conditional covenant.

It has been argued that since Pompey's time the Romans had acquired prescription. It would be difficult to prove, in the first place, that the Romans maintained their system of taxation throughout that time. But those who thus argue forget for the moment that the political right of Israel was not subject to prescription, being divine. The people might be temporarily punished by servitude ; the human rule of the Theocracy was nevertheless an indefeasible right in a more than human sense. That the sceptre of His race should be handed down to Christ belonged to the absolute covenant. Christ, therefore, acknowledged the conditional right of Cæsar, without prejudice to His own. And those of the people of God who had kept the covenant were destined to hail their King at the proper season : "Blessed be the kingdom of our Father David that cometh."

We may now consider :—

How the Jews Reversed the Terms of the Conditional Covenant.

The Jews, as St. Chrysostomus observes, were never punished by God, except when they forsook the Faith and worship of God. Whatever, therefore, may have been the precise cause of their fear of the Romans, during the time of Christ's public ministry, whether it was feigned or sincere, the truth remains that Christ, as the God Incarnate and the heir of the kingdom of Israel with its twofold inheritance, henceforth to be known as "the kingdom of God," was the natural and sworn protector of Israel. He was bound to protect the Church-nation by the terms of the conditional covenant. What, then, must we think of the deliberate sentence uttered by the chief priests and the Pharisees before a Council especially convoked : "If we let Him alone so, all men will believe in Him : and the Romans will come, and take away our place and nation."* We know that the Pontiff's reply was couched in prophetic terms indicating

* St. John xi. 48.

the salvation of mankind by the death of Christ, although it voiced the secret wish and suggestion of the Council, which was murder. The Evangelist lived to see the fulfilment of that prophecy : " Neither do you consider that it is expedient for you that one man should die for the people, and that the whole nation perish not. And this he spoke not of himself ; but being the high priest that year, he prophesied that Jesus should die for the nation." But the previous utterance of the assembled Council was characterised, like that of the Pontiff, by being prophetic of the future, whilst deliberately conveying a falsehood. The event foretold was : " The Romans will come, and take away our place and nation." And so it came to pass, for the Romans inherited the twofold power of the Roman Pontificate with all the privileges of the Mistress Christian Church. The deliberate falsehood conveyed was the assertion that to allow full freedom to the Heir of the vineyard of Israel would cause them to forfeit their place and nation to the Romans. This was a direct reversal of the terms of the conditional covenant, according to which they should have said : " If we let Him *not* alone so . . . the Romans will come and take away our place and nation ;" or, " If we let Him alone so . . . the Romans will *not* come and take away our place and nation." Another instance of the reversal of the terms of the covenant by the carnal Jews may be quoted from the words which Christ puts into their mouth, in the parable of the vineyard : " This is the Heir ; come, let us kill Him, and we shall have His inheritance." According to the conditional covenant, the following saying would have been true : " Come, let us kill Him, and we shall forfeit His inheritance ;" or again : " Come, let us acknowledge Him, and we shall have His inheritance." From which we may, therefore, conclude that the succession of the Roman Pontiff-Kings to the double line of David and Aaron in the ancient Theocracy rests not only on the positive foundation supplied by the association of St. Peter in the twofold sovereignty and independence of Christ and on the translation of "the kingdom of God" to the Roman Church; but that it has a rational basis also, although of a negative character, in the logical outcome of an unfulfilled but legitimate hypothesis, which was also a condition of the covenant.

THE NOTES OF THE CIVIL PRINCEDOM AND THE READING OF THE FATHERS.

THE early writers of the Church, whose united testimony is of such weight to determine the meaning of the Scripture and the *mens ecclesiæ* frequently speak of "the kingdom of God" as being entirely spiritual and heavenly. They reprobate the idea of the carnal Jews that God's kingdom is to be founded on the subjugation by force of arms of the enemies of His people. It would be easy to infer from their language that the Sovereign Pontiff is possessed by right of no Temporal Kingdom, and that, as a matter of expediency, his government would be all the more spiritual for being separated from his Civil Sovereignty.

I have had occasion already* to distinguish between two kingdoms described in Holy Scripture as of Divine institution. "One," I insisted, "is universal and the other is circumscribed. The former is spiritual, and the latter is both spiritual and temporal. And to both kingdoms is pledged an everlasting destiny. The corruption of their tradition by the Jews did not consist in their belief in a Temporal Kingdom of the Messias, but in mistaking the character of the Messias and assigning Him a temporal instead of a spiritual empire. A proof of this lies in the fact that one of their deadly errors consisted in rejecting Christ as their legitimate King, and charging it against Him, that whereas He was not King, He pretended to that title." In reality, the two kingdoms here spoken of are merely two aspects of "the kingdom of God."

* Page 94.

The kingdom of David is "the kingdom of God" by anticipation,† It becomes properly "the kingdom of God" when inherited by Christ. God acquires a human title, and takes His place among the kings of the earth in virtue of the Incarnation. This circumscribed kingdom necessarily prepared for Christ was inherited by the Roman Church, as Mistress Christian Church, together with all the privileges of the direct succession to Christ. This is the first aspect, and "the kingdom of God" in its strict, proper, local, and theandric sense. As a consequence of God's becoming a human king, there is begun a spiritual conquest of the Gentiles, who are to be inherited by the Theocracy and ingrafted with their several nations. This is the spiritual extension of "the kingdom of God" : the Catholic Church.

In order to avoid all possible confusion in the reading of the Fathers or later writers, it will be useful to have recourse to a sub-distinction in reference to the local and circumscribed kingdom of God, or rather to its Temporal Power called the Civil Princedom.

When it is considered that its object is to subserve the interests of Christendom, that its character in the New Testament, as well as in the Old, has always been stationary and non-aggressive ; that its destiny is to supply neutral, because common ground to all Christians ; that it is not, as in pagan Rome, the scene of carnal pomp and triumph ; that it depends not on the weapons of carnal warfare, although it might rightfully invoke them in self-defence, but relies, as of old, on God's peculiar protection and singular Providence—it will be easily admitted that if such be a temporal or secular kingdom it is not a profane one. If, then, in reading the Fathers we meet with the note " spiritual," expressly or equivalently applied to the royalty of Christ, or to His kingdom, or to Rome the Papal city, we shall have to be guided by the context to ascertain what is meant by that expression : Whether by " spiritual " " sacred " be meant or " non-political."

† I Chron. xvii. 14.

The following quotation is from St. Augustine: "Has ei laudes turba dicebat: Hosanna, benedictus qui venit in nomine Domini, rex Israel. Quam crucem mentis invidentia principium Judæorum perpeti potuerit, quando regem suum Christum tanta multitudo clamabat? Sed quid fuit Domino Regem esse Israel? Quid magnum fuit Regi sæculorum, Regem fieri hominum? Non enim rex Israel Christus ad exigendum tributum, vel exercitum ferro armandum, hostesque visibiliter debellandos: sed rex Israel, quód *mentes regat*, quód in æternum consulat, etc."*

A true king is not denied by St. Augustine, yet a king is proclaimed whose object is spiritual. Such is the kingdom of the Papacy. That the expression spiritual or celestial is not intended to exclude a Temporal Kingdom may be illustrated again by the following words from St. Leo, Pope, on the foundation of Christian Rome: "Isti sunt patres tui, verique pastores, qui te *regnis cœlestibus inserendam* multo melius multoque felicius *condiderunt*, quam illi, quorum studio prima mœnium tuorum fundamenta locata sunt: ex quibus is, qui tibi nomen dedit, fraterna te cœde fœdavit. Isti sunt qui te ad hanc gloriam provexerunt, ut *gens Sancta, populus electus, civitas sacerdotalis et Regia*, per sacram beati Petri sedem caput orbis effecta, latius prœsideres religione divina, quam dominatione terrena."†

Whilst St. Leo claims for the holy Apostles that they laid a better foundation than that of Romulus, and ingrafted Rome into the heavenly kingdom of Christ, he vindicates also the Royal and Sacerdotal character of the city privileged to contain the See of Peter, showing it to have succeeded to the privileges of "the kingdom of God" in the old Theocracy by using the words of the conditional covenant to Israel.‡

We shall see in reference to the covenant that "the two families" of priests and kings were to endure for all

* Tr. 50 in "Joann." † S. 1 in "Nat. S. Pet. et. Paul."
‡ Exodus xix. 4, 6.

time.* This Divine pledge could not refer only to a genealogical succession, which was to cease with Christ and the translation of the law and the priesthood. It had reference also to the sucession *sine genealogia* or virginal succession of the Christian Pontiffs. In them, as Pontiff-Kings, the functions of " the two families " are united, which union constitutes the order of Melchisedech.

If the expressions, " Priestly Kingdom " or " Royal Priesthood " are applied sometimes to the Christian Church generally, it is, therefore, because the Church is characterised principally by its Head, the Pontiff-King.

Thus, the succession of the Roman Church to the Theocratic government is expressed by the following words : " Thronus David et regia sedes est Sacerdotium in S. Ecclesia, quam dignitatem regiam simulque Pontificiam conjunctim largitus est Dominus Sanctæ Ecclesiæ suæ, translato in ipsam throno David non deficiente in æternum."†

Once more, the order of Melchisedech is that of the Incarnation, because it united for ever the spiritual and temporal powers of the Theocracy, before typically kept asunder.

We may conclude these quotations taken at hazard by the salutation of St. Tharasius to the Mother of God : " Tu Regni et Sacerdotii Melchisedech perillustris splendor."‡

The Absolute Covenant with " the two Families " fulfilled in the Papacy.

There was nothing conditional in the covenant made with Abraham. It included a temporal as well as a spiritual promise. Whence it might have been concluded that the two kinds of promises would be fulfilled together.

We have learned, it may be hoped, to look upon the land of promise as something more than a country with

Jeremias xxxiii.   † S. Epiphan. hœresi 29.   ‡ Hom. S. Tharasii episc.

large clusters of grapes, "which *in very deed* floweth with milk and honey, as may be known by these fruits."* It has been the writer's most earnest endeavour, resulting, no doubt, in the feeblest of attempts, to point out that the Divine promise and the Divine gift of land was an essential condition of the Incarnation, and not a mere accessory determinable by fortuitous causes or dependent on the will of man. It was pre-ordained by the most absolute covenant to secure to Messias the inheritance of a Civil Sovereignty of immediate Divine right. It was foreseen as the indispensable instrument to usher into this world " the kingdom of God."

The promises to Abraham, because they referred to Christ and to the Christian Church, included all the prerogatives granted to St. Peter and to the Roman Pontiffs. For thus was Abraham constituted " heir of the world."† Hence the successor of St. Peter is in direct line the heir to the promises, both spiritual and temporal. Whether we compare this doctrine to that which has been delivered concerning the Civil Princedom, or to the Scripture evidence of the association of St. Peter in the twofold Sovereignty and independence of Christ, we are forced to admit that the witnesses point the same way and sound the same note. And that which might have been concluded *a priori*, viz., that the two kinds of promises to Abraham would be conjointly fulfilled is discovered to be true by the event.

The duration of the Jewish nation unto the time of Messias, which was unconditionally foretold by the Patriarch Jacob, included three essential elements :—

1. The uninterrupted succession of the tribe of Juda and of the family of David, or a sufficient remnant thereof to constitute a nation, with kings or rulers to hand down the sceptre to Christ. This is the immediate scope of the patriarchal blessing.

2. The uninterrupted succession of the tribe of Levi and of the family of Aaron, which was necessarily im-

* Numbers xiii. 28.   † Romans iv. 13.

plied in the national prophecy of Jacob. For without the priests and Levites the Jews could not have held together as a nation under the Mosaic law.

3. The possession of land without which Israel could not have been a nation, and Messias could not have introduced " the kingdom of God."

The prophecy of Jacob foretells the duration of the Jewish nation unto the time of Messias, and it does not go beyond ; except that by indicating the translation of the sceptre from Juda, it implies the translation of the priesthood from Aaron, thus betokening the beginning of a new order. In other words, the sceptre was not taken away from Juda by fortuitous causation, but by the law of the absolute covenant, which constituted Christ King and Pontiff, and heir of the twofold authority of the Church-nation.

But nowhere does the absolute covenant with the two families of kings and priests, typifying the sacrificing and sacrificial elements of the sacred humanity together with the twofold power of Christ and of His Vicars, appear enshrined in more lofty and divine language than in the thirty-third chapter of Jeremias, verses 14 to 22 :—

" Behold the days come, saith the Lord, that I will perform the good word that I have spoken to the house of Israel, and to the house of Juda. In those days, and at that time, I will make the bud of justice to spring forth unto David, and he shall do judgment and justice in the earth. In those days shall Juda be saved, and Jerusalem shall dwell securely ; and this is the name that they shall call him, the Lord our Just One. For thus saith the Lord : ' There shall not be cut off from David a man to sit upon the throne of the house of Israel. Neither shall there be cut off from the priests and Levites a man before My face to offer holocausts, and to burn sacrifices, and to kill victims continually.' And the word of the Lord came to Jeremias, saying : ' Thus saith the Lord : " If My covenant with the day can be made void, and My covenant with the night, that there should not be day and night in their season. Then may also My covenant with David My servant be made void, that he should not have a son to reign upon his throne, and with the Levites and priests, My ministers. As the stars of Heaven cannot be numbered, nor the sand of the sea be measured: so will I multiply the seed of David My servant, and the Levites, My ministers ; " ' etc."

It is admitted by all that the words, "Neither shall there be cut off from the priests and Levites a man before My face, to offer holocausts and to burn sacrifices, and to kill victims continually," refer to the New Testament and to the everlasting order of Priesthood. But if Temporal Power were not equally covenanted to the Sovereign Pontiff of the Christian Church for all time, what need was there of the promise to David conveyed in similar terms : " There shall not be cut off from David a man to sit upon the throne of the house of Israel." Thus the twofold power of the Vicars of Christ is pledged as " a man to sit upon the throne of the house of Israel," and " to offer holocausts, etc." The extension of "the kingdom of God " by the ingrafting of other kingdoms with their local churches is likewise pledged and foretold : " As the stars of Heaven cannot be numbered, nor the sand of the sea be measured : so will I multiply the seed of David My servant, and the Levites, My ministers."

Thus the order of Melchisedech, which is that of the God Incarnate, unites the two powers, which is the perfection of authority and the fulfilling of the Divine Government.

This, then, is the true meaning of the absolute covenant with the two families, not to be made void any sooner than the covenant of the same God with the day and the night. Hence we understand that the law which Christ declared He came not to destroy was the law of the Theocracy. And those words, which express the judgment of the enemies of the Jewish nation, or the wail of the people of God, will ever convey a falsehood: "The two families which the Lord had chosen, are cast off and they have despised My people, so that it is no more a nation before them."* The Church-nation still subsists, and is destined with its Pontiff-Kings to endure as long as the covenant of God "between day and night" and the laws He hath set "to Heaven and earth."

The Divine Right of Kings.

It has been admitted in these pages that Civil Sovereignty is of Divine origin, because, according to Suarez: "All things, which are by the law of nature, are from God, the Author of nature."

It has been denied that the Civil Princedom is in no other sense of Divine origin than ordinary Civil Sovereignties. It has been shown that the Civil Princedom transcends the law of nature, because in virtue of Church legislation it is in every sense inalienable, or if the expression be preferred, it is constitutionally everlasting, which implies a superadded Divine sanction. On the other hand, that which is the outcome of authentic teaching, or its emphatic meaning, that which Catholic tradition has handed down embodied in the Papal states, is likewise the conclusion which Holy Scripture unfolds : " the kingdom of God," however wide its spiritual empire, however sacrosanct its sway or heavenly its prospect, must be traced primarily to the human right of the Son of Man, which was a local, territorial, and well determined right. That is the proper and original meaning of "the kingdom of God." The expression signifies the Incarnation with its birthplace, its family, its tribe, its country and sovereign social position at home and in relation to the kingdom s of the world. It signifies the Incarnation covenanted and legislated for, and the Incarnation fulfilled, translated, inherited by the Gentiles and continued through all time and eternity. Temporal Power may be only " one jot or one tittle" in the Theocratic law, yet

* Jeremias xxxiii. 24.

has it been fulfilled. "And it is easier for Heaven and earth to pass, than one tittle of the law to fall."*

And now, what means the Divine Right of Kings? Is it a natural divine right, or a Theocratic right, that was claimed for their respective sovereigns by Anglican divines at home and by Josephist divines or Gallican canonists on the Continent. It must be admitted by the candid student of history that it was not merely the natural divine right that was claimed by Court theologians. Church history teems with instances of the more or less successful resistence of Catholic Bishops and Roman Pontiffs to the Theocratic pretensions of kings and emperors. And if half Europe is given over at least to schism at the present day, it is due to those pretensions which finally evolved the doctrine of the Divine right of kings. Whilst trampling on the rights of conscience, the most sacred of popular rights, and sowing the seeds of future spiritual and political revolt, the crowned Heads of Europe, abetted by anti-Roman divines, encroached on the lawful jurisdiction of the Roman Pontiffs, and obscured by their false tradition the only Theocratic right vouchsafed to this world.

To pretend, therefore, at this hour of the day to confound the Divine right of the Roman Pontiffs to Civil Sovereignty with the right of the dynastic princes of France, and to condemn as "an error of judgment the (supposed) abjuration by His Holiness in France of a principle which he perseveringly labours to uphold in Italy, the principle of Divine right," would hardly seem to be an innocent perversion of facts and principles. The anonymous writer, from whom these words are quoted, practically appeals, whatever may be his motive, to Protestant or political prejudice all the world over against a spectre of his own conjuring up ; "the policy of the Pope."† The affected moderation of style and un-

---

* St. Matthew v. 18 ; St. Luke xvi.

† "The present high-handed assertion of the Pope's right to sway all Catholic politicians will, it is feared, be productive of equally lamentable

sustained dignity, the show of regard for the Holy
Father's good intentions and profession of respect for
his person are too thin to disguise a charge of wholesale
betrayal of Catholic interests, such as was never hurled
at the head of the most unworthy of Popes.
To the unbiased Catholic mind it must be a source
of unspeakable satisfaction that the Holy Father has not
only acknowledged the French Republican Government,
but has bidden French Catholics do the same. It is not
merely that the interests of the Church in France are
more likely to be consulted by the union of all Catholics.
to promote them. What is of more importance, as affect-
ting the Universal Church, is that men should cease to
identify the so-called Divine right of kings with the
Roman Theocracy. Nothing could be more conducive
to that end than the recent policy of Leo XIII. The

results in Ireland (where in view of Home Rule the religious question is once
more prominent), in England, and in America. It is not enough that the
doctrine is implicitly contained in the decree of Infallibility. Why dot the
i's and cross the t's as the organ of the Vatican does in the following
authoritative declaration?

"Politics," we read in the *Osservatore Romano*, "are neither more nor
less than morals applied to the social acts of Governments and to the public
life of peoples. Now, the Pope is admittedly the infallible teacher of faith
and of morals. It follows, therefore, that he is the unerring judge in both
spheres (politics and religion), inasmuch as the practical application of
morals by individuals and peoples must not be allowed to run counter to the
commands, interests, and rights of the Faith. It is clear, therefore, that as
the Pope is an infallible teacher in all that concerns what we should believe
in the religious sphere and what we should do in the domain of morals, *he
is in like manner the unerring judge of what we should do or leave undone
in public as well as in private life.*"

This extract I quote (says the anonymous writer) as a proof of a sad want of
tact rather than error of judgment. If there be an error of judgment any-
where it is to be found in the abjuration by His Holiness in France of a
principle which he perseveringly labours to uphold in Italy—the principle
of Divine right. For the frank acceptance of the French Republic involves.
acquiescence in the doctrine on which it is based, and to which the Pope
rightly attributes his loss of the Temporal Power, viz., that all power is from
the people, in whom is invested the right of giving and of taking away.
With what face can Catholics uphold that principle in France at the cost
of most heavy sacrifices, *in order* to combat it the more successfully in
Italy? Surely, from a worldly point of view, the tactics of the Vatican
seem as short-sighted as those of the good Auvergnois, who let go the
parapet of the bridge from which he was hanging by his hands, in order
to take a firmer grip."—*The Contemporary Review for October*, 1892, *p.* 465.

result will be, whether France returns to the monarchical form of government or not, that Catholics will perceive more and more that the Civil Princedom has a foundation and a character of its own, that it is an inheritance of the Incarnation, and the solid nucleus of "the kingdom of God." The Christian nations will learn more and more to look up from the midst of their native instability to the rock of St. Peter, and to seek the friendly alliance of the only everlasting kingdom.

DANIEL, THE SPOKESMAN OF THE THEOCRACY, AND THE LAW OF NATIONAL CADUCITY.

"*And Daniel made answer before the King, and said: 'The secret that the King desireth to know, none or the wise men, or the philosophers, or the diviners, of the soothsayers can declare to the King. But there is a God in Heaven that revealeth mysteries, who hath showed to thee, O King Nabuchodonosor, what is to come to pass in the latter times. Thy dream, and the visions of thy head upon thy bed, are these: Thou, O King, didst begin to think in thy bed what should come to pass hereafter; and He that revealeth mysteries showed thee what shall come to pass. To me also this secret is revealed, not by any wisdom that I have more than all men alive; but that the interpretation might be made manifest to the King, and thou mightest know the thoughts of thy mind. Thou, O King, sawest, and behold there was as it were a great statue; this statue, which was great and high, tall of stature, stood before thee, and the look thereof was terrible. The head of this statue was of fine gold; but the breast and the arms of silver, and the belly and the thighs of brass; and the legs of iron, the feet part of iron and part of clay. Thus thou sawest, till a stone was cut out of a mountain without hands; and it struck the statue upon the feet thereof that were of iron and of clay, and broke them in pieces. Then was the iron, the clay, the brass, the silver, and the gold broken to pieces together, and became like the chaff of a summer's threshing-floor, and they were carried away by the wind, and there was no place found for* *them; but the stone that struck the statue became a great mountain, and filled the whole earth. This is the dream: we will also tell the interpretation thereof before thee, O King. Thou art a king of kings: and the God of Heaven hath given thee a kingdom, and strength, and power, and glory; and all places wherein the children of men and the beasts of the field do dwell: He hath also given the birds of the air into thy hand, and hath put all things under thy power: thou, therefore, art the head of gold. And after thee shall rise up another kingdom, inferior to thee, of silver: and another third kingdom of brass, which shall rule over all the world. And the fourth kingdom shall be as iron. As iron breaketh into pieces, and subdueth all things, so shall that break and destroy all these. And whereas thou sawest the feet and the toes, part of potter's clay and part of iron: the kingdom shall be divided, but yet it shall take its origin from the iron, according as thou sawest the iron mixed with the miry clay. And as the toes of the feet were part of iron and part of clay, the kingdom shall be partly strong and partly broken. And whereas thou sawest the iron mixed with miry clay, they shall be mingled indeed together with the seed of man, but they shall not stick fast one to another, as iron cannot be mixed with clay. But in the days of those kingdoms the God of Heaven will set up a kingdom that shall never be destroyed, and His kingdom shall not be delivered up to another people: and it shall break in pieces, and shall consume all these kingdoms, and itself shall stand for ever. According as thou sawest that the stone was cut out of the mountain without hands, and broke in pieces the clay, and the iron, and the brass, and the silver, and the gold, the great God hath shown the King what shall come to pass hereafter; and the dream is true, and the interpretation thereof is faithful."—*Daniel ii. 27—45.

The statue represents the principal monarchies which succeeded one another whilst Israel was a nation ; namely, those of the Babylonians, of the Persians, of the Greeks, and of the Romans. They are grouped together under the appearance of one statue, not only because they succeed one another without interruption, like its varying parts, but because it is the intention of the King's dream to signify their simultaneous contact with the fifth kingdom, which overthrows them. That simultaneous contact of the symbolised monarchies with a fifth kingdom, which overthrows them, marks not only their contemporaneous existence with the fifth kingdom, but the continued action of overthrowing and surviving of the latter. The full significance of the dream centres in this point, that Daniel, a type of Christ, of the blood royal, fitly representing the Jewish monarchy, and its sceptre in captivity, and apparently at the mercy of the King of Babylon, is called upon to proclaim the character and destiny of the Theocracy : the smallest of kingdoms, but God's own ; and therefore symbolised not by the metal which dazzles, nor by the metal which superficially reflects, nor by the metal which resounds, nor by the metal which deals death, but by the stone, the most lasting and the most constructive of substances. The stone, it is true, was not yet cut out of a mountain without hands ; that is, Christ's sacred humanity was not yet cut out of the mountain of His race by a conception wrought without the operation of man. But He Who, without hands, cut the stone out of the mountain of Israel, becoming its abiding firmness, God Himself, was in anticipation governing His chosen people. In anticipation God acted like a man and became King of Israel. Hence the original and proper meaning of " the kingdom of God."* King is a human title, and was proper to Christ. It is not God's own name nor proper to Him alone. Thus anticipating the Incarnation of His Son, God protected that fifth kingdom when the human

* 1 Chron. xvii. 14.

sceptre was in the dust and the best part of the people in captivity. He handed the Imperial rule from one monarchy to another, and broke them down in succession, manifesting their human origin. He upheld Israel in spite of its weakness and infidelity, for it was the predestined kingdom of His Son. May I be forgiven if I interpret wrongly the words of the Mother of God ; but her vision, who was familiar with the Scripture of Daniel, must have swept a wider horizon than that of her country, when she sang : " He hath put down the mighty from their seat . . . He hath received Israel, His servant . . . As He spoke to our fathers, to Abraham, and to his seed for ever."* "When the fulness of time was come God sent His Son, made of a woman, made under the law,"† and therefore destined at the fit moment to exercise full supremacy over the law, such as it came forth from the hands of Moses, with its civil and religious enactments, under a single legislation.

But if the prophetic interpretation of the royal dream indicates a simultaneous contact of the Theocracy leaning upon the stone, with the four principal monarchies of the Old World, it contains a provision which belongs only to the future : " And His kingdom shall not be delivered up to another people." The Jewish Church-nation had no unconditional guarantee against forfeiting " the kingdom of God." That was reserved for the local Church of the Vicar of Christ, which alone is spiritually and temporally inalienable : " in the days of those kingdoms, the God of Heaven will set up a kingdom that shall never be destroyed, and His kingdom shall not be delivered up to another people : and it shall break in pieces, and shall consume all these kingdoms ; and itself shall stand for ever." The hysterological character of the language in which the future stands also for the present, marks the *actually established* kingdom of God : *suscitabit regnum*, and its then existence "in the days " of the first monarchy

* St. Luke i. 52.   † Galatians iv. 4.

as well as its continued relation thereto and to the succeeding monarchies, and finally its indissoluble union with a central and Universal Church, when the metaphorical stone becomes a great mountain and fills the whole earth.

This exposition shows the agreement so far between the character of the fifth kingdom and the notes of the Civil Princedom as developed from the Church's authentic teaching. It also points to their identity. We may not, consistently with Catholic doctrine, trace the essential right or origin of the Civil Princedom to any epoch between St. Peter and Leo XIII., because that right is not adventitious. We must, in quest of that right, look to St. Peter and to his relation with the Divine Founder of the Church. The non-fortuitous character of the Civil Princedom, in other words, makes it reach up to the time when the fifth kingdom, symbolised by the stone, struck and destroyed the mystic statue. On the other hand, the Civil Princedom is constitutionally everlasting, being, as we have seen, spiritually and temporally inalienable and thus raised above the law of national caducity ; whereas, of the fifth kingdom, we read that, "itself shall stand for ever." The fifth kingdom, like the Civil Principality, is strictly analogous to the monarchies in that it is a temporal kingdom—yet is it a sacred kingdom, with a sacred object and a world-wide purpose.

The identity of the Civil Princedom with the fifth kingdom is further shown from other Scripture testimonies :—

1. It is the twofold kingdom of the Pontiff-King prefigured by Melchisedech and proclaimed by the inspired pen of David to be everlasting.

2. It is the spiritual and temporal inheritance promised to the ancestors of Christ, whereof He was the principal heir.

3. It is the twofold sovereignty conferring twofold independence which the Roman Pontiffs have inherited from St. Peter, associated in the twofold sovereignty of Christ.

4. It is "the kingdom of God" taken from the Jews and "given to a nation yielding the fruits thereof."

5. It is, with its people and territory, the "peculiar possession" of the God Incarnate, "a priestly kingdom and a holy nation."

6. It is the law of the Theocracy, which Christ came not to destroy, but to fulfil.

7. It is the translation of the law, of the priesthood, and of the sceptre of Juda: the throne of David, and his everlasting kingdom.

St. Peter and his successors, during the centuries of persecution, were therefore *de jure* the Sovereigns of Rome, although the Roman Emperors continued to be its *de facto* rulers with powers fortuitously obtained and permissively exercised: in the same way as the ancestors of Christ were *de jure* the owners of the land divinely promised to their fathers, although more than four centuries elapsed from the time of their entering that land until David had vindicated the full extent of their right.

THE SURVIVAL OF THE ROMAN EMPIRE OR THE CIVIL PRINCEDOM.

AGAINST these conclusions we have the authority of Cornelius à Lapide, not surely a Father of the Church, but a giant of erudition, and the most careful collator of patristic testimony, the prince of commentators.

1. He declares that the Roman Empire is still standing, and is destined to endure until the end of the world: *adhuc durat*, etc.

2. On the other hand, that no kingdom can be everlasting in this world, *nullum enim regnum in terris potest esse æternum;* and therefore he interprets the words of Christ to Pilate, "My kingdom is not of this world," not as the Catechism of the Council of Trent, to signify the heavenly or divine origin of the kingdom of God, but to exclude the idea of a terrestrial sovereignty of divine origin.

3. And consistently he adds: "Although, therefore, the Pontiffs have a Temporal Dominion, they possess it not as Vicars of Christ, but as something *accessory* from the donation of Constantine? of Charlemagne," etc., etc.

If the gifted and loyal mind which dictated these lines had lived in this second half and latter end of the nineteenth century, he might possibly have written: *unum regnum in terris potest esse æternum :—*

1. Because the Catholic doctrine of the necessity of the Civil Princedom is binding for all time, and, therefore, the Civil Princedom is *de jure* and constitutionally everlasting.

2. Because, as we have seen, that constitutional right has a divine guarantee for its normal translation into a concrete fact, since the local Church of the successor of St. Peter, together with the Universal Church, cannot fail to assent to Catholic doctrine, and their joint action to triumph in the end over the law of national caducity.

3. Because that kingdom being the inheritance of the Incarnation is the terrestrial expression of a right essential to the sacred humanity of Christ, which does not end with this world.

Again, understanding from a Sovereign Pontiff, and from the Bishops' authentic interpretation of his words, that the Civil Principality did not originate from fortuitous causes, he would have paused before interpreting the words of Christ to Pilate to mean that He had no Temporal Kingship of divine origin and bestowal.

Or had he, before the Pontifical Acts of Pius IX., and the joint declaratory assent thereto of the Bishops of the whole world, committed those words to writing: " Licet ergo Pontifices jam habeant dominium temporale, id tamen non habent qua vicarii Christi, sed quasi *accessorium ex donatione* Constantini, Caroli Magni, Mechtildis et aliorum piorum principum ;" he would, no doubt, have been startled at the opposite and contradictory character of the authentic utterance : " Ab omnibus igitur nobis esse pro certissimo tenendum non fortuito hoc regnum temporale Sanctæ Sedi accessisse." . . . Maybe he would have torn that paper and consigned the fragments to the same luck as "the iron, the clay, the brass, the silver, and the gold," which were " broken to pieces together, and became like the chaff of the summer's threshing-floor, and they were carried away by the wind."

And, finally, judging from the same authentic teaching, that since the Roman Pontiff's Civil Sovereignty is not adventitious or fortuitous like the kingdoms of this world, but inherent to his office and involving a superadded divine sanction, it must be traced through St. Peter to Christ, he would not have substituted the Roman Empire for the Civil Princedom. He would not have been led into the error of supposing that a portion of the mystic statue remained standing, namely, the legs and the feet, with one point of rest in the east and the other somewhere in the west. He would have drawn the more natural conclusion, that the broken pieces were so carried away by the wind that " there was no place found for them."

The reader may in fairness expect a more extensive quotation from this commentary. It will serve to put the question in a clearer light. The commentator inquires why other contemporary nations are not mentioned by Daniel, and concludes that the statue represented only the kingdoms about which Nabuchodonosor was concerned in the interest of his own monarchy, whilst the figure of the everlasting kingdom of Christ served to wean his mind from perishable kingdoms : " Quod illa omnia caduca sint et mortalia ; hoc sempiternum."

Commenting on the words "the feet part of iron and part of clay," he shows that we are not to understand that one foot was of clay, the other of iron ; or that a part of one foot was of clay, another part of iron ; because such distinction would indicate not different states of the one empire, but different empires. And, therefore, we are to understand that the feet were a mixture of clay and iron forming with the legs of iron one empire.

Then follows a learned dissertation on the charac teristics of the three first monarchies as symbolised by the gold, the silver, and the brass as well as by their respective positions in the statue.

On the words : "And the fourth kingdom shall be as iron," he comments thus : "Hoc est regnum, ait S. Hieron. et alii passim, Romanorum, armis et fortitudine inclytum, quod v. 33, assimilatur tibiis : quia ultimum fuit et firmissimum, idque duabus : quia imperium hoc apud plures fuit, scilicet, primo, apud duos consules ; secundo, apud duumviros ; tertio apud duos imperatores, unum in Oriente, alterum in occidente ; unum Constantinopoli, alterum Romæ, vel in Germania agentem. Hinc ejus insigne est aquila biceps, sive duorum capitum : inde in castris vexillifer dictus est aquillifer, et vulgo voce contracta alfiero."

Here occurs the first suggestion that the Roman Empire still exists. It should be observed that if the commentator had referred only to the Holy Roman Empire, we need not have demurred. The Holy Roman Empire is a creation of the Popes, and not a lineal descendant of the old pagan empire, which disappeared in right, when St. Peter settled in Rome, and, in fact, when Constantine embraced the Christian faith and withdrew to form a new, because a Christian, empire in the East. If the ancient standard is preserved, it is no longer the ensign of pagan power and still less of pagan right. The *aquila biceps* is now claimed by Austria and Russia, but the most likely eagle of our day rejoices in but one head and spreads its mighty wings to the setting sun. The supposed dualism of the Roman Empire, as typified by the legs of iron, is more apparent than real. Besides the fact that there were triumvirs as well as duumvirs in the Roman Empire, we must remember that the mystic statue was that of man,

with a twofold character running through its whole
physical being. There were two arms, and two breasts
of silver, and two thighs of brass, besides two eyes and
ears of gold, not to mention other outward and inward
twofold parts. Yet the commentator does not insist on
the dual position or character of the other monarchies.

APOSTASY OR CONVERSION A BAR TO POLITICAL CONTINUITY.

FOR reasons that we shall see, . the convert Roman
Empire continued to be spoken of as politically identical
with its pagan predecessor. It is useful to examine
whether this were a reality or a mere fiction. When
we speak of a kingdom being superseded by another
kingdom, we mean that that which is essential to such
kingdom, and not that which is merely accessory, is
supplanted. Many things conspire to fill up the compound idea of kingdom : the rulers, the political scope,
the race, the territory, the language, the religion, the
ensign of war ; but they are not all equally essential.
When the change of religion involves so complete a
transition as the turning from the worship of devils to
the worship of the living God, the convert kingdom is a
new foundation. The three centuries of persecution of
the followers of Christ sufficiently indicates that the
old Romans considered their gods as essential to their
Empire, and that their policy was wedded to their
religion. It has been remarked that a kingdom is
temporally alienated from the Church in proportion as it
is spiritually alienated; it is equally true that a kingdom or
empire is temporally alienated from the enemy of Christ
when it embraces the Christian faith. As with the
baptism of individuals, so with that of nations, there is a
new birth and a new foundation. The new nation, like
the new man, belongs spiritually and temporally to Christ.
ngdoms are, therefore, subject to the law of national
·city, either by surrendering to Christ or surrendering to His enemy ; instability being shown in either case.

I conclude that not only the Civil Princedom with its transcendent right was a new foundation at the headquarters of the old pagan empire, but that the other Christian kingdoms which arose in the East and in the West were new foundations, whose connection with the old Roman Empire was merely transient and superficial. We shall return to the fiction of a political continuity of the old Roman Empire.

The sentence, "The kingdom shall be divided," having been construed by the Rabbins to signify "the fifth kingdom" of the Turks, who made up a divided empire with the Romans, à Lapide points out that the Turks, being the sworn foes of the Roman Empire, cannot be said to be a part of that Empire.

Pursuing, he points out that the toes indicate the inequality of the princes who contended for the Roman Empire. But he declares the breaking up of the Roman Empire into various Christian monarchies to be foreshadowed by the same figure.

Glancing again at the three first monarchies, he determines the duration of each one and the time of its fall, and then adds : " Quarta Romanorum, quæ cœpit a Julio Cæsare et Augusto, adhuc durat.   . . ."

The Civil Princedom and the "Temporal Kingdom of the Romans" Incompatible.

Finally, the concluding sentences of the prophetic interpretation are commented on : " But in the days of those kingdoms the God of Heaven will set up a kingdom that shall never be destroyed, and His kingdom shall not be delivered up to another people : and it shall break in pieces, and shall consume all these kingdoms : and itself shall stand for ever."

On the words, " In the days of those kingdoms," occurs the following commentary : " Cum scilicet quatuor regna jam dicta suum tempus, sua spatia regnandi habuerint, eaque evoluta fuerint usque ad ultimum, hoc est, Romanis jam regnantibus, ' suscitabit Deus cœli regnum,' etc." And further on the same words are interpreted as follows: "Stabit enim, ut ait Daniel, Romanorum regnum usque ad finem mundi. Ergo Messias suum regnum triumphans et gloriosum non habebit in hoc mundo, sed in cœlo. Quocirca ait Daniel hic ' *In diebus regnorum illorum,*' q.d. Stante adhuc regno temporali Romanorum, orietur regnum spirituale Christi."

Therefore the overthrowing of the fourth kingdom was, according to the commentator, only a spiritual affair: "Quintum hoc regnum est Christi, quod alia omnia regna evertit, non quoad temporale regimen, sed quoad idololatriam, etc. Unde hoc regnum non temporale est, sed spirituale et æternum. . . . Licet enim Christus, qua homo, . . . esset etiam temporalis rex orbis ; . . . tamen ipse hoc regno et hac potestate regali uti noluit. . . ."

To which interpretation and commentary exception may be taken on the following grounds :—

1. The enduring "until the end of the world " of a " Temporal Kingdom of the Romans," which is not identical with the Civil Princedom, is incompatible therewith, and therefore, with Catholic doctrine.

2. Christ was "made under the law," which was twofold, spiritual and temporal ; but in His public ministry He exercised supremacy over the law ; therefore, He *used or exercised regal power*, not over the whole world, which belonged not to Him, as son of David, but over Israel, which belonged to His sacred humanity.—For it was essential to Him as man, not to take other kings' sceptres, but to possess His own.

3. Of the fourth kingdom, which is understood to be " the Temporal Kingdom of the Romans," Daniel does not say : " itself shall stand for ever." These words are said of the fifth kingdom. The fourth kingdom meets with the same fate as the preceding monarchies. It belongs to the statue, the whole of which was admittedly carried away at the first coming of Christ.

4. The co-existence with the spiritual kingdom of Christ " until the end of the world " of a " Temporal Kingdom of the Romans " not identical with the Civil Princedom would involve unequal dealing with the four kingdoms, which is not warranted by the dream or its interpretation :—

For the fifth kingdom symbolised by the stone is either a purely spiritual kingdom, whose destroying power was exercised for the breaking up of the idolatrous worship of the four monarchies ; or it is a temporal as well as a spiritual kingdom bearing analogy to the monarchies, and whose contact therewith, not necessarily violent, annihilated all the four. Whether the process of breaking into pieces and consuming be of a purely spiritual or of a compound nature, it applies certainly to all the four monarchies, and it is of the same nature in respect to all. About this there can be no question.

We may not, therefore, conclude that the fifth kingdom dealt only a spiritual blow to the Roman Empire, but a physical or political one to the previous monarchies ; that it wrought the spiritual conversion of the kingdom of the Romans, whilst leaving it untouched in its temporal character ; whereas it left the kingdoms of the Babylonians, of the Persians, and of the Greeks plunged in idolatry, but broke them up politically and annihilated them.

The purely spiritual relation or contact of the fifth kingdom with the fourth would involve this unequal dealing. No spiritual treatment, including the overthrow of their idolatrous worship and the preservation of their political character, was meted out to the three first monarchies ; therefore, the Temporal Kingdom of the Romans was not so treated, but was overthrown entirely by the fifth kingdom and met the same fate as its predecessors. God, to whom belongeth the fifth kingdom, " changeth times and ages : taketh away kingdoms and establisheth them."*

* Daniel ii. 21.

The commentator remarks that the stone seen by Daniel (or rather by the King of Babylon) being small, could not overthrow such a statue " bodily or physically," and that we should conclude that the overthrowing was " mystical, spiritual, and symbolical." The whole dream, no doubt, was symbolical, but the symbolism consists in physical agents and physical agency; whereas the thing symbolised is the "taking away of kingdoms" and the "establishing of them."*

In order that the fifth kingdom should have physically or politically overthrown the four previous monarchies, it is only required :—

1.   That it should have existed "in the days of those kingdoms."

2.   That it should be God's own kingdom, not only before the Incarnation, but after.

3.   That the action of God, Who "taketh away kingdoms and establisheth them," should be ascribable to this kingdom, in view of the Incarnation and of the ancestral right of Christ.

Those who with à Lapide exclude the temporal relations and power of the fifth kingdom, seem to have been prompted by the thought that political dominion essentially implies the recourse to physical force, the raising of tribute, the clanging of broadswords, and the pomp of war and carnal triumph. This may be practically the case with the kingdoms of the world ; not so, however, with " the kingdom of God." Even the defensive wars of Israel were not the cause of its political survival.

But if some exclude the Temporal Power of " the kingdom of God," neither here nor elsewhere is the spiritual power ever excluded when speaking of the temporal. The survival of " the Temporal Kingdom of the Romans," besides being an hypothesis incompatible with the Civil Princedom was fated to supply a convenient handle to the Jewish doctors.

The commentator introduces thus the rabbinical

° *Ibidem.*

objection founded on this passage of Daniel : " This stone is said to have broken the gold, silver, brass, and iron of the statue, that is, the empires of the Chaldees, of the Persians, of the Greeks, and the Romans ; now we see that the empire of the Romans is not yet broken, but still stands : therefore, the stone, that is Messias, who will break it, has not yet come."

The reply that Messias spiritually broke the empire of the Romans is not, as we have seen, in keeping with the treatment of the other monarchies.

Will it suffice to reply that Christ will completely destroy all the kingdoms of the world on the last day ? The commentator, after quoting two early Fathers for that opinion, declares that such is not the meaning of Daniel, who points to the destruction in question as being effected at the first coming of Christ. And he insists again on its purely spiritual nature.

QUODNAM EST HOC (QUINTUM) REGNUM ?

A LAPIDE has recourse to the seventh chapter of Daniel, containing the vision of the four beasts, in confirmation of the view that the Roman Empire will stand until the end of the world, that is until Antichrist. It is remarkable that such is the evidence of the Temporal Kingdom of Christ in that chapter, that the commentator is constrained to admit that at least for a time after Antichrist, Christ and His Saints will hold such a kingdom on earth. The commentary is on the twenty-seventh verse : " And that the kingdom and power, and the greatness of the kingdom, *under* the whole Heaven, may be given to the people of the Saints of the Most High : whose kingdom is an everlasting kingdom, and all kings shall serve Him, and shall obey Him."

And he says : This is the fifth monarchy or kingdom of the Saints. You will inquire which shall this kingdom be ? And quoting Porphyrius, who declares it to have been the kingdom of the Machabees, he points out that the Asmonean kingdom was not everlasting, *non fuit æternum*, since it only lasted under Judas, Jonathan, and Simon, and later on until Herod under their un-worthy descendants. (Elsewhere I have shown that the Machabees were in no sense kings, although their successors illegitimately put the diadem on their heads.)

The commentator rejects also the millenium, as a reply to this question, declaring that it is not everlasting. He then says : " Dico ergo, certum est hoc regnum fore Christi et Sanctorum, illudque non tantum spirituale, quale fuit in terra, cum ipsi persecutionibus, martyriis **et** morti essent obnoxii : sed etiam corporale ac gloriosum, quo scilicet Sancti et corpore et anima beati, cum Christo in cœlis gloriose regnabunt in sæcula sæculorum. *Porro hoc regnum inchoabit Christus et Sancti in terra*, mox post necem Antichristi : tunc enim Antichristi regno everso Ecclesia ubique terrarum regnabit, et fiet tam ex Judæis quam ex gentibus unum ovile et unus pastor : et hoc innuitur hîc, cum ait, non, *quæ est super*, sed, *quæ est subter omne cœlum*, etc.

Bearing in mind the doctrine of the Church in reference to the Civil Princedom, namely, that it has been constantly, licitly, necessarily, legitimately, and not fortuitously associated with the universal and spiritual kingdom of Christ, there is no doubt about the value of the word *subter* "under the whole Heaven." It keeps our subject well anchored to this planet under the moon and the stars. In consequence, we have the admission that Christ and the Saints, that is the Catholic Church, will begin on earth this everlasting yet temporal kingdom. The only point, then, where we diverge is in reckoning the time of the beginning of that kingdom on earth. If it is to exist after Antichrist, one may inquire why not before ? Whatever may be the time of the death of Antichrist, whether he be human or demoniacal, one adversary or many, whether ever in opposition to Christ, or only destined to oppose Christ at the end of the world ; one thing appears certain from the vision of the mystic statue, that Christ, typified by the stone, established His kingdom over the ruins of the four previous monarchies even at His first coming. His kingdom, including the limited but twofold inheritance of the ancient kingdom of God, together with the inheritance of the Gentiles and their kingdoms, had not to wait for Antichrist to vindicate its twofold right.

"CECIDIT, CECIDIT BABYLON MAGNA."*

THE belief that the chief Apostle brought to Rome and settled there a civil sovereignty limited in extent as well as a universal spiritual power is warranted, as we have seen, both by Church teaching and by the witness of Sacred Writ.

We have seen also that the Civil Princedom is incompatible with the survival of "the Temporal Kingdom of the Romans." Two civil sovereigns cannot exercise their sovereignty over one territory because a sovereign is not a duumvir. We should consistently expect, then, that pagan Rome fell, forfeiting all natural or human sovereign right when its first Pontiff-King settled there the sceptre, the priesthood and the law of the Theocracy of the God Incarnate, his crucified Master. And reading those words, "Cecidit, cecidit Babylon magna," whether first shouted in Heaven or only re-echoed there from Peter's voice, we should understand them of the fall of pagan Rome. Was that, then, the moment when "the stone cut out of a mountain without hands" struck the base of the statue, which symbolised the monarchies? *De facto* that statue had not entirely crumbled before the withdrawal of Constantine to found a new and Christian empire in the East. But these were, without doubt, "the times or moments, which the Father (had) put in His own power," and which it was not for the Apostles "to know."†

That such was the time when the stone, that is the man-God, whose divine power had not ceased to be exercised in respect to the previous monarchies, now

* Apoc. xviii. 2.   † Acts i. 6, 7.

struck the base of the statue, appears from this, that such must have been the moment of the final translation of the Theocracy from Jerusalem to Rome. With Christ's death, no doubt, legal observances became dead, *mortua ;* but most theologians hold that they became not deadly, *mortifera,* until the destruction of the Temple seventy years after Christ. The Temple was open to St. Peter and St. John, and, no doubt, to others for the working of miracles and preaching the Gospel of " the kingdom of God." Mosaic observances might still be justified, because ignorance and prejudice could not be at once dispelled. God had not withdrawn, nor commanded the withdrawal of the Faithful from the Temple and the city of the great King. That supreme moment of national agony for everyone that felt as a Jew, that most cruel of nations' falls, the thought of which brought tears to the Saviour's eyes, was now at hand. The sceptre had been translated, and the priesthood, not only legally but locally, and now God Himself, who had been the King and protector of Israel for fourteen centuries, was about to withdraw for ever from that Temple, from that hitherto Holy City, from the land promised to Christ and to His Jewish ancestors. For now came Vespasian before Jerusalem. It was the spring of the year of Our Lord 68, the year of St. Peter's martyrdom in Rome. The Roman general had reduced the whole of Judea, and could be seen with his army camping before Jerusalem. The Christians had not to wait for Titus. This was the signal. Now was the time fixed by Christ for fleeing the city, and the time foretold by Daniel for the supreme desolation of the people of God. The Faithful withdrew; God withdrew. " When, therefore, you shall see the abomination of desolation, which was spoken of by Daniel the Prophet standing in the holy place "—not exclusively the Temple—or " standing where it ought not " according to St. Mark : " He that readeth let him understand. Then they that are in Judea, let them flee to the mountains.*

* St. Matthew xxiv. 15, 16.

The year that witnessed St. Peter's matryrdom seems, therefore, to be the epoch of the foundation of Christian Rome, since it was the year of the final translation of the Theocracy from Jerusalem. The Faithful, as bidden, had fled from the doomed city. God did not remain for the wicked, but passed over to their enemy. Thus "the kingdom of God" was, in fufilment of divine prophecy, "taken from the Jews and given to a nation (destined to yield) the fruits thereof" (St. Matthew xxi.)

Whether the first words of the eighteenth chapter of the Apocalypse should be ascribed to an angel, or to St. Peter, or to both, he must then have known that God would "restore again the kingdom to (Christian) Israel," and that the stone, which through his ministry had struck the statue, had brought down the last overwhelming enemy of the people of God. "Babylon the great is fallen, is fallen."

St. Peter, writing from Rome to his Eastern converts, uses the same language: "The Church that is in Babylon, elected together with you, saluteth you."*

Alcazar, quoted by à Lapide, says: "Nil aptius Romæ templo S. Petri pro foribus inscribi posset, quam hic hujus angeli titulus : angelo descendenti de cœlo, habenti potestatem magnam, et terra illuminata est a gloria ejus."

The fall of pagan Rome, through the ministry of St. Peter, is not the doctrine of those who hold with the survival of "the Temporal Kingdom of the Romans." They, therefore, postpone that fall of pagan Rome till the end of the world, and are, as we shall see, cruelly reduced to make Rome apostatise.

It was the common belief in the first centuries that the Roman Empire was destined to last to the end of the world. Tertullian's prayer is an indication of this. The same belief has been handed down almost to our times. Had the object of that natural belief been a political reality, such belief would have been at most a political

* 1 St. Peter v. 13.

forecast, although apparently the result of the interpretation of the Jewish prophets; but its object was a political phantom. The pagan Romans had gathered the earlier tradition which they feared, viz., that some would come from the East who should become the masters of Rome. The Christian Romans seem to have forgotten the old tradition and to have adopted an opposite one. Was not the wish in many noble and patriotic Romans father to the thought?

Those who, through not being conscious of the inherent right of the Roman Pontiffs to the Civil Princedom, have handed down a natural belief in the political continuity of "the Temporal Kingdom of the Romans," have to account for the non-destruction of Babylon, that is, of pagan Rome, whose fall in the midst of its abominations and its corrupting influence over the whole world is graphically described by St. John. No slight difficulty to grapple with, it must be confessed.

Pagan Rome, which was predestined to fall, has not yet fallen; therefore at the end of the world it must fall. But Rome is now Christian and has been Mistress Christian Church throughout the Christian Era; therefore, Rome must apostatise, nay, become once more the polluted and corrupting centre from which every error and blasphemy may go forth to the world: a rather unexpected end for the *Sancta ecclesia Romana.* And, therefore, commenting on the words, *Cecidit, cecidit Babylon magna,* à Lapide says: "Excidium enim Babylonis per Cyrum, quod describit Isaias c. 13 allegorice significabat *excidium Romæ ethnicæ in fine mundi.*"*

* From the words of St. Matthew xxiv. 21: "For there shall be then great tribulation, such as hath not been from the beginning of the world until now, neither shall be," we may judge that the fall of Jerusalem and the destruction of the Jewish nation have no parallel in the past and are not destined to have in the future. Whatever, therefore, Antichrist may effect in the world now or at the last day, we may infer from these words that nothing similar will happen to Christian Rome. L'Abbé Bergier quotes as follows from a treatise on Antichrist by Raban-Maurus, Archbishop of Mayence.

Those, therefore, who believe in the future apostasy of the Eternal City will understand the following words of the second verse : " And is become the habitation of devils, and the hold of every unclean spirit, and the hold of every unclean and hateful bird "—together with the following verses of the same chapter to describe that apostasy. On the other hand, those who are guided by the Catholic doctrine in reference to the Civil Principality will see that the sacred page contains a description of ancient pagan Rome at its worst stage of corruption, which fell, not through the invasion of Anti christ, but through the advent of him who was empowered to lay afresh its spiritual and temporal foundation.

In reference to the first verses of this chapter of the Apocalypse we read the following commentary : " Romæ paganæ in fine mundi excidium prædicit hîc Johannes ; sed tacito nomine, imo mutato ; vocat enim eam Babylonem." . . . On the words of the third verse : " And the kings of the earth have committed fornication with her : and the merchants of the earth have been made rich by the power of her delicacies,"

The author proves from St. Paul that the complete overthrow of the Roman Empire, which he supposes to be that of Germany, will precede Antichrist, and he thus concludes : "Ce terme fatal pour l'empire Romain n'est pas encore arrivé. Il est vrai que nous le voyons aujourd'hui extrémement diminué, et pour ainsi dire détruit dans sa plus grande étendue : mais il est certain que son éclat ne sera jamais entièrement éclipsé ; parce que, tandisque les rois de France, qui en doivent occuper le trône, subsisteront, ils en seront toujours le ferme appui. Quelques uns de nos docteurs assurent que ce sera un roi de France, qui à la fin du monde dominera sur tout l'empire Romain."

Bergier adds : "Il ne parait pas que nos rois aient jamais compté beaucoup sur cette prédiction." The learned author of the " Dictionnaire de Théologie " then reviews the treatise of Malvenda, a Spanish theologian, whose work is divided into thirteen books. He concludes with the remark : "Il ne manque à toutes ces belles choses que des preuves et du bon sens."

He adds : "Il est fort douteux si, dans la seconde épitre aux Thessaloniciens, St. Paul, par l'homme de péché, a voulu designer l'Antéchrist. . . . Nous n'avons ancune preuve certaine que St. Jean, par l'Antéchrist, ait entendu un seul homme puis qu'il dit qu'il y a eu plusieurs Antéchrist, etc. Enfin l'on ne peut pas prouver qu'il est question de ce personnage dans l'Apocalypse."

we read the commentary : " Romam vocat hîc primo, meretricem, secundo, mercatricen, tertio, cauponam," etc. And again, " Idque Romæ paganæ maxime congruit et congruet in fine mundi."

Again : " Alcazar addit, in voce mercatoris et meretricis notari Romanos imperatores et Judices qui ob sua peculiaria lucra Christianos in jus vocabant. . . . Rursum Christianas virgines in judiciis ad suam libidinem pellicere satagebant. . . . Similiter in fine mundi Romani, Pagani et tyranni opibus fidelium sese ingurgitabunt, ut avari mercatores, et ut lenones suam insaturabilem libidinem cum eis explere satagent."

And speaking of the wealth of pagan temples, with their marble columns ; of the statues and idols of gold and silver ; of their plays, and the gladiatorial fights, with which the pagan Romans sought to draw men to the worship of their false gods, the commentator says : " By the same means will they at the end of the world seek to draw men: " et in fine mundi pellicent." " Hasce enim delicias mercatores Romam advehebant, careque vendebant, itaque divites fiebant ; et rursum fient in novissmis temporibus."

All of which supposes not a partial nor transient usurpation of error, not mere heresy or schism, which may leave a foundation of Christian truth ; but a complete apostasy, the going over once more to the worship of devils, and for so long as to permit the rebuilding of pagan Rome.

This surely is an inconvenient outcome of the theory of the survival of " the Temporal Kingdom of the Romans," when put in juxtaposition with the words of Christ to St. Peter, of whom the Bishop of Rome is the successor : "Thou art Peter, and upon this rock I will build My Church, and the gates of hell shall not prevail against it ; " or with the familiar words occurring in this day's office : *
" Cum tanta sit ejusdem Ecclesiæ dignitas atque auctoritas, quanta illi omnino debetur, quæ est catholicæ veritatis et

* " Offic. Imm. Concs. die iii. infra Oct."

unitatis centrum, in qua solum inviolabiliter fuit custo-
dita Religio, et ex qua traducem fidei reliquæ omnes
ecclesiæ mutuentur oportet."

Next come the words : "Go out from her, My
people, that you be not partakers of its sins, and that
you receive not of her plagues." This was wholesome
advice for early Christians to keep themselves unspotted
in the midst of the wicked world around them. It is
understood by à Lapide to be a similar warning to that
given to the Faithful to leave Jerusalem before its destruction. But the Church of Rome is not to meet the fate
of the Church of the Synagogue.

On the words : "I sit a Queen" (verse 7), he
remarks that Rome will return to her ancient Imperial
splendour resulting from her wealth, her power, and her
pomp. Thus pagan Rome says : "Quamvis Pontificem,
qui vir meus erat, ejecerim, non sum tamen vidua, sed
plena populo." Here, again, a state of things is presented,
which is incompatible with the words of the Divine
promise, "the gates of hell shall not prevail against it."

The twentieth verse runs as follows : "Rejoice over
her, thou Heaven, and ye holy Apostles and Prophets, for
God hath judged your judgment on her ;" and is thus
commented on : "Puniet prisca Romanorum peccata, im-
pleta corum mensura in fine mundi : unde gravius puni-
entur Romani tunc futuri." If the succession of human
events be witnessed in Heaven with anything analogous to time as we seem to understand it, then the
Apostles including St. John, and the holy Prophets including Daniel, must find it long to wait for the ratifica-
tion of their judgment on pagan Rome.

"THE KINGDOM OF GOD" AND THE STABILITY OF THE NATIONS.

CIVIL Sovereignty has ever belonged to the Roman
Theocracy. For it is the temporal inheritance of "the
kingdom of God," translated from the Jewish nation.
We are now in a position to point out that not only is

there a common standard of right and truth for the nations, as we hinted in the beginning of the previous chapter; but provision has been made for the political as well as for the spiritual union and stability of Christendom.* The Roman Pontiff, being by Christ's appointment a civil ruler, holds direct relations with the Civil Governments of the world. The Theocracy is not a one-sided institution. It deals directly with both bishops and kings. It is the one perfect Government with unlimited authority, being spiritual and temporal, human and divine. Therein is the remedy against national caducity, whether in the religious or in the political order. For in spite of recent criticism† the successor of St. Peter " is the unerring judge of what we should do or leave undone in public as well as in private life." In other words, Christ in His Vicar is "appointed King over Sion" with twofold power. Thither must rulers and nations go, if they would learn heavenly and earthly wisdom, the divine science of faith and morals, the precepts of the positive law and those of the natural law. National stability will be the result of the observance of both. National caducity will follow the violation of either. A nation may sin more against the precepts of the Faith and of the positive Divine law, such as England ; or like our neighbours across the Channel, a nation may offend the Divine Government of the world by the more conspicuous violation of the natural law, under which I include the law of marriage and the law of the Sabbath. A corresponding breaking up of the spiritual or political unity and peace of the respective nations is the foreseen and foregone conclusion : " And whosoever shall fall on this stone (the kingdom of God) shall be broken ; but on whomsoever it shall fall, it will grind him

---

* Jos. Carrière, speaking on the origin of prescription, takes it for granted that in the civil order no common legislator exists to whom the nations are subject : " Cum nullus sit in ordine civili legislator communis cui gentes subjiciantur. . . ."—" De Justitia," Parisiis, 1869.

† Vide p. 146, " Policy of the Pope," etc.

to powder." The process of breaking up or grinding to powder will be in the spiritual or political order according as the nation has offended against "the kingdom of God." So that of two nations most favoured by God, each one, looking across the Channel, laughs at the other's insanity, while God laughs at both : " He that dwelleth in Heaven shall laugh at them." And yet may we hope that God Almighty is not entirely displeased with either nation. Where is the Church more worthily represented than in France and in her missions? And where is Civil Government more fitly exhibited than in the British Empire? We may yet learn, then, on both sides of the Channel, to take note of the presence of "the kingdom of God," of which it was foretold that "the nation and the kingdom that will not serve Thee shall perish."* And the day is, perhaps, not far distant, O Holy Roman Church, when "the children of them that afflicted thee shall come bowing down to thee; and all that slandered thee shall worship the steps of thy feet, and shall call thee the City of the Lord, the Sion of the Holy One of Israel.'

* Isaias lx. 12.   + *Ibidem*, 14.

THE THEANDRIC KINGDOM.

*"And from the days of John the Baptist until now, the
kingdom of Heaven suffereth violence, and the violent
bear it away. For all the prophets and the law
prophesied until John."*—St. Matthew xi. 12, 13.
*"The law and the prophets were until John; from that
time the kingdom of God is preached, and every one
useth violence towards it."*—St. Luke xvi. 16.

A Retrospect.

In the preceding dissertations on the Civil Principality
of the Vicar of Christ, the order of Melchisedech was
first considered, because like a mirror lifted up to Abraham and to all the Faithful, it reflected the figure of
Christ and the characteristics of His Royal Priesthood.
To the patriarchs it inspired the confidence that Christ
and His succession of Vicars would not be pilgrims and
wanderers over the face of the globe. It confirmed the
promise that they would inherit a fixed abode in their
own land with a posterity to surpass the stars of Heaven.
To David it gave the assurance, that although his Lord
and successor should assume the High Priesthood and
dispense with genealogical succession, his throne and
Royal Sovereignty should endure for ever. To the
Aaronic priesthood it was a warning that their office
and functions were preliminary. To the twelve tribes
it was prophetic that their distinctions would cease, be-
ca use tribal inheritance throughout Israel having been
or dained as a rampart to the ancestral time of Christ,
would eventually fulfil its destiny.

Next came the analysis of Scripture evidence relating to the declaration and vindication by Christ of

exemption from the national tribute to the Temple, viz., the didrachma, wherein St. Peter was associated. It was conclusively proved that both the Master and the disciple being "made under the law" could enjoy no right to exemption except on the score of twofold Sovereignty within the land promised to them and to their fathers.

It may be useful at this point to make a remark, although of a prefatory nature, which may indicate the sequence of thought and the order of writing in the original thesis. In the first meditations,* on the finding and payment of the stater, that coin was taken to be the profane tribute payable to Cæsar, which many commentators have held. There seemed to be no difficulty in raising a superstructure of argument in favour of "the Temporal Power" upon the exemption from foreign tribute in the successor and son of David, which was declared and vindicated in identical terms on behalf of the Chief Apostle. Howbeit, after much thought bestowed on this passage and on various commentaries, and after not a little writing, the conviction came that the coin was not profane, but sacred. The painful discovery seemed to leave no hope. For was not the didrachma a purely spiritual affair? The result was a bonfire, and the turning of the mind to more every-day duty. Time went on, and although the thesis seemed for ever cremated, two ghosts came hovering nearer and nearer to the mind. They pursued it at home in times of rest and in times of duty. They pursued it abroad, when riding or driving carried one on the bridle-track across the mountains, or along the level banks between the waving sugar-cane, and the wide stretch of the lower Clarence, with its broads and creeks: one kingdom belonging to a Pontiff-King among the kingdoms of this wide world was singled out for the peculiar government of Divine Providence.

* The first records on the subject in the possession of the writer are a printed lecture and correspondence, dated Sydney, September, 1885.

ab initio. That was an authentic utterance, which cured the imagination once for all from fancying anything adventitious in the conception of the Temporal Kingdom of the Papacy. But if so, Melchisedech rose in response, and nodding across the distance of space and time, he seemed to say : his order is mine with a twofold power. And then, how quickly does the mind lapse to the things of sense ! The next thought may have been in a lover of nature : how many times the age of yonder giant gums would reach to the day of Abraham and of the Pontiff-King ? Why are the Flora and Fauna of this island-continent so different to those of other lands ? How long will it be before Australasia is powerful enough to return the protection of the old country ? And our late expedition to 'Africa, now also an island-continent. A bet with the Colonel that the British Government would never give up Suakin, verified up to date. And the ghosts would be laid for that day, and by a similar process for many another day. But across the distance of space and time rose that figure again. It said : I am King, and for a like reason is the Roman Pontiff King. The result was not only the quickening from its ashes of the Scriptural order of Melchisedech, but the reconstruction of the whole thesis. The reflection of the Royalty of the Incarnation was cast back upon the sacred records of the past, and became the text of Apostolic teaching for the future. How came it then that Christ who exercised sovereign power in Israel during His public ministry, meant nothing by declaring His own and Peter's independence, and vindicating the same ? Was it a purely spiritual exemption that He declared and vindicated ? At last the truth flashed forth. In the Hebrew Commonwealth the power of the Prince and of the Pontiff were distinct, but there was no distinction of legislation. That was single and Divine, and co-ordained both the spiritual and temporal powers to one Theocratic Government. Hence the tribute payable to the Temple, although spiritual in its object, had the sanction of the whole law with its twofold human power. The declaration of exemption from such tribute and its vindication, could only be the sovereign act of a legislator holding twofold human sovereignty together with Divine power. Hence the first Roman Pontiff inherited twofold Sovereignty from His Divine Master. And, finally, Church teaching was borne out both by the type and the Reality.

Once the twofold Sovereignty and independence of Christ and of His Vicar had come into view, justifying both Church teaching and the ancient type of Royal Priesthood, the promise of land in the day of Abraham was understood to relate to Christ. That which was reflected in the Pontiff-King had to come out of Abraham, and was impossible in concrete existence without the land. A land was preordained for the Incarnation in view of its royalty. A peculiar people, a holy nation, a priestly kingdom, were to establish beforehand the home, the social position, the national right to eventual supremacy of Messias. "To thy seed will I give this land," was a promise corresponding with the type of Royal Priesthood, and indicating how its realisation would be performed in the fulness of time.

In this argument two points were principally insisted on : (1) That at the extinction of the Church of the Synagogue there was no earthly nor heavenly reason for the cancelling of God's gift of land to the children of the promise, since to the Mother Church of Christendom territorial independence would not only be suitable but necessary ; and (2) that Christ, besides being the principal inheritance promised to Abraham, in Whom all nations should be blessed, was also the principal Heir of the Promised Land, henceforth destined to be inherited for all time as " the kingdom of God."

The next argument was based on the Parable of the Vineyard, revealing a threefold eviction of the Jews : a political and spiritual eviction, which cast them out of the high office of sheltering the human and vicarious authority of the Theocracy, and an eviction from God's peculiar ownership. It was shown that the forfeited inheritance of Israel passed to another nation, viz., the Holy Roman Church, which enables us to account even for the spiritual inheritance with its exalted privileges, not extending to all Churches, but remaining circumscribed within a definite centre of Theocracy.

Finally, Church documents were studied and commented on. The notes of the Civil Princedom evolved from authentic teaching were found to correspond with the Fathers on the one hand, and with the Scripture evidence of the imperishable nature of the kingdom of the God of Heaven. Other Governments were discovered to be subject to the law of caducity in the spiritual or political world. The Civil Princedom of the Roman Pontiff is an exception: "to all the fowls he seems a Phœnix."*

The second Psalm was chosen as a text as well as Daniel's interpretation of the dream of the King of Babylon, because Christ is there represented as "constituted King over Sion," not merely for three years of most prudent exercise of power and partial recognition, ending with a mocking coronation and a torturing enthronement, but for the inheriting and ruling of the Gentiles during all time. The words *dirumpamus vincula eorum* have been put into the mouth of the Apostles by some commentators. They have not the Apostolic ring, but the rebellious accent of the disciples of Antichrist. And seeing that the psalm reveals God's provision for Christ's kingly inheritance of the Gentiles during all ages, and easy victory over their opposition, the words *dirumpamus*, etc., inciting to rebellion, may be legitimately ascribed to the enemies of Christ, not only before the Resurrection, but after that glorious event. It is now time to give a special attention to the nature of Christ's kingdom on earth, to distinguish between that which is limited and that which is universal, between that which

* "Paradise Lost." Book V.

belonged to His manhood during His mortal career and that which afterwards became His inheritance. The influence of Royal potentates on theological learning, since the Renascence, may be traced not only to courtiers, but to the most holy writers of the last centuries. Even the reaction against the worldly pomp and national pride of modern European Courts must have been unfavourable to a clear perception of the Royalty of Christ and of His Vicar, and led many a writer to etherealise Christ's Kingship. Against such etherealism this paper is directed.

CHRIST'S ROYAL SUCCESSION.

THE first chapter of St. Matthew shows two things : (1) the Royal succession of Christ through St. Joseph from David and Juda and the patriarchs, and (2) that Christ was conceived by the Holy Ghost. This is a remarkable testimony of the inspired word to the Royalty of Christ, which precludes the possibility of an illusory or nominal dignity. The natural genealogy of Christ, although not excluded, is passed over, and the regal succession through St. Joseph is thereby not only insisted on, but singularly emphasised. Those who are desirous to learn how the prophecies, which foretold Christ's natural descent from David, were fulfilled, must go elsewhere. Here a page is open to those who are willing to ponder on the care God took, not only to record, but to secure a rightful succession and well defined national and social position for the Son of Man. If in the Divine plan a natural descent without Royal succession from David had been intended, the natural genealogy of Christ, which was the legal genealogy of St. Joseph, as given by St. Luke, would have sufficed, and alone been appropriate. There was only one line of Royal succession, and it came down through St. Joseph, who fulfilled all the duties and enjoyed all the privileges of a lawful husband and a Royal father compatible with the Incarnation. The Royal succession of Christ, in view of the exercise of His public ministry, may be said to be God's reverential provision for the conformity of Christ to the laws of His own creation. God, the author of all order and national legislation, whether natural or Theocratic, was the author of the law under which Christ was made. The manhood of Christ could only be subject to that law or endowed with sovereign and local legislative power. The fact of His being King of the whole world, in virtue of the hypostatic union and the supposition that only in that sense He was King of the Jews, will afford no escape from the imperious necessity of a local Kingship. If you derive Christ's authority in Israel from His Godhead, so as to exclude what He was capable of as man, you curtail His manhood without justification. The one thing human incompatible with the hypostatic union is a human personality. The substitution of the personality of the Son of God was Christ's perfection. The idea of any other Divine substitution can only be an error outrageous to the perfection of Christ's sacred humanity. Therefore, since Christ exercised supreme power in Israel during His public ministry, let us ascribe it, where we can, to the human and limited rule He was capable of as man, and which belonged to the perfection of His manhood.

No doubt Christ was and is King of the whole world. Even the overthrowing of the monarchies before the Incarnation was, as we have seen, attributable to Christ, (1) because the attributes of Christ as God can be predicated of Him as man ; and conversely, provided we speak not of the Divine and human natures in the abstract. And (2) because the motive power of the Incarnation was anticipating in Israel the work of "the kingdom of God." But one thing is to govern by the natural law—"taking away kingdoms and establishing them"—another to be King in a particular land and therein to exercise legitimate power. One thing that Christ should have full power in Heaven and on earth, another thing that by purely human succession He should exercise the local powers vested in Him as Son

of David and last bearer of the sceptre of Juda. The
Royal succession of Christ was therefore a Divine provision to harmonise Christ's manhood with the essentially
necessary exercise of sovereign power in Israel. The
Royal succession contained in the first inspired record
in the New Testament writings came down to Christ
through that noble and trustful personage, St. Joseph.
This point has been controverted, but with singularly
feeble argument.

Le Blanc, commenting on the second Psalm, inquires
whether Christ by hereditary and purely human right
were temporal King of the Jews. He proceeds to
quote authorities for that opinion, some tracing His
Royal succession through Mary, the others through St.
Joseph. In refutation of the Royal descent through St.
Joseph, held by à Lapide, he questions whether St.
Joseph were the eldest among his brethren, whether his
father, grandfather, and other ancestors were the first-
born among their brethren. From which mere doubt he
concludes that the words of Christ, "I am constituted
King by Him over Sion," are to be understood of the
Church over which He is a spiritual King. The latter
conclusion is, of course, true in any case, since Christ
holds twofold human power. But the negative argument
employed by Le Blanc to etherealise Christ's Temporal
Kingship is of no value in the presence of positive
evidence of an opposite character. No doubt, like other
modern commentators, he was impressed with the carnal
nature of the kingdom expected by the Jews, and the
worldliness of many Christian kings, and failed to realise
that a temporal kingdom may be sacred by reason of
its purpose, and necessary at the seat of a universal
spiritual kingdom.

The Subjection of Christ.

The first chapter of St. Matthew prepares us, therefore,
for the birth of the King of the Jews recorded in the
second. We shall see more in detail how and when

Christ began to exercise the legitimate power that de-
volved upon Him within His own country, a power which,
by God's special permission and most wise counsel, had
fallen from the hands of His predecessors in spite of the
provision made for the Prince from the days of Captivity.*
For the present, "as long as the Heir is a child, He
differeth nothing from a servant, though He be Lord of
all; but is under tutors and governors until the time
appointed by the Father." Fully conscious that that
Child is God, let us continue to watch jealously over the
belongings of His humanity. Not that the Divine nature
of the God-man could obliterate or attenuate anything
essential to our humanity in Christ; but that the human
mind, in contemplation of this mystery, may, in assigning
rights to the sacred humanity in virtue of the hypostatic
union, leave out something of the subjection and limita-
tions which are essential to man. Such would be birthright in one country, nationality, limitation of inheritance,
local subjection, local citizenship, or local sovereignty.
Thus, to say that Christ was born "King of the whole
world," which He was, no doubt, in virtue of the hypostatic
union, to the exclusion of the local title as "King of the
Jews," is an invasion of His human rights, and an error
no longer excusable, but most pernicious in our day.
Those who, like Le Blanc, derive Christ's authority in
Israel from a source exclusive of His Jewish birthright
and local sovereignty, which it was the perfection of His
manhood to exercise when called upon, make no distinction between the time of Christ's subjection and the time
of His assumption of power. Hence confusion reigns in
their ideas of His subjection, just as in their ideas of His
Sovereignty.

If we be guided by the knowledge that Christ had
all the attributes of man on the one hand, and by the rules
of the *communicatio idiomatum* on the other, we cannot
get astray from Catholic doctrine. What are the essential relations of man born into this world and into the

* *Vide* Ezechiel.

society of other men. Well, first to be assigned a
definite social position, and first of all to be subject.
Subjection to parents, subjection to civil and ecclesiastical rulers, subjection to the laws of the country, subjection to God, are the normal condition of human
existence. Was Christ subject to His parents? " He
was subject to them."* In what sense? Essentially as
man, condescendingly as God, Who in assuming our
nature assumed all that is essential to our nature.
Therefore we may say Christ was subject to His parents,
whether we mean as God or man, provided we mean
condescendingly as God and essentially as man. For
the same reason we may say that Christ was not subject
to His parents, nor to rulers, nor to the law, even considered as the interpretation of the natural Divine law,
provided we mean not essentially subject as God. The
same rule applies to Christ's subjection to His Heavenly
Father. He was subject to His Father in Heaven
essentially as man, voluntarily and condescendingly as
Son of God. For as such he was co-equal with the
Father. Through not strictly adhering to these rules,
some authors have improperly distinguished between the
obedience yielded by Christ as man to His Heavenly
Father, to civil and ecclesiastical rulers, to His parents, and to the law, commencing with circumcision.
Thus, whilst they consider Christ's obedience to His
Father in Heaven a matter of obligation as man, they
declare that the same human obedience to civil or ecclesiastical rulers was without any obligation whatsoever,
whereas they hold that Christ acknowledged some jurisdiction in His father and mother. There is confusion
of ideas in all this. Christ, as man, was essentially subject to the law, insomuch as the law was the interpretation of the natural law. Christ, as man, belonged to
the order of human society. Hierarchical order reigns
among the unfallen angels. Some kind of social organi-
sation is essential to the rational creature, whether fallen

* St. Luke ii. 5.

or unfallen. But Christ was not subject to the law inso-
far as it related to a sinful race, and prescribed a remedy
for sin. In His subjection to such prescriptions He
condescended also as man. He was, therefore, subject
to His parents and to rulers in the same sense that He
was subject to the natural Divine law. So long as He
remained in subjection to the law as man, He was, therefore, capable of inferiority in respect to parents and to
rulers ; the only distinction being that obedience was
tendered with love and gratitude to the former, and with
mixed feelings corresponding with the merits or demerits
of the latter. The time of Christ's subjection seems to
have lasted twenty-nine years. For He was to receive
not only royal, but prophetic, doctrinal, and sacerdotal
authority. Now, according to the custom of the law,
"the Levites were numbered from the age of thirty
years and upwards."*

Inauguration of the Jewish Theandric Kingdom.

We read in St. Luke iii.: "Now it came to pass, when
all the people were baptised, that Jesus also being baptised, and praying, Heaven was opened : and the Holy
Ghost descended in a bodily shape as a dove upon Him ;
and a voice came from Heaven : 'Thou art My beloved
Son, in Thee I am well pleased.' And Jesus Himself
was beginning about the age of thirty years. . . ."
This last act of subjection to legitimate human
authority immediately prepared Him, Who was constituted "King over Sion," for beginning His public
ministry of preaching the mystery of the Incarnation :
the advent of "the kingdom of God," the accession to
power. on earth of a Theandric Ruler, Whose Royalty
was an earthly title, unabridged by the hypostatic union.
St. Matthew thus records His first preaching in
Galilee : "From that time Jesus began to preach and to
say : 'Do penance, for the kingdom of Heaven is at
hand.'" The words "is at hand" may both mean is near

° 1 Par. xxiii. 3.

or is present. I take the latter meaning to be the adequate rendering of *appropinquavit*, has come nigh.   For
the sentence does not refer to what occurred three years
later, the opening of Heaven by Christ after His death,
which enabled the repentant thief to pray thus : " Lord,
remember me when Thou comest to Thy kingdom."
No doubt the Son of Man, before He opened Heaven to
the soul of the good thief, was already in Heaven as
God : " And no man hath ascended into Heaven but
He that descended from Heaven, the Son of Man, Who
is in Heaven."*   To be both on earth and in Heaven,
was a Divine attribute belonging to Christ before " He
ascended into Heaven."   Hence Israel, the first Christian
Church, was fitly termed the kingdom of Heaven, that
is, " the kingdom of the God of Heaven," the expression
used by Daniel.   And no hailing of His kingdom on
earth could be acceptable to Christ unless it were accom-
panied with the recognition by faith and repentance of
His kingdom in Heaven.   Hence the proper recognition
even of His earthly kingdom began with faith.   Even
the coming of that earthly kingdom was not observable
to the carnal eye, as the kingdoms of this world, founded,
for the most part, on violent conquest.   It was not fit
that Christ's Royalty should be hailed before its formal
object, the Incarnation or " kingdom of God."   Therefore, to those who lacked the necessary faith, and inquired when the kingdom of God should come, He
answered them and said : " The kingdom of God cometh
not with observation ; neither shall they say : ' Behold
here, or behold there.'   For the kingdom of God is
within you."†   But those, like Nathanael, whose heart
was prepared as a throne for the Heavenly King by the
obedience of the faith, were welcome to proclaim His
accession to an earthly kingdom : " Rabbi, Thou art the
Son of God, Thou art the King of Israel."‡   The preaching of Christ was then His assumption of power and the

---

* St. John iii. 13.   † St. Luke xvii. 20, 21.   ‡ St. John i. 49.

earthly accession of the Son of God connecting, under
one personal rule, the kingdom of Israel and the kingdom of Heaven. The same meaning is expressed by
the words of Christ : " If I, by the Spirit of God, cast
out devils, then is the kingdom of God come upon you."*
And again : " If I, by the finger of God, cast out devils,
doubtless the kingdom of God is come upon you."†
Sometimes the expression like that of the last quotations
signifies the kingdom of the God-man established on
earth. Sometimes, as in the following quotation, it
refers to the near future of the kingdom of Heaven
above : " For I say to you, that I will not drink of the
fruit of the vine, till the kingdom of God come."‡ The
coming state of the blessed in the kingdom of Heaven,
and the actual state and position of the faithless Jews
upon whom "the kingdom of God" had come on earth,
are expressed in the two following verses of St. Matthew : "And I say unto you that many shall come from
the east and west, and shall sit down with Abraham,
and Isaac, and Jacob, in 'the kingdom of Heaven :' But
the children of ' the kingdom ' shall be cast out into the
exterior darkness."§ A similar meaning is conveyed by
the text "the kingdom of God shall be taken from you.
. . ." It was not the spiritual kingdom of the Faith
that they were children of, and that was to be taken from
them, since they had not the Faith. Neither was it the
kingdom of Heaven, wherein the blessed sit down with
Abraham and the patriarchs. Wherefore it could only
be the Temporal Kingdom of Israel, now become " the
kingdom of God."

A Lapide, commenting on the words : " And Jesus
Himself was beginning about the age of thirty years,"
takes care to point out that the word beginning is not to
be referred to the age of Christ, but to the public ministry for which He was sent by the Father. He says:

---

* St. Matthew xii. 28.   † St. Luke xi. 20.   ‡ St. Luke xxii. 18.
§ St. Matthew viii. 11, 12.

"το incipiens non referas ad το annorum triginta : sic enim redundaret vox *quasi*, sed ad prædicationem publicam Jesu, ad quam missus est a Patre, q.d. Jesus quum in baptismo per columbam et vocem Patris declaratus est Messias, Orbis Doctor, legislator et Salvator, ideoque hoc suum munus et officium exercere, ac publice legem evangelicam docere et prædicare inciperet, *erat quasi annorum triginta*. Patet ex Græco, qui habet : ' Et Jesus erat quasi annorum triginta incipiens,' id est, cum inciperet officio fungi et prædicare. Ita Jansenius, Baronius, et alii."

Such was the inauguration of the Jewish Theandric kingdom : a kingdom in complete harmony with Jewish law and with all types and prophecies, which brought down the God of Heaven to succeed to the throne of Israel, and enthroned the Son of David in the kingdom of God.

Besides the Evangelist's narrative we have a record of Christ's own testimony to His assumption of power in the following words : " And from the days of John the Baptist until now, the kingdom of Heaven suffereth violence, and the violent bear it away. For all the prophets and the law prophesied until John."* And again : " The law and the prophets were until John ; from that time the kingdom of God is preached, and every one useth violence towards it"—*et omnis in illud vim facit.*† These words must not be understood as though every one were using spiritual violence to bear away the the prize of Heaven above. This is a mystical accommodation of the text, but I cannot honestly give it as the proper and literal interpretation. I look upon it, indeed, as dangerous, and belonging to that etherealism of the "kingdom of God" so injurious to the Papacy in our day. *Every one* in Israel at the time of Christ's public ministry was very far from possessing such spiritual energy. Whatever violence there was in the nation, whether in the will or in the execution, was

* St. Matthew xi. 12, 13.   † St. Luke xvi. 16.

directed against "the kingdom of God," since it was heralded by John the Baptist. At the time Christ gave this testimony St. John was in prison, awaiting further violence, and the preaching of Christ was transferred to Galilee by reason of the same violent opposition to "the kingdom of God." The whole generation of that day was a violent one, deaf to any appeal, whether by lamenting or by piping. On occasion of the former, they said, " He hath a devil "; and of the latter, " Behold a man that is a glutton and wine drinker, a friend of publicans and sinners." Corozain used violence against " the kingdom of God." Bethsaida did the same. Christ's choice of Capharnaum as the city of His residence, the mighty works that He did therein, should have brought its people under the sway of the King of Heaven ; but the violence of their opposition drove back the kingdom of God and bore it away.

But we are not so much concerned with the meaning of the violence used towards " the kingdom of God," as with its inauguration declared in the following words recorded by St. Luke : " The law and the prophets were until John : from that time the kingdom of God is preached . . ." and these other words recorded by St. Matthew : " For all the prophets and the law prophesied until John." Whatever testimony he produced to show that Christ by these words indicates His assumption of power in succession to the law and the prophets, will be so much testimony that the violence in question was used, not in reference to the Heaven of the blessed, but towards " the kingdom of God " then proclaimed in Israel.

THE SUCCESSION OF "THE KINGDOM OF HEAVEN" TO THE LAW AND THE PROPHETS NOT A MERE PREACHING OR FOLLOWING OF A MORE HEAVENLY DOCTRINE.

A LAPIDE, after explaining these passages in a purely spiritual sense (perhaps I should express myself more

2

correctly by saying, in a sense exclusive of the Temporal Power of Christ), namely, that whereas Moses and the prophets prophesied obscurely concerning Christ and His kingdom of Heaven, promising earthly goods, that is abundance of wine and corn and oil and a peaceful Temporal Kingdom, the precursor clearly pointed to the kingdom of Heaven to be opened by Christ, proceeds to give a different testimony, saying : " Paulo aliter Maldonatus. Omnes prophetæ, inquit, et lex prophetaverunt, id est officio suo functi sunt, et durarunt usque ad Joannem ; non quod tunc statim omnino lex desierit, ut volunt Centuriatores Magdeburgenses sed quod mori et desinere cœperit ; lex enim vetus, ejusque obligatio duravit usque ad promulgationem legis novæ, quæ facta est post resurrectionem et ascensionem Christi in Pentecoste."

Maldonatus clearly perceives in the testimony of Christ concerning the succession of John and of " the kingdom of God " to the law and the prophets an evidence of Christ's assumption of power, concurrently with the law and the prophets and in fulfilment of them. This principle lies at the foundation of the whole thesis. The violence used towards "the kingdom of God " or " the kingdom of Heaven " was not, therefore, identical with the repentance of a small remnant on the banks of the Jordan, nor with the faith and loyalty of the timid disciples, but consisted in the opposition of the Church-nation to their heavenly and earthly King, already partaking of a physically violent character in the imprisonment of St. John. Christ, on His accession to power, whether in the spiritual or temporal order, was met with violent opposition, not only on the part of Herod, who had cast the herald of His kingdom into prison, or on the part of the Roman power curtailing, as a punishment from God, the sovereignty and independence of the nation, but on the part of the Synagogue and the spiritual masters of Israel, and, worse still, on the part of the majority of the people, who would not have this man to reign over them.

When contemplating "the kingdom of God" on earth, we must, therefore, take the utmost care never to separate the three powers—temporal, spiritual, and Divine. For the violence towards the temporal rule is a consequence of the opposition to the spiritual kingdom and to God's own Sovereignty. Hence the seriousness of the violent opposition to the Temporal Power of the Pope at the present day, which is due no longer to a passing fit of anger in a rebuked monarch of some Catholic land, but to the apostasy of a whole section of the peninsula.

From the evidence of the Royal succession of Christ, of His subjection and eventual accession to power, we gather that in a logical sense Christ was first earthly King, then King of Heaven, and, finally, priest according to the order of Melchisedech. For although God had been, according to the law, the high ruler of Israel even before kings were established, yet the title king was borrowed by God from the earthly sovereigns. Kingship is the attribute of a human being and the title of a limited power. It could not properly belong to God before the Incarnation. For it belongs not to the Divine nature, but to the human nature of the Son of God Incarnate. Logically, therefore, Christ was first "King of the Jews." On the other hand, an earthly title applied to God's ruling in Heaven comes logically in the second place. He was, therefore, secondly, "King of Heaven," and "the kingdom of God" came logically after the kingdom of Israel. But the preaching of the mystery of "the kingdom of God" Incarnate, embracing both the kingdom of Israel and "the kingdom of Heaven," was the function of Christ's holy soul or spiritual power, for which testimony He lived and died. Hence He was ordained from the beginning Pontiff-King. The spiritual dignity was, however, logically in the third place. The first preaching of the Royal Pontiff and Theandric King was then a doctrinal definition of the fundamental mystery of the Christian religion: the Incarnation, together with a proclamation of its kingly rule. Such was "the gospel of the kingdom."

It may be further remarked that the word kingdom is not the special designation of the spiritual power. It belongs rather to the order of nature, which is antecedent to that of grace. A kingdom has a direct reference to the body, whereof it is the sovereign extension. Man's earthly rights begin with his body. They can be traced first to food and clothing, then to his bed, and cell, and house. Maybe to his grounds or estates, to his earldom, or dukedom. If he be a sovereign, his earthly rights are only limited by his kingdom or empire. Hence, when the Church of God throughout the world is designated " the kingdom of God " we must admit, unless we are accustomed to wrestle with the transparency of logical truth, that a temporal kingdom—viz., that of Israel—was the foundation of " the kingdom of God " throughout all space and time.

The Prophecy of Jacob.

THE succession of Christ's kingdom to the law and the prophets throws light on the prophecy of Jacob, and confirms more and more the interpretation given to it in these pages. Of the prophetic words, "The sceptre shall not be taken away from Juda, nor a ruler from his thigh, *till He come*," it was said. This does not mean that the sceptre should be taken away before Christ could inherit it, nor that violence could snatch away a Theocratic right. The national prophecy evidently alludes to the termination of the old order of things, when both the law and the priesthood should be translated. The sceptre then was safely carried down to Christ. The tribe of Juda had endured as a nation for that purpose.

The hypothesis that the sceptre had been taken away from Juda by the usurpation of Herod the Great, who had reigned thirty-five years before the coming of Christ, leaves a gap of more than a third of a century between the failing of the sceptre and the coming of Messias the King. The succession of the King of Heaven to the law and the prophets, or, in other words, to "the kingdom of Israel," was, as we have seen, without any break whatsoever. Besides which there was no kingly usurper at the time of Christ's assumption of power. Judea was tributary to the Romans, but not yet a Roman province. Which interpretation seems more in accordance with sound exegetics? But we may further inquire on what principle are the words *donec veniat* interpreted to mean a time before *the birth of Christ*. His coming, as we have seen, had not reached its full meaning before His accession to power. Then, indeed, He inherited the sceptre with the kingdom, succeeding to the law and the prophets. At the outset of His public ministry He had said : "Do not think that I am come to destroy the law and the prophets ; I am not come to destroy, but to fulfil."* His fulfilment of the law was the meaning, and the measure, and the time of His coming. That was not consummated till He expired on the Cross. Then was the sceptre taken away from Juda. For with the priesthood it passed to the Apostle Peter, who was not of the Royal succession. "For the priesthood being translated, it is necessary that a translation also be made of the law."

À Lapide examines the meaning of the words *et dux de femore ejus*, which he interprets of the leaders who followed the kings after the Captivity, such being Zorobabel and the Machabees. But the Machabees were not of the stock of Juda, but of Levi. How, then, are they to be ranked in the succession, not only from Juda, but from David?

I have no difficulty in saying that the Machabees were not included in the succession of leaders foreseen by the prophet and foretold as the posterity of Juda. But the line of Royal succession so carefully preserved by God and recorded in the first inspired page of the

* St. Matthew v. 17.

New Testament, was foreseen and foretold by the prophetic blessing of the patriarch Israel. In other words, the ancestors of Christ from the time of the Captivity were leaders with a Theocratic right of succession, to whom God for most wise reasons had, in fact, denied the sacred unction, and whom He allowed to fall by degrees from the splendour of their forefathers. Provision, however, had been made for the Prince, as we see from Ezechiel; but in the absence of any prophet to come forth as of old on behalf of the secular ruler, the priests were allowed to monopolise the twofold power of the Church-nation. And the nation was allowed to make choice of the Machabees, and to confer, not a Theocratic, but a natural right of succession upon their family, " till there should arise a faithful prophet."

The Jewish Kingdom in Abeyance.

And what can have been the reason in the all-wise Providence of God for the retirement of the Royal descendants of David? God, Who can not only foresee and foretell, but make provision in the sacrificial rites of a nation for, its future corruption and apostasy and murderous design, without interfering with man's free will, could also foresee the incompatibility between the reigning of holy monarchs and the temper of a rebellious nation at the time of the coming of the Saviour. It is to be presumed, from the disinterested conduct of Zorobabel and his successors, who sought not to vindicate their hereditary right that seventy years of captivity had left its impress upon their minds, and that they bowed to God's special appointment. Certain it is that the immediate ancestors of Christ were among the beloved ones of God. Had they been constrained to mount the throne of their forefathers, could they have quelled the insubordination of a wicked race, which deserved rather the lashing of a Herod than the government of a David. God was too careful to preserve the most precious ancestry of the Redeemer, to expose them to the fury of a race of vipers. A king after the pattern of David, anxious to share with God the government of His people, could only have fallen a premature victim to their perversity. Let the destined Victim accede to power, be saluted Son of God, and King of Israel, and restorer of the kingdom of David; here was no un-wisdom. It was according to the Divine plan. The sceptre had reached its appointed goal. It will appear in the hand of " the King of the Jews " in the form of a reed, whilst the triple crown, which they plaited, will proclaim the three powers of Redemption.

Thus the succession of "the kingdom of Heaven" to the law and the prophets could not bring to Christ less power than belonged to the law and the prophets. We have seen that the perfection of His manhood required that He should inherit and exercise in Israel whatever powers a Jewish Prince was capable of, if called upon, and that the hypostatic union did not etherealise any of His human rights.

We read in Ezechiel* the following words to the wicked King Sedecias: " But thou profane wicked Prince of Israel, whose day is come that hath been appointed in the time of iniquity : thus saith the Lord : ' Remove the diadem, take off the crown : is it not this that hath exalted the low one, and brought down that was high ?' I will show it to be iniquity, iniquity, iniquity, but this was not done, till He came to Whom judgment belongeth, *and I will give it Him.*"

The removal of the diadem from the Royal succession was due to iniquity, as we have seen. The iniquity of kings before the Captivity, and the iniquity of the people in later times. But if the diadem was removed, either as a punishment for the iniquity of kings, or as a measure of precaution against national iniquity for the safety of the ancestors of Christ, not so the Theocratic right of succession.

Le Blanc, in his exposition of the sixth verse of the

* Ezechiel xxi. 25-27

second Psalm, *Ego autem*, etc., although etherealising the local and territorial right of Christ as a Jewish king, is forced to admit that the passage quoted from Ezechiel may be explained of the temporal kingdom of Christ: "Itaque locus hic tam de regno Christi temporali quam de spirituali exponi potest." "*And I will give it Him*," is eloquent enough, both of the nature of the crown and of the Person entitled to it.

The secret of the removal of the diadem and crown from the Royal succession by the Providence of God, the high Ruler of Israel, was thus only made manifest after the accession to power of Christ, the King of Israel and King of Heaven. He, the high One, was brought down by the coronation, which had exalted the low one. It was necessary for the redemption of the world. "I will show it to be iniquity, iniquity, iniquity; but this was not done till He came to Whom judgment belongeth, and I will give it Him." This exposition is not out of harmony with that of à Lapide, who in his Commentary on Ezechiel xxi. 27 has these words: "Simplicius, æque ac planius posset iniquitas tam proprie pro culpa, quàm figurate accipi pro pœna iniquitatis." The deprivation of the crown in the immediate ancestors of Christ was the penalty of iniquity, although a most merciful appointment. And the assumption of the kingly power by Christ followed by His coronation became the penalty of iniquity.

LIMITATION OF SPIRITUAL RIGHT.

IF the mystery of the Incarnation left untouched the human rights that the sacred humanity of Christ was capable of possessing and exercising ; if, on the other hand, God provided a Royal succession for the Son of Man, and if "the kingdom of Heaven" did at the appointed time succeed to the law and the prophets, until it fulfilled them, what have we to conclude? Without going back to Christ's sovereign declaration and vindication of right on His own behalf and on behalf of St.

Peter, and other sources of Scripture evidence, we might legitimately conclude from this evidence alone that Christ succeeded to the twofold human power over the people of God. The kingdom of David, whose limited inheritance was provided by the law and the prophets for Christ, was a sacred kingdom. The two human powers of that kingdom, unlike the two powers of the ordinary Christian nation, were equally under immediate Divine control and possession. From this we should infer that Christ, in virtue of His Jewish birth and local inheritance, was possessed, not only of a limited territorial right, but also of a limited spiritual power, extending to the confines of Israel, and coextensive with His Royal succession. That which we find ourselves in duty bound to yield to the sacred humanity is equally vouched for in Holy Writ. We read in St. Matthew these words of Christ to His disciples, who had besought Him in favour of the woman of Chanaan : " I was not sent but to the sheep that are lost of the house of Israel." Compare these words with the declaration He made after His resurrection, " All power is given to Me in Heaven and in earth," and it becomes apparent that Christ's personal mission, by which, in contradistinction with the Apostolate, I mean the mission entrusted to Him as man during His mortal career, being limited, had a special relation to His own country and kingdom. In other words, the hypostatic union, far from obliterating His human right and local kingdom, emphasised it, by restricting the preaching and spiritual mission of Christ to the limits of Israel. For the preaching of Christ was of a kingdom, which is a human and limited attribute distinct from the Priesthood. The preaching of that kingdom was the preaching of the Incarnation. For the Royal attribute, with every other human attribute, was assumed by the Son of God under His one personality. Hence the expression, " the kingdom of God," or " the kingdom of Heaven."

Now we may seek in vain for any intimation, whether in the Scriptures or in the Fathers, or in the tradition of the Roman Church, that the personal inheritance of Christ was undone by the assumption of world-wide powers. The kingdom does not necessarily disappear with the growth of an empire. Neither does the Mother Church become confounded with the Church Universal. She retains her local privileges. We have seen elsewhere that the local "kingdom of God" was destined to pass to another nation, yielding the fruits thereof. The land of which Jerusalem is the capital is no longer "the land of Israel." The spiritual prerogatives of the local Roman Church belong to a special inheritance, which explains, independently of other evidence, her spiritual indefectibility. Just as the temporal inheritance of "the kingdom of Israel" and "kingdom of God" explains the vitality in right and in fact of the Civil Princedom. THE number twelve of the Apostles belongs to the limited and national mission of Christ. It was destined to disappear with the disappearance of genealogical right of inheritance, whether in the spiritual or temporal order. The ecumenical office presupposed the amalgamation of the tribes among one another, and with the Gentiles. When the faithful Israelites had learned that the law no longer insisted on their genealogies, which were a preparation for the Incarnation, and that the Christian law bade them regard the convert Gentiles as brethren, a fusion of Jewish and Gentile blood took place in all the first Christian communities. St. Paul's discharge of this Apostolic teaching is on record. He writes to Timothy : "As I desired thee to remain at Ephesus, when I went into Macedonia, that thou mightest charge them not to teach otherwise, nor to give heed to fables and genealogies without end, which minister questions rather than the edification of God, which is in faith." And to Titus : "But avoid foolish questions and genealogies, and contentions, and strivings about the law : for they are unprofitable and vain."

St. Peter's Limited and Ecumenical Power.

St. Peter was the only Apostle associated in the two-fold Sovereignty and independence of his Divine Master. If that sovereignty and independence have been handed down to the Vicars of Christ, St. Peter, besides an ecumenical mission and a universal flock scattered among the nations, must have received a limited mission to a peculiar flock. A question then arises: Where was that peculiar flock before St. Peter finally established the Roman Church? Was there a solution of continuity in the spiritual government of the centre of Theocracy? We can understand the Sovereign Pontiff of the new law being without a *de facto* civil government, just as we understand the captivity of the leaders of Israel in Babylon. The Temporal Power is not proof against passing violence. But no persecution which the gates of hell can raise may cause even a temporary breakdown of God's central spiritual government. The infallibility of the Pontiff, in virtue of Divine promises, is bound up with the indefectibility of His own particular Church. We may, perchance, then discover some traces of the limited mission of St. Peter, and of his peculiar flock, before the final establishment of the Holy Roman Church. Let it be premised, however, that a limited mission does not exclude a wider one, or one without limits. The Bishop, besides his diocese, has a Cathedral parish, with a peculiar flock of his own, distributed over a well-defined district. St. Paul, then, shall be our first authority. In his Epistle to the Galatians he says: "When they had seen that to me was committed the Gospel of the uncircumcision, as to Peter was that of the circumcision (for he who wrought in Peter to the apostleship of the circumcision wrought in me also among the Gentiles), and when they had known the grace that was given to me, James and Cephas and John, who seemed to be pillars, gave to me and Barnabas the right hands of fellowship: that we should go to the Gentiles, and they to the circumcision."

In reading this text we must bear in mind that all the Apostles had ecumenical power, that Peter addressed himself to the Gentiles and St. Paul to the Jews. "For He is our peace, Who hath made both one, and breaking down the middle wall of partition, the enmities in His flesh. . . ." We must, therefore, with St. Jerome, discard the idea of a division of power between the two Apostles and interpret the words of St. Paul as to a general division of labour. A division of power if wrought by God between the two Apostles would have implied a limited mission in each one, as in the case of two ecclesiastical provinces. and that was incompatible with ecumenical power. But if one Apostle, besides ecumenical power, possessed a special limited power and a peculiar flock, such limitation would not curtail the ecumenical power in the other Apostles, but would constitute the additional power and special province of the Bishop of the Mother Church. We can easily discover the reason of the Apostleship of St. Paul among the Gentiles. His previous Jewish zeal and the natural reaction that would follow after his conversion, his Greek culture fostered at the schools of Tarsus, made him a most fit medium to bridge over the chasm between the Hebrew and Gentile worlds. He was fitted by God for his special work. But we cannot discover a similar reason for the assigning to St. Peter the Apostleship of the Jews. For to begin with, St. Peter was the leader in the conversion of the Gentiles; and, again, he was not alone in "going to the circumcision," since James and John shared the same work. We shall not be far out, then, in saying that if St. Peter is singled out for an Apostleship in contradistinction with himself by the Apostle Paul, the latter witnessed in the Chief Apostle some special fitness and power to govern the Jewish remnant which he did not see in others and did not feel conscious of himself. Of that special fitness and power to govern the Jewish flock there seems no other cause but St. Peter's sovereign association with the King of the Jews and the Saviour. They, the faithful remnant of the ancient Theocracy, whether at home or abroad, were not left after Christ's ascension without a pastor and a Prince of their own. They were associated with him in the ecumenical work of laying the foundation of the early churches, just as our national Apostles were deputed by Rome. They knew St. Peter to be the Prince. They were attached to him as a particular flock, not for a negative reason, because he wounded not their traditional susceptibilities, but for a positive reason. They knew him to be the plenipotentiary vicar of Messias, their Lord. If further confirmation of the promises made unto their fathers were to be expected, they had not to hark back to Jerusalem, the doomed city, but to follow the traces of the principal heir. Hence St. Peter was the Apostle of the circumcision, as a special inheritance, because His Divine Master had been its minister. "I say," says the Apostle,* "that Christ Jesus was minister of the circumcision for the truth of God, to confirm the promises made unto the fathers." If, by the withdrawal of genealogical distinctions, their descendants became merged into the Christian and Gentile communities, they had the honour of being associated with St. Peter in bridging over the distance between Jerusalem destroyed and Christian Rome founded, and the interval between those events and the translation of power from the Cross.

Besides the witness of St. Paul, there is some intimation in the Epistles of St. Peter, addressed principally to the faithful Jewish remnant or to converts from Judaism in dispersion, and, no doubt, also to the Gentile communities in which they mixed and intermarried, of the peculiar relation to them of the Chief Apostle. That is, he designates them with the same attributes which Moses ascribed to the people of God in the old law, and which constant tradition has since ascribed to "the Holy Roman Church." He, moreover, designates them as "a

* Romans xv. 8.

purchased people," in contradistinction with the carnal Jews, of whom Christ had said, through the prophet : " Who is my creditor to whom I sold you." " But you are a chosen generation, a kingly priesthood, a holy nation, a purchased people." The whole Church being governed by a kingly priest partakes of his Royal Priesthood, but not in the special sense of his particular flock. Moses had said in the name of God : " If, therefore, you will hear My voice, and keep My covenant, you shall be My peculiar possession above all people : for all the earth is Mine. And you shall be to Me a priestly kingdom, and a holy nation." And St. Leo, voicing the tradition of the Roman Church on the foundation of Christian Rome declared : " These are they (the Apostles) who have promoted thee (Rome) to such a degree of honour, that having been made the holy nation, the chosen people, the sacerdotal and Royal city, and the capital of the world, by the sacred See of Peter, thou shouldst by Divine religion enjoy a wider sway than by earthly domination." The particular flock of St. Peter having been once established in the pagan city of the emperors, continued to enjoy its special attributes and prerogatives until the late capital of the pagan world became the *Holy City* and its province the *Holy Roman Church* As for its Royal attributes, they were signified by various names, such as the " Royal City," the " territorial rights of St. Peter " *(justitiæ St. Petri)* " the imperial power of the Pope," the " Holy Roman Empire," the " Patrimony of St. Peter," the " Royalty of St. Peter," and, in later times, the " Temporal Dominion of the Holy See," the " Pontifical States," the " Temporal Power " and the " Civil Principality."

As Christ at the outset did not directly claim that He was King and God, but with admirable delicacy preached of " the kingdom of God," so St. Peter mentions not his attributes directly, but reflects them on his particular flock in dispersion. It may be remarked, in connection with the special flock of St. Peter. that had the twelve Apostles witnessed for Christ at Rome, their ecumenical power would not have interfered with the Chief Apostle's special pastorate, nor with the unity of succession in the ecumenical line. There was, on the other hand, a special fitness in the co-operation of St. Paul with the Prince of the Apostles in the foundation of Christian Rome. The unity of the Apostolic See was thus marked in more ways than one. The Gentiles could not claim a distinct Apostolic See, nor the Jews exclude from the See of Peter the ecumenical pastorate of the Gentiles. The work of the ecumenical office had been divided, and would require much more division of labour as time went on. But the power of the ecumenical office was handed down to one line of succession, and together with it the special prerogatives of St. Peter. Thus, although it was most fit that the cessation of tribal right and genealogical succession should be preached by twelve Apostles on the one hand, and that a special Apostle should be sent to announce the Gentile inheritance on the other, yet the number twelve, so carefully restored after the treason of Judas, was destined to disappear with the cessation of genealogies, and the additional number for the Apostolate to the Gentiles with the preaching : " There is neither Jew nor Greek."* What remained was the continued subdivision of the Apostolic succession and labour throughout the world, and the preservation of ecumenical unity in the " Royal Priesthood " *sine genealogia* of the Vicar of Christ.

The Triple Crown.

We have seen that the inauguration of the Theandric Kingdom consisted in the preaching of the union between our human nature, attended with the Royal attribute, and the Divine nature, in the Person of the preacher and in the proclamation of the united kingship arising therefrom. Should we wish to symbolise the powers of the Incarnation and redemption, three crowns will be found adequate, no more and no less. We cannot divide the

* Galatians iii. 28.

Divine nature, nor the one Person of the Son of God. Therefore the kingdom of Heaven should be expressed by one crown. The kingdom of Israel, the human and Royal attribute, from which the previous Theandric appellation is communicated, should be designated by another crown ; and the preaching of " the kingdom of God " consummated in death, which is the office of the spiritual and sacrificing power, should be expressed by the mitre or spiritual crown. I cannot help thinking, therefore, that the crown of thorns, which the soldiers plaited for Christ was significant of the powers of redemption, and was, therefore, a triple crown, and that the artists who so represent it were rightly inspired. No one will question that the Romans and Jews, bent upon mockery, were carrying out a programme pre-arranged in Heaven. Man may strive against God—he will never compass but a feature of God's plan. " Licet in irrisione coronent," says St. Bernard, "tamen ignor-antes et irridentes coronatum regem fatentur. Ergo Rex eorum, vel ab ipsis nescientibus demonstratur."† That which gives weight to this conclusion is the minute and extreme care taken by God in the clothing of the Aaronic Pontiff, to express his relation to God and to the twelve tribes. God could not have taken less care in bridling the powers of evil on the day of Christ's coro-nation, in comparison with Whom the Jewish Pontiff was but a faint adumbration and the Jewish King an ordained ancestor. The Holy Ghost cannot have bestowed a less minute or extreme care upon the externals of the Christ-ian public worship, which surround not a figurative sacri-fice, but the real commemorative action instituted by Christ; nor have symbolised the powers and mission of the Head of the Christian Church with less perfection than the functions of the Jewish Pontiff. The Roman Pontiff, let it be remembered, wields no power of his own : he is only the Vicar of Christ. The triple crown, which he wears on certain occasions, represents the powers of the

† St. Bernard, " De Passione," cap. xix.

Incarnation and redemption. The name of God was written in gold on the tiara of the Jewish high priest. There is more reason to remember that God has a share in the government of the Christian Church. As for the spiritual and temporal crowns they are not always worn together. In purely episcopal functions he wears the mitre only. The following quotation is from Innocent III.‡ " Romanus Pontifex in signum imperii utitur regno : et in signum Pontificii, utitur mitra, sed mitra semper utitur, et ubique : regno vero nec ubique nec semper, quià Pontificalis auctoritas, et prior et dignior et effusior est, quam imperialis." We may find it useful to dwell a little more on the Scripture evidence of the import of the Christian triple crown. Daniel and his people in captivity had learned from the vision of the statue and of the four beasts that "the God of Heaven" would set up a "kingdom" that should never be destroyed, nor delivered to another people, and that it should break in pieces and should consume all the kingdoms that strove against it. The stability of the Theocracy before and after the Incarnation having been revealed to one of the blood Royal in the shape of the " stone" or kingdom set up by the " God of Heaven," it was natural that the priesthood of the Aaronic line should be informed by one of their tribe how their office would be perpetuated in that "kingdom of Heaven," and how; after seventy years of captivity, it was destined to be exercised in a new temple until the coming of the God of Heaven. The prophetic message delivered by Daniel for the admonition or consolation of Royalty had its counterpart in the office discharged by Zacharias, a prophet of the Levitical race, in the typical crowning of Jesus, the son of Josedec, the high priest. And we shall see that on the same occasion the conditional covenant is insisted on not without interest for our thesis.

‡ Serm. I. in Festo St. Petri.

THE TYPICAL CROWNING OF JESUS, THE SON OF JOSEDEC,
THE HIGH PRIEST.

IN commenting on the sixth chapter of Zacharias it will
not be sought, any more than elsewhere, to supply full
explanations of the text, which may be found in our
commentaries, but to dwell more particularly on what is
said or left unsaid in respect to our subject. The chapter
begins with the vision of the four chariots. The reader
who would insist on verifying the allusions of this prophet
to the visions of Daniel, or ascertain the interval between
the delivery of his prophetic message and that of Daniel,
and the exact historical period of both, may be referred to
à Lapide. What we have to keep in view is the Theocracy, whether before or after the Incarnation. As in
Daniel the kingdom of the God of Heaven leaning on the
stone that is depending on the Incarnation, holds good
against the four monarchies, removes them, and takes
their place in the whole world, so in Zacharias the
"kingdom of God," albeit the smallest of kingdoms, is
foreshadowed by a triple coronation of the high priest
to signify to the successors of Aaron and Levi that the
seventy years of captivity was only a phase in the history
of Israel, that the nation is once more set free to take up
its work of preparation for Messias, that the Priesthood
has to pursue its work in building a new Temple, and that
no kingdom on earth can frustrate the promises to the
Messianic kingdom. The four chariots with differently
coloured horses represent the four monarchies of the
Chaldeans, Persians, Grecians, and Romans. The
prophet, after describing the vision as signifying the
judgments of God on the empires contemporary with
Israel, passes suddenly from the vision to describe a
command received from God : " And the word of the
Lord came to me, saying : ' Take of them of the captivity,
of Holdai, and of Tobias, and of Idaias : and thou shalt
come in that day, and shalt go into the house of Josias.

the son of Sophonias, who came out of Babylon. And thou shalt take gold and silver : and shalt make *crowns*, and thou shalt set them on the head of Jesus, the son of Josedec, the high priest. And thou shalt speak to him, saying : 'Thus saith the Lord of Hosts, saying : " Behold a man, the Orient is His name : and under Him shall he spring up, and shall build a temple to the Lord. Yea, he shall build a temple to the Lord : and he shall bear the glory, and shall sit and rule upon his throne : and he shall be a priest upon his throne, and the counsel of peace shall be between them both. And the crowns shall be to Helem, and Tobias, and Idaias, and to Hem, the son of Sophonias, a memorial in the temple of the Lord. And they that are far off shall come, and shall build in the temple of the Lord : and you shall know that the Lord of Hosts sent me to you. But this shall come to pass, if, hearing, you will hear the voice of the Lord your God." ' "*

The typical coronation of the high priest commanded by God is a presentation of the figure of Christ and of His Vicar under Him in the Christian Church. It includes the spiritual and temporal powers of His manhood, which is in accordance with the main thesis ; but it includes more. For the word *crowns* in the Hebrew is in the plural and not in the dual number. It matters little whether or how the *crowns* were joined together, so long as we are agreed that they were placed on the head of the high priest. What is more important is to see that they were figurative of the *crowns* destined for Christ, and that they were not intended for the son of Josedec. On this point à Lapide has the following : " Jam sensus est, *q.d.* Hanc coronam impono tibi, O Jesu fili Josedec, non propter te, sed propter Orientem, id est, Christum, ut scilicet ejus typum geras, ejusque sacerdotium et principatum repræsentes." That the crowns were figurative of the triple crown of Christ and of

---

* Zacharias vi. 9-15.

His Vicar, à Lapide gives the following testimony after quoting Paschalius on the majesty of the triple diadem : "Similes ergo videntur fuisse hæ coronæ Jesu filii Josedec, quia repræsentarunt coronas et regnum Christi, æque ac illud idem repræsentat corona triplex Pontificis : illa itaque hîc in coronis Jesu Pontificis fuit typicè figurata et adumbrata, præsertim quia *Ataroth*, id est, coronæ, est plurale, non duale, ac proinde plures, puta tres potius, quam duas significat." In confirmation of this evidence the following testimony in the vision of St. John may be quoted : " And on His head were many diadems."*

In spite of this, however, à Lapide, apparently overlooking the Divine element in the powers of redemption prefigured in this coronation, remains uncertain as to whether the crown was double or triple. On the words : " Thou shalt set them on the head of Jesus, the son of Josedec," he comments thus : " Itaque ad litteram jubet hîc illi Deus, ut coronam duplicem, vel triplicem imponat capiti Jesu, quasi Pontifici et Principi ; tum ut ad litteram significet, eum in novo hoc templo fore gloriosum, itaque eum ad fabricam ejus perficiendam et ornandam animet, tum, ad mysterium, scilicet ut typus sit Jesu Christi Pontificis et Regis, ejusque sacerdotium et regnum repræsentet. Christum enim fuisse regem patet Psalmo ii.: ' Ego autem constitutus sum Rex.' Et Luca I. : ' Dabit ei Dominus sedem David patris ejus et regnabit in domo Jacob in æternum.' Eumdem fuisse Pontificem patet ex Psalmo cvii.: ' Tu es sacerdos in æternum secundum Melchisedec.' " À Lapide, Le Blanc, etc., hold, of course that Christ was " King of the whole world," in virtue of the hypostatic union, but not King of the Jews in virtue of Royal succession and local right. They, moreover, hold that Christ did not exercise universal kingship. I have made it plain elsewhere that Christ did exercise power in Israel, that He could not exercise it without the sanction of the law, which was twofold, and that the

---

* Apoc. xix. 12.

twofold human power that He necessarily exercised must not be ascribed to the hypostatic union to the detriment of His human attributes ; and, finally, that the supposition that the hypostasic union abridged Christ's natural kingship is incompatible with Catholic doctrine.

But to return to the point, how are the three crowns to be accounted for, which à Lapide admits belong to Christ, and are signified by the literal meaning of the sacred text. Not, assuredly, from their similitude to the tiara, on the assumption that the Pontiff wears it, because as Vicar of Christ he presides over Asia, Africa, and Europe. The world has grown since this supposition was made. Not even because he represents the Blessed Trinity, whose Priest and Pontiff he is. The commentator is surely nearer the mark when he says of the crowns, as already quoted, "that they represented the crowns and 'the kingdom of Christ,' just as the triple crown of the Roman Pontiff represents them."

The kingdom of Christ is the "kingdom of God." In that kingdom there is more than the sovereign human powers spiritual and temporal. There is included with them the Divine power ; all three powers of redemption coming under the one personal possession and exercise of the *Orient*. Such is the kingdom of the Incarnation, as we have seen. And such was the presentment of Christ, when the prophet, having crowned the high priest with a triple crown, said, as he was bidden : " Behold a man, the Orient is His name." The production of a picture of the crowned figure of the Pontiff by the action of light could not have handed down to our day a more faithful likeness. Pictures fade and are not so faithfully reproduced as the written word. And the sense of sight alone takes in but little of the moral features. We seem to gaze five centuries before his coming on the figure of the Incarnate God and King of the Jews, as they led Him forth : " So Jesus came forth, bearing the crown of thorns and the purple garment.

And he saith to them : '*Behold the Man.*'"* We cannot
separate in that Divine figure either of the human powers,
nor the Divine power of redemption. Had Christ been
debarred during His public ministry (for what reason
passes human wits to espy) from the possession and
exercise of Temporal Sovereignty over Israel, its eventual
and eventful mockery would not have constituted so
heavy an item of the Passion. The fulness of the
Divine condescension appears in this very truth, that the
Divine Saviour lacked nothing human, whether subjection or sovereignty, such as they affect mankind. He
was a pattern to all, and sanctified the social position of
all. Such was the Divine figure "when the goodness
and kindness *(humanitas)* of God our Saviour appeared."†
" For we have not a high priest who cannot have com-
passion on our infirmities (whether we be subjects or
whether we be spiritual or temporal rulers): but one
tempted in all things like as we are, yet without sin."‡

The presentment of Messias, under the name of
Orient, covered with the triple crown, for whom the
Temple should be built, was to the Aaronic priesthood
what the "stone cut out of a mountain without hands "
was to the Royal succession of Israel. More persecut-
ing monarchies would arise and succeed one another,
but they are shown to be destined to caducity and to
be removed by Him Who now exercises Theocratic
rule in "the kingdom of Israel," and will presently
exercise Theandric rule over "the kingdom of God."
Here, as in many other places, à Lapide comes very
near the conclusion of the thesis : " Et ipse, Oriens, non
Zorobabel, ut volunt Hebræi et Theodor. Sed Christus,
' portabit gloriam,' puta coronam gloriæ, scilicet gloriosi
pontificatus et. regni. Unde explicans subdit : ' Et
sedebit, et *dominabitur* super solio suo, et erit sacerdos
super solio suo.' Hanc autem gloriam inchoatè Christus
adeptus est in hac vita : unde significat hîc propheta

* St. John xix. 5.   † Titus iii. 4.   ‡ Hebrews iv. 15.

quatuor quadrigas, id est, monarchias, desiisse in regnum Christi, de quo ait : ' Dominabitur super solio suo.' "

THE SOURCE OF PEACE WITH LIBERTY BETWEEN THE TWO POWERS OF THE CHRISTIAN STATE.

"AND he shall be a priest upon his throne, and the counsel of peace shall be between them both." The words " between them both " refer to the two sovereign human powers of the Prince and the Pontiff, so frequently at war with one another in ancient Israel and in the Christian Church, and yet to be religiously kept apart, when vested in fallible hands, for the sake of liberty and the rights of conscience. " The counsel of peace shall be between them both," because the Pontiff and the Prince are the one person of Christ, the unseen Head of the Church, and the one person of His Vicar on earth wielding both powers. The worst of tyrannies—that of forcing erroneous doctrine and false religions upon the human conscience—can find no place at the centre of Theocratic government. The Petrine prerogatives repose upon emphatic Divine promises, which stand out conspicuously even among the clearest of Divine records. It is sometimes objected that under the Pontifical Temporal Sovereignty the Romans are deprived of the civil liberty claimed by other nations. Aye, but they are not on the same footing as other nations, since spiritual tyranny can never affect them. Here, then, is the source of peace with liberty not only for the Romans, but for the spiritual and temporal powers of the world.

After giving full scope, as usual, to the opinions which he quotes, à Lapide concludes : " Vel potius majisque appositė ad rem, æque ad versionem Latinam, το *illos* demonstrat principem, qui, ut præcessit, 'sedebit et dominabitur super solio suo' et pontificem, de quomox subdit : ' Et erit sacerdos super solio suo,' *q.d* . In Christo summus erit consensus et concordia inter principem sedentem in solio regali et pontificem sedentem in solio Pontificali : quia Christus utrumque

erit, et utramque dignitatem Pontificatus et Regni in se
conjunget : cujus rei typo Jesus filius Josedec duplicem.
accepit coronam, sacerdotii scilicet et principatus, ut
utramque potestatem in Christo uniendam portenderet."
The typical coronation of the son of Josedec thus
explains some of the blessings to flow from the order
of the typical Pontiff-King, who in the person of the
Father of the Faithful blessed all the covenanted ancestors of the Incarnate God.

It is said that the Christian Church is a perfect
society of itself. This does not mean that the spiritual
power is in every sense independent of the temporal.
One thing is that the temporal power should be subordinate to the spiritual power, as the body should be
subject to the soul ; another thing that the spiritual
power should be in every sense independent of the
temporal power, which is as impossible as the soul's
independence of the body during its earthly life. The
Church cannot dispense with Christian families and
Christian provinces, which belong to the State and
constitute a part or even the whole of the temporal
power. Yet these powers are distinct, and, according
to the Christian law, should be, except in Rome,
vested in different hands. Whereas in pagan times and
pagan lands the union of the two powers in the civil ruler
ultimately developed into the worst of tyrannies. In
Christian lands, where the spiritual power has been
ursurped by the civil ruler, there is either peace without
liberty, or license with religious discord. As a remedy
against spiritual tyranny, the two powers are vested in
different hands ; as a remedy against religious strife,
the two powers have their respective communion with
the bearer of the triple crown. No king or civil ruler
can say, as Seba, the son of Bochri : " We have no part
in David."* The two powers of the Christian state are
destined to constitute one society, just as man, compounded of body and soul, enjoys one individual life. It

* 2 Kings xx. 1.

would be, however, a sad misconception of the meaning of Christian peace to suppose that it can be purchased without effort, even without frequent misunderstandings between the two powers. History teems with the records of strife between bishops and kings, and pontiffs and kings. But the history of the Catholic nations is a record of liberty. If there were intervals of strife, it was the strife of human nature in conflict with the spiritual power. And when submission was tendered to the Church by individuals or nations, it was not submission to brute force, but to the powers of persuasion. The result was genuine peace. Let us ever bear in mind that the Christian Pontiff represents spiritual and temporal powers that are Theandric. That mystery is not only the source of our Sacraments and Sacrifice, of Divine grace and infallible truth, it is a source of sacred peace for the Christian state. Sponsa is compounded of a spiritual and temporal nature. If the law be duly observed, and that creature meets her destiny, which is union with Sponsus, peace will reign between the spiritual and temporal powers of her being. But let that destiny be frustrated, Sponsa will become a world of strife ; her spiritual nature striving for the mastery, and her subordinate nature not unnaturally rebelling— " For these are contrary to one another : so that you do not the things that you would."† In virtue of the sacramental union between Christ, represented by His Vicar and Christian society, civil rulers have their special share of the blessings of a Theandric Kingship, just as ecclesiastical princes receive their special blessing from communing with a Theandric Priesthood. God cares for the temporal order as well as for the spiritual, and has made provision for both. And if the sacred tie between the spiritual power and its Theandric centre have been frequently broken off by the violence of secular princes, the spiritual powers have

† Galatians v. 17.

not always respected the sacred tie between the temporal powers and the vicar of a Theandric king. Witness the opposition of Josephists to the appointment of nuncios ; witness, again, the liberties of the Gallican Church in the vindication of which the laity were much less concerned than the clergy. I am not here dilating on the origin of power, whether spiritual or temporal, whether *mediante papa* or *mediante republica.* The counsel of peace between the spiritual and temporal powers, whether of the individual or of Christian society, resides, then, in the Royal Priesthood of the Incarnation. And the harmony of this prophecy and typical coronation of Jesus, the high priest, with other facts of Scripture showing the reality of the Royal Priesthood of Christ and its inheritance by the Chief Apostle, is, therefore, what we should expect. The only thing really surprising in connection with this our thesis is the gratuitous character of modern etherealism. By this I mean the spiriting out of existence of Christ's "Temporal Power," than which no doctrine was ever more intrinsically unwarranted. We cannot expect to find in the Fathers a treatise on the Temporal Power of the Pope, which was never denied before the latter half of this nineteenth century. The most eloquent tribute of the Catholic tradition is the concrete existence from the times of persecution of the Temporal Sovereignty of the Papacy. That was not usurped, but forced on to the shoulders of the Roman Pontiff by the Catholic populations and confirmed by the intervention of Catholic princes. Neither were the powers of redemption usurped by Christ. " So Christ also did not glorify Himself, that He might be made a high priest." *   " Ecce altera major invidia," says St. Augustine, commenting on the words : " He ought to die, because He made Himself the Son of God," "parva illa videbatur affectasse regnum ; *et tamen neutrum sibi Jesus mendaciter usurpavit :* est enim Dei

---

* Hebrews v. 5.

unigenitus, et rex a Deo constitutus super montem Sion, et utrumque demonstraret nunc, nisi quanto erat potentior, tanto mallet esse patientior."

The Hypothesis of the Faithful Keeping of the Conditional Covenant and its Doctrinal Consequences.

It might seem superfluous to set about proving that the faithful keeping of the conditional covenant was a possible eventuality, and that the opposite doctrine is Calvinistic. Yet, because the consequences of such hypothesis throw much light on our subject, as we have already seen, it may be useful to point out that, hypothetical though the ground may be, it is none the less Catholic on that account.

The doctrine of Calvin includes the absolute predestination of the wicked, not only to everlasting perdition, but to rebellion and sin before any prevision of their demerits. This cruel doctrine seems to be the result of the unguided reading of the prophecies which foretold Christ's Passion and the reprobation of the Jews. Calvin, Beza, and others failed to see that man's actions, good or bad, are not bound by prophecy, but that prophecy is bound by man's freewill. Had the Jews repented and been gathered to Christ the event would have been reflected back in the light of prophecy. Had the Romans been principally guilty in the hypothesis of Christ's death, no reprobation of the Jews would have been foreseen or foretold. Commenting on the words of the second chapter of the First Epistle of St. Peter, " Nec credunt in quo positi sunt," à Lapide says : " Beza ex hoc loco contendit, reprobos ante prævisionem operum et peccatorum a Deo positos, id est, destinatos esse ad inobedientiam et rebellionem, sicut electi a Deo solo ante prævisionem meritorum destinati sunt ad fidem, obedientiam et salutem. Additque ; hoc enim ait hic Stus. Petrus, scilicet eos positos esse, utique a Deo, ad hoc, ut non credant." The children of Abraham, who as a nation had prepared the way for the Incarnation of the Son of God, were the first called to believe in that mystery. Moreover, they were called to be the principal believers and to constitute the Mother Church, since by nature and position they were the most closely united to the Founder and foundation of the Christian Church. But, unlike their father Abraham, they resisted their vocation to the Faith. The Divine Founder of the Universal Church became to them "a stone of stumbling, and a rock of scandal, to them that stumble at the word, neither do believe, whereunto also they are set." But the faithful remnant, who at once acknowledged the Messias; or the convert Jews, who, like St. Paul, were brought back from their Judaising; or the convert Gentiles of St. Peter's flock, took the place of the faithless nation, and were set to that corner-stone represented by St. Peter. And hence they became "a chosen generation, a kingly priesthood, a holy nation, a purchased people."

If the hypothesis of the faithful keeping of the conditional covenant be, therefore, strictly legitimate, it is useful to consider what would have been the consequences so far as they affect our thesis. We have already seen that "the kingdom of God" would not have been taken from the Jews. They would have retained their privileges as the Mistress Church of Christendom. Genealogies would have disappeared, the Royal Priesthood would have succeeded to the two families of kings and priests. Jerusalem would not have been destroyed. The Apostles would not have turned to the Gentiles, to the prejudice of those to whom it "behoved them first to speak the word of God." Simon, although invested without universal power and full doctrinal authority, as Vicar of Christ, would not necessarily have been called Peter; for no fresh foundation would have been required. And, finally, " the kingdom of God," or Mother Church of Jerusalem, would not have been deprived of "the temporal power"

promised to the patriarchs. All this has been substantially enunciated before, but one point of criticism has
not been directly dealt with. It was asserted by the
Jesuits, who kindly undertook the criticism of my fundamental thesis, that " the conditional covenant made with
the Israelitish nation, with its temporal endowments,
has been absolutely made void." In reply to which it
has to be said that the covenant was not conditional *in
se*, but only in respect to the Jews, and consequently
that it has been made void not *in se*, but in respect to
that people. The Jews, had they been faithful, would
have remained the centre of the Christian Theocracy.
This, I think, will be admitted by all but Calvinists.
But the centre of Theocracy, with its exalted Christian
privileges, has not been made void in spite of Jewish infidelity. It still admittedly exists as a spiritual centre. If
the spiritual inheritance has not been made void by the
infidelity of the Jews, why should the temporal inheritance
have been made void? The same critics add : "The
absolute covenant made with Abraham and David has
been translated, not to another geographical centre, such
as Rome, but to the heavenly Jerusalem, the city of God,
the spiritual kingdom of Christ, the rule of which embraces all nations." This sounds much like the doctrine
of Protestant Acephalists, who require no further commission than the army and navy. But they, at least,
have prophesied, in designating Catholics as "an Italian
mission," whether, in the spirit of Balaam, or in the
spirit of Caiphas, need not be too closely scrutinised, and
have pointed to Central Italy as the geopraphical
centre from which *our* mission comes. God covenanted from the beginning things spiritual and things
temporal. Which of these have been translated, not to
another geographical centre, but to the spiritual kingdom
of Christ, the rule of which embraces all nations? Surely
the spiritual headship, the source of unity in the Christian
Church, is reflected on the map of the world, as well as
the dual authorities of Mount Sion and Mount Moriah.

The special prerogatives of St. Peter were included in the absolute covenant, and yet they have been translated to the Apostolic See, which is certainly another geographical centre. And, once more, if the spiritual power and right of inheritance of the Chief Apostle could be translated to Rome, why not the temporal right and its corresponding inheritance ? As for the new covenant, which was the fulfilling of the old, it was first intended for the Jewish people : "'Behold, the days shall come,' saith the Lord, 'when I will make a new covenant with the house of Israel, and with the house of Juda,'" etc.*

ZACHARIAS ON THE HYPOTHESIS OF THE FAITHFUL KEEPING OF THE CONDITIONAL COVENANT.

IT would be easy to multiply testimonies as to the absolute character of the temporal promises, and to show that the covenant of land was only conditional in respect to the Jewish people. But to appreciate these promises, we must get rid of the notion that the promise of land referred principally to abundance of corn, and wine, and oil, and not to the political independence of the Theocracy. The Jews were not better off, as regards the good things of this life, than Christian people ; and we should be sorry if it were otherwise. And if the good things aforementioned, to which others might be added, are a hindrance to the spiritual life, then are the Christian nations worse off in this respect than any others without exception. Then, again, when the Royalty of Christ or of His Vicar is insisted on, we may be too pre-occupied with the idea that glory is the object of Temporal Sovereignty, whereas duty and conformity to law is the principle underlying the temporal promises. And, once more, the magnificence of the temporal promises, as re-echoed by the prophets, may seem out of proportion with the little corner of land allotted to Israel or to the Vicar of Christ. A corrective for this illusion will be found in the contemplation

* Hebrews viii. 8 ; Jeremias xxxi. 31.

of the territorial right of Christ and temporal inheritance of the Incarnation, with its overflowing blessings
for the Christian nations. In the following words of
Ezechiel among the captives, the promise of land is no
more conditional than when addressed to the patriarchs.
It can either apply to the Jews under the new covenant,
in the hypothesis of their repentance, or it can apply to
the new centre of Theocracy. " Because they say of you :
'Thou art a land that devourest men, and that stiflest thy
nation ;' therefore thou shalt devour men no more, nor
destroy thy nation any more, saith the Lord God.
Neither will I cause men to hear in thee the shame of
the nations any more, nor shalt thou bear the reproach
of the people, nor lose thy nation any more, saith the
Lord God."* Again, after the miracle of the joining
of the two sticks, representing Juda and Israel, and por-
tending the disappearance of genealogies : " ' Behold, I
will take the children of Israel from the midst of the
nations whither they are gone ; and I will gather them
on every side, and will bring them to their own land.
And I will make them one nation in the land on the
mountains of Israel, and one king shall be king over
them all; and they shall no more be two nations, neither
shall they be divided any more into two kingdoms.
Nor shall they be defiled any more with their idols, nor
with their abominations, nor with all their iniquities :
and I will save them out of all the places in which they
have sinned, and I will cleanse them : and they shall be
My people, and I will be their God. And My servant
David shall be king over them, and they shall have one
shepherd ; they shall walk in My judgments, and shall
keep My commandments, and shall do them. And they
shall dwell in the land which I gave to My servant
Jacob, wherein your fathers dwelt, and they shall dwell
in it, they and their children and their children's children, for ever : and David My servant shall be their
prince for ever. And I will make a covenant of peace

* Ezechiel xxxvi. 13, *et seq.*

with them, it shall be an everlasting covenant with them : and I will establish them, and will multiply them, and will set My sanctuary in the midst of them for ever.'"† Thus in Holy Scripture there are temporal promises belonging to the everlasting covenant. On the other hand, there are terrible threatenings that the nation shall be cast out from their land and its threefold inheritance, if it should forget its Lord and God. It was natural that God should hold out either prospect, and therefore we must guard ourselves against the error of Calvinists, who conceived the Jews to be necessarily excluded from the new covenant, and their nation and city to be unconditionally foredoomed. And as a further consequence, we must guard ourselves from applying exclusively to the Gentile Mother Church that which was first intended for a Jewish Mother Church. For instance, the promise : " Nor shalt thou bear the reproach of the people, nor lose thy nation any more. . . ."

But let us return to Zacharias. The prophet winds up the account of the typical coronation of the high priest, with its portent of peace for the Christian world, with the following words : " But this shall come to pass if, hearing, you will hear the voice of the Lord your God." On these words we read in à Lapide the following commentary : " Erit autem hoc *q.d.* Hæc prospera et gloriosa templi et consequenter vobis, O Judæi, obvenient, sub hac conditione, nimirum, si Dei legi vocique obedieritis, sin ei sitis inobedientes et rebelles, nolite me falsitatis accusare, si sua meaque promissa revocet Deus. ita Theod." In his mystical interpretation he adds : " Sin eum repuleritis, ipse bona hæc sua a vobis revocabit, *et transferet ad gentes.*" Though à Lapide, as we have seen, admits the Royal succession of Christ through St. Joseph, and commenting on the words, "dominabitur super solio suo," grants that Christ

† Ezechiel xxxvii. 21-26.

began to obtain the glory of His twofold kingdom in this life, which put an end to the four monarchies, yet we know that he and Le Blanc, through their peculiar view of the hypostatic union, absolutely refuse to Christ an hereditary power over the Church-nation. Hence, when the prophet holds out the bright prospect of a threefold coronation of the Orient in Jerusalem, and the enjoyment of its glory and peace by the Jewish people on condition of their fidelity, the commentator etherealises the nature of the temporal crown and holds out to the Gentiles, on account of the transgression of Israel, nothing beyond the translation of spiritual power.

In the light of more modern and authentic teaching, which attributes the Civil Principality of the Vicar of Christ to "a singular decree of Divine Providence," or to a non-fortuitous cause, we may gather without hesitation the evidence of the Temporal Kingship of Christ, and consider how it was first destined for the place and people in the midst of which it naturally originated, giving its very name to the rule of the God Incarnate ; and how, belonging to the everlasting covenant, it was translated to the new centre of Theocracy. Therefore, brushing out of existence the false view that Christ's manhood was deprived of its hereditary Royal attribute, let us cling to the conditional promise to the Jews, in reference to their thrice crowned King. The prophet thus expresses the condition : "This shall come to pass, if, hearing, you will hear the voice of the Lord your God." The condition does not affect the coming of the Orient, nor His triple coronation, nor its meaning throughout all time. Whether that were done in mockery and in death, or whether it were done in honour, it was predestined to be done. It belonged to the absolute covenant. The condition of the Jewish fidelity referred to their own share, and to the share of Jerusalem, as Mistress Christian Church, in the "glory" and "peace" of the local coronation of the Orient. In other words, only through their perversity could "the kingdom of

4

God," with its three powers of redemption, be taken from them and from Jerusalem, and be given to "a nation yielding the fruits thereof." That which the Jews forfeited belonged to the everlasting covenant. Let none be surprised, therefore, if the centre of Theandric Government, although translated, retains its temporal kingdom. And woe to him who would detract from the majesty of the triple diadem!

AN APPEAL AND PETITION TO THE BISHOPS AND THEOLOGIANS OF THE BRITISH ISLES, AND OF THE ENGLISH-SPEAKING WORLD, FOR THE THEOLOGICAL DISCUSSION AND DEFINITION OF THE CIVIL PRINCIPALITY OF THE VICAR OF CHRIST.

In submitting this series of papers on "the Temporal Power" to the Bishops and theologians of the English-speaking world, the writer may be permitted to inquire, whether in the defence of the rights of the Holy See we have hitherto exhausted the whole armoury of Divine truth placed at our disposal. No doubt, the Roman Pontiff has the most ancient historical title to sovereignty, the questioning or unsettling of which is dangerous to all civil powers. No doubt, in the exercise of his universal pastorate, he can neither be, nor certainly appear, free from the influence of other powers, if he be not himself a temporal sovereign. No doubt, but that no small State was ever confiscated under such revolting circumstances, including the violation of a solemn treaty signed by the Sovereign of France and the King of Piedmont and their respective ministers ; a violation which took place as soon as the other signatory power was seen to be overwhelmed. No doubt *Italia unita* presents no other unity but the conspiracy of sacrilege, and may be judged by the crop of misery daily increasing throughout the country. All this and much more may be urged against the spoliation and in favour of the restoration of "the States of the Church."

And yet, in spite of what has been urged in defence

of the rights of the Holy See, is it not plain that some
Catholics remain doubtful. The necessity of the Temporal Power standing alone implies no more than a
natural or political right. The venerable antiquity of the
title does not constitute an absolutely inalienable right.
The stain of treachery and deceit may lower the Italian
name and character before the nations, so long as the
conspiracy lasts ; but it proves nothing to those who
have no interest in the maintenance of ancient dynasties,
but the fall of an exceptionally noble institution, in the
general passing away of the old European *régime.* Given
a Temporal Power founded on mere human right, it is
subject to caducity. As far as the writer can make
out, these are substantially the thoughts of some
Catholics, both priests and laymen. They may be
comparatively few, but their influence is felt. The
writer had occasion some years ago to complain to one
of the directors of a large company about the remarks
in their guide-book referring to the Civil Sovereignty
of the Roman Pontiff, and to add that such was not
fit reading for Catholics. The reply of the Com-
modore, who had inquired whether there were any
complaints, came quick and ready : " But some of your
own cloth have advised me differently." Whether
they were Italians or British I know not, and it
matters not. I will only submit, in extenuation of their
sin, that they most probably had never seen the text
of the Apostolic letters bearing on the subject of the
Civil Principality. The text, with its translation, is in
the hands of the French clergy, and why should it not
be in our hands in England and elsewhere ? Who can
well venture to write or to speak on the subject of the
Temporal Power for the Catholic or Protestant public,
without being familiar with the teaching of the Sovereign Pontiff?

But we have further to inquire into the meaning of
that Apostolic teaching and the Bishops of the world
assembled in Rome in 1862, or represented there on

the occasion, have given their authentic interpretation of the Pontifical utterances. To the writer it seems that the conjoint teaching of the *ecclesia docens* has struck the rock and fetched the true foundation for a "tractatus de civili Romani Pontificis principatu." The little work now submitted, when expurgated from possible errors, may be of some small service to encourage theological inquiry. It will not be a task of literary excitement, but of filial duty. It will not unduly interfere with those whose minds are deeply engaged with the German subjectivism of the so-called higher criticism. It only asks to have a share of attention from those who prosecute more fascinating studies. It may be said on its behalf, that it proceeds by "leaving the word of the beginning of Christ,"* such as "the origin, integrity and authority of each (sacred) book,†" and seeks to keep pace with every living and growing kingdom in nature, by pointing to "strong meat" for the perfect. It is a doctrine of growth and progress, not duly ordered, but merely suggested and requiring better manipulation ; a doctrine "hard to be intelligibly uttered,"‡ not from want of intelligent hearers this time, but from lack of grappling power and the gift of enunciation. It concludes to the necessity of the restoration of every inch of the Pontifical territory, which may appear an insurmountable difficulty to those who do not believe in a Divine institution, and it re-echoes the voice of the despoiled Pontiff : "ac civilis, quo Romana pollet ecclesia, principatus *integritatem*, ejusque jura, quæ ad omnes catholicos pertinent, etiam atque etiam reclamamus, et reclamare nunquam desistemus."§

The petition humbly shows and submits :—

1. That the authentic utterances of the Vicar of Christ in respect to the Civil Principality and the joint

* Hebrews vi. 1.   † Late Encyclical on Holy Scripture.
‡ Hebrews v. 11.
§ Allocution of Pius IX. after the Battle of Castelfidardo.

declaratory assent thereto of the Bishops of the whole Catholic world in 1862 have the following effect :—

(a) Of differentiating the Civil Principality from the Civil Governments of the world, by attributing it to "a singular decree of Divine providence."

(b) Of marking its origin as non-fortuitous.

(c) And as a consequence of removing its rightful origin back to a Divine institution and to the foundation of the Christian Church.

2. That the twofold Sovereignty of Christ and of His Vicar on earth was typified by a Royal Priesthood.

3. That the twofold Sovereignty aforementioned was typified by a triple coronation expressing and including the three powers of the Incarnation and of man's redemption.

4. That the foundation of Christ's kingdom was the Theocratic Temporal Power consisting :—

(a) In the land unconditionally promised to the seed of Abraham as "an everlasting possession."

(b) In the succession *de jure* and *de facto* to the sceptre of Juda.

(c) In the Royal succession to the throne and kingdom of David unconditionally covenanted for all time.

5. That the kingdom of Christ, or of God, or of Heaven, did actually succeed to "the law and the prophets."

6. That Christ did exercise power in Israel.

7. That the power exercised by Christ in Israel was not merely sacerdotal, but Royal and Theandric.

8. That Christ's Temporal or Royal attribute, whereby He, as man, succeeded to David, was not abridged by virtue of the hypostatic union.

9. That Christ's sovereign independence in Israel was a consequence of His sovereign authority as Heir of the Theocracy, which was intimated to the Jews who questioned His authority, first by His refusal to reply to their question, and secondly by the recitation of the

parable revealing that they were cognisant of His title and claims.

10. That the declaration of Christ in reference to the payment of tribute to the Church of the Synagogue, "then the children are free," was a declaration of twofold sovereign independence belonging to twofold earthly Sovereignty. And that the vindication of such independence was a sovereign act.

11. That the association of Peter in both declaration and vindication of sovereign independence reveals the translation to Peter and his successors of the twofold human sovereignty of the Divine Master and the fulfilment of all types and prophecies concerning the Royal Priesthood.

12. That Christ allowed to the Faithful the acknowledgment of His Kingship over Israel and before His Passion prepared the way for its general recognition.

13. That the coronation of Christ done in mockery was not merely an exhibition respectively of malice and of patience, but a predestined event full of legal and prophetic import.

14. That the translation of the Royal Theandric Priesthood from Jerusalem to Rome was foretold by Christ to the Jews in the Parable of the Vineyard.

15. That the tradition of the Roman Church, as gathered from the Fathers and the Roman Pontiffs, includes the Royal inheritance of David and the inheritance of the Royal Priesthood of Christ.

16. That the testimony of the Fathers does not exclude the sacred kingdom of Christ or of His Vicar, but only the profane kingdom or empire expected by the carnal Jews.

17. That there exists a perfect agreement between the teaching and tradition of the Roman Church, and of the Fathers on the one hand, and the witness of Sacred Writ on the other, in reference to the Civil Principality.

18. That it is opportune at the present day, in view of the position of the Roman Pontiff, to discuss and

elucidate the subject of the " Temporal Power " from its
theological standpoint.

19. That it is opportune to catalogue and censure
the errors respecting the Civil Principality which have
crept into some of our standard books and commentaries,
in order that the clergy and laity may cease to be mis-
informed and confused by conflicting doctrines.

20. That the most powerful and abiding assistance
to be tendered by man to the Holy See will spring not
merely from the protection of one or two European
states, but from the moral suffrage of the Catholic
world, when strong convictions become possible by the
removal of all cause of doubt and confusion.

21. That before asking for the judgment of Rome
on this thesis, it is desirable to discuss it elsewhere.

SOME PROPOSITIONS WHICH, ACCORDING TO THE THESIS,
SEEM TO DESERVE CONDEMNATION.

1. No temporal or secular kingdom can be *de jure*
or *de facto* everlasting.

2. Therefore the kingdom of Christ is a purely
spiritual kingdom.

3. And the temporal dominion of the Papacy i
adventitious.

4. A secular kingdom is necessarily a profane one,
or at least a purely natural one.

5. The words of Christ, " My kingdom is not of
this world," are exclusive of temporal power in Christ
and in His Vicar.

6. A temporal kingdom can be at the same time
adventitious, that is *de jure humano* and yet be exempt
from the law of national caducity.

7. Christ was neither, in turn, subject to the law
nor local sovereign.

8. The sceptre of Juda was taken away before
Christ's public ministry.

9. The ancient Temporal Kingdom of the Romans
still subsists.

10. And Christian Rome is fated to apostatise.

11. The Roman Pontiff can temporarily yield some portion of his territorial right in virtue of a Concordat.

12. In virtue of the hypostatic union, Christ exercised no local and ancestral right of sovereignty.

13. The sovereign political independence of the Roman Pontiff can exist without territorial independence.

14. " The conditional covenant made with the Israelitish nation, with its temporal endowments, has been absolutely made void, and the absolute covenant made with Abraham and David has been translated not to another geographical centre, such as Rome, but to the heavenly Jerusalem, the city of God, the spiritual kingdom of Christ, the rule of which embraces all nations."

EXCERPTA FROM THE PONTIFICAL ACTS.

ALLOCUTIO

Habita in Consistorio Secreto Gaïetæ XX Aprilis Anni MDCCCXLIX.*

Quibus, quantisque . . .

Atque inter hæc Nostra ardentissima desideria haud possumus eos non monere speciatim, et redarguere, qui decreto illi, quo Romanus Pontifex omni civilis sui Imperii honore ac dignitate est spoliatus, plaudunt, ac decretum idem ad ipsius Ecclesiæ libertatem, felicitatemque procurandam vel maxime conducere asserunt. Hic autem palam publiceque profitemur, nulla Nos dominandi cupiditate, nullo temporalis Principatus desiderio hæc loqui, quandoquidem Nostra indoles, et ingenium a quavis dominatione profecto est alienum. Verumtamen officii Nostri ratio postulat, ut in civili Apostolicæ Sedis Principatu tuendo jura possessionesque Sanctæ Romanæ Ecclesiæ, atque ejusdem Sedis libertatem, quæ cum totius Ecclesiæ libertate et utilitate est conjuncta, totis viribus defendamus. *Et quidem homines, qui commemorato plaudentes decreto tam falsa, et absurda affirmant, vel ignorant vel ignorare simulant, singulari prorsus divina Providentiæ consilio factum esse, ut Romano Imperio in plura regna, variasque ditiones diviso, Romanus Pontifex, cui a Christo Domino totius Ecclesiæ regimen et cura fuit commissa, civilem Principatum hac sane de causa haberet, ut ad ipsam Ecclesiam regendam, ejusque unitatem tuendam plena illa potiretur libertate, quæ ad Supremi Apostolici ministerii munus obeundum requiritur.* Namque omnibus compertum est, fideles populos, gentes, regna nunquam plenam fiduciam et observantiam esse præstitura Romano Pontifici, si illum alicujus Principis vel Gubernii dominio subjectum, ac minime liberum esse conspicerent. Siquidem fideles populi et regna vehementer suspicari ac vereri nunquam desinerent, ne Pontifex idem sua acta ad illius Principis vel Gubernii, in cujus ditione versaretur, voluntatem conformaret, atque idcirco actis illis hoc prætextu sæpius refragari non dubitarent. Et quidem dicant vel ipsi hostes civilis Principatus Apostolicæ Sedis, qui nunc Romæ dominantur, quanam fiducia

---

* Pius IX. from Gaeta on the Roman Revolution.

et observantia ipsi essent excepturi hortationes, monita, man-
data, constitutiones Summi Pontificis, cum illum cujusvis
Principis aut Gubernii imperio subditum esse cognoscerent,
præsertim vero si cui subesset Principi, inter quem et Romanam
Ditionem diuturnum aliquod ageretur bellum ?

ALLOCUTIO

<small>Habita in Consistorio Secreto Die XX Maii Anno</small>
MDCCCL.*

Si semper antea, . . .

Quocirca iis quoque omnibus debitas meritasque habemus et
agimus gratias, atque ipsis Nos summopere gratos esse profitemur.
Qua quidem in re nemo admirari non potest summam illius
omnia fortiter suaviterque regentis et moderantis Dei provi-
dentiam, qui in hac quoque tanta temporum perturbatione et
acerbitate effecit, ut vel ipsi Principes cum Romana Ecclesia
minime conjuncti *civilem ejusdem Ecclesiæ Principatum susti-
nerent, defenderent, quo Romanus Pontifex singulari ejusdem
divinæ providentiæ consilio per tot jam continentia sæcula optimo
quoque jure potitur,* ut in universæ Ecclesiæ regimine sibi divinitus commisso supremam suam Apostolicam auctoritatem toto
orbe ea plane libertate possit exercere, quæ ad Summi Pontificatus munus obeundum ac totius Dominici gregis salutem
procurandam tantopere est necessaria.

DAMNATIO

Et prohibitio Operis cui titulus *Juris Ecclesiastici Institutiones Joannis
Nepomuceni Nuytz in Regio Taurinensi Athenæo Professoris*—Itemque
—*In Jus Ecclesiasticum universum Tractationes—Auctoris ejusdem.*

<small>Ad Perpetuam Rei Memoriam.</small>

Ad Apostolicæ . . .

Quandoquidem palam, et aperte in editis dicti Auctoris libris
asseritur, "Ecclesiam vis inferendæ potestatem non habere,
neque potestatem ullam temporalem directam, vel indirectam.
. . . Nihil vetare alicujus Concilii generalis sententia, aut
universorum populorum facto, Summum Pontificatum ab Romano
Episcopo, atque Urbe ad alium Episcopum, aliamque Civitatem
transferri ; nationalis Concilii definitionem nullam aliam ad-
mittere disputationem, et civilem administrationem, rem ad hosce
terminos exigere posse: doctrinam comparantium libero Principi
Romanum Pontificem, et agenti in universa Ecclesia, doctrinam

* Allocution of Pius IX. on his return to Rome.

esse, quæ medio ævo prævaluit, effectusque adhuc manere : de temporalis regni cum spirituali compatibilitate disputare inter se Christianæ, et Catholicæ Ecclesiæ filios."

SS. DOMINI NOSTRI PII IX.

LITTERÆ APOSTOLICÆ.*

PIUS PAPA IX.

AD PERPETUAM REI MEMORIAM.

Cum Catholica Ecclesia a Christo Domino fundata et instituta, ad sempiternam hominum salutem curandam, perfectæ societatis formam vi divinæ suæ institutionis obtinuerit, ea proinde libertate pollere debet, ut in sacro suo ministerio obeundo nulli civili potestati subjaceat. *Et quoniam ad libere, ut par erat, agendum, iis indigebat præsidiis quæ temporum conditioni ac necessitati congruerent, idcirco singulari prorsus Divinæ Providentiæ consilio factum est, ut quum Romanum corruit Imperium et in plura fuit regna divisum, Romanus Pontifex, quem Christus totius Ecclesiæ suæ caput centrumque constituit, civilem assequeretur principatum.* Quo sane a Deo ipso sapientissime consultum est, ut in tanta temporalium Principum multitudine ac varietate Summus Pontifex illa frueretur politica libertate, quæ tantopere necessaria est ad spiritualem suam potestatem, auctoritatem et jurisdictionem toto orbe absque ullo impedimento exercendam. Atque ita plane decebat, ne Catholico Orbi ulla oriretur occasio dubitandi, impulsu fortasse civilium potestatum, vel partium studio duci quandoque posse in universali procuratione gerenda Sedem illam, ad quam "propter potiorem principalitatem necesse est omnem Ecclesiam convenire."

ALLOCUTIO

HABITA IN CONSISTORIO SECRETO DIE XXVIII. SEPTEMBRIS ANNO MDCCCLX.†

Novos, et ante . . .

In hac igitur tam injusta, tam hostili et horrenda civilis Nostri et hujus Sanctæ Sedis principatus aggressione et occupatione a Subalpino Rege ejusque Gubernio contra omnes justitiæ leges et universale gentium jus peracta, Nostri officii probe memores in hoc amplissimo vestro consessu, et coram universo catholico orbe Nostram vocem denuo vehementer attollimus, ac omnes nefarios

---

* Bull of Excommunication signed on March 26th, 1860.

† Pius IX. after the Battle of Castelfidardo.

sacrilegosque ejusdem Regis et Gubernii ausus reprobamus, penitusque damnamus, omnesque actus plane nullos et irritos declaramus, decernimus, ac civilis quo Romana pollet Ecclesia principatus integritatem, ejusque jura, quæ ad omnes catholicos pertinent etiam atque etiam reclamamus, et reclamare nunquam desistemus.

. . . *Agitur de violenta direptione illius principatus, qui singulari divinæ Providentiæ consilio Romano Pontifici datus est ad Apostolicum suum Ministerium in universam Ecclesiam plenissima libertate exercendum.* Quæ profecto libertas summæ omnibus Principibus curæ esse debet, ut Pontifex ipse nullius civilis potestatis impulsui subjaceat, atque ita spirituali pariter catholicorum in eorumdem Principum dominiis degentium tranquillitati cautum sit.

ALLOCUTIO

HABITA IN CONSISTORIO DIE IX. JUNII ANNO MDCCCLXII.*

ADSTANTIBUS ETIAM PATRIARCHIS, PRIMATIBUS, ARCHIEPISCOPIS, EPISCOPIS, SOLEMNIS SANCTORUM MARTYRUM IN JAPONIA ET MICHAELIS DE SANCTIS CANONIZATIONIS CAUSA ROMA CONGREGATIS.

Maxima quidem lætitia . . .

Nihil item dicimus de impia conspiratione, et pravis cujusque generis molitionibus ac fallaciis, quibus civilem hujus Apostolicæ Sedis principatum omnino evertere ac destruere volunt. Juvat potius hac de re commemorare miram prorsus consensionem, qua vos ipsi una cum aliis Venerabilibus Fratribus universi catholici orbis Sacrorum Antistitibus nunquam intermisistis et epistolis ad Nos datis, et pastoralibus litteris ad fideles scriptis hujusmodi fallacias detegere, refutare, *ac simul docere, hunc civilem Sanctæ Sedis principatum Romano Pontifici fuisse singulari divinæ Providentiæ consilio datum*, illumque necessarium esse, ut idem Romanus Pontifex nulli unquam Principi aut civili potestati subjectus supremam universi Dominici gregis pascendi regendique potestatem auctoritatemque ab ipso Christo Domino divinitus acceptam per universam Ecclesiam plenissima libertate exercere, ac majori ejusdem Ecclesiæ, et fidelium bono, utilitati et indigentiis consulere possit.

* Pius IX. to the Bishops assembled in Rome in 1862. The Bishops' declaration in reply is given elsewhere.

CORRIGENDA.

FOR paragraph (p. 124) beginning thus : *It may be useful here* . . . read : It has been said that it could not be defined that the Temporal Power is necessary (*vide* p 99), and that it could not be raised to the dignity of a dogma, referring, as it does, to the contingent element of historical circumstances, which is not to be sought for in revelation *(ibid.)*. Nevertheless, the utility and necessity of the Civil Principality, as shown in ecclesiastical law, " constitute Catholic doctrine infallibly proposed by the Church, as the Church is infallible, not only in proposing dogma, but in all those things which are connected with the conservation and evolution of dogma itself and of the Church ; *ex. gr.*, the Council of Trent is ecumenical." It will be seen by referring to the Appendix of Pontifical Acts that "the present circumstances," under which the Civil Principality is judged necessary, are the division of the ancient Roman Empire into several kingdoms. We may fairly judge that a return of the whole civilised and Christian world, now no longer identical with the old world, but including every nation of the globe, to the sway of one sceptre, is a practical impossibility. And even though such a wild dream became realised, reasons would still exist, showing the necessity of the Civil Principality amidst the provinces governed by men appointed by a universal emperor. The nations would still retain their racial sympathies or prejudices, and their governors might still be suspected of partiality. The civil governor of the Roman province, if the Civil Principality were undone, might be suspected of influence upon the Roman Pontiff, injurious to the interests of other peoples and other governors. It may be useful here to remark, for the sake of any reader unacquainted with the language of the Church on this point, that the word *relative*, as applied to the necessity of the Civil Princedom, is used in contradistinction with absolute necessity. The Civil Princedom is not absolutely necessary, since the Church existed and made headway during the centuries of violent persecution, and is making headway without the Civil Princedom at the present day. But in relation to the normal state of the Church, which is not that of violent persecution, the Civil Princedom is necessary. Hence the term *relative* necessity, which applies to the Civil Principality in the present circumstances of the world.

After the words : *That was reserved for the local Church of the Vicar of Christ, which alone is spiritually and temporally inalienable* (p. 152), close the sentence, and add : The previous interpretation of the words : " And His kingdom shall not be delivered up to another people," supposes that the text may refer to the eternal alliance with the Roman Church after the divorce of the Synagogue and Church-nation and its annihilation by the Roman power. But the contrast established by Daniel's prophetic interpretation is not between the Church of the Synagogue and the Holy Roman Church, but between the kingdom of God and the monarchies. The text: "And His kingdom shall not be delivered up to another people," manifestly denies of the kingdom of the God of Heaven (His kingdom) what has been foretold of the monarchies, viz., that they should be delivered up to one another in succession. This interpretation, which seems the only true one, is in full conformity with the thesis. It shows that the unfaithful nation of the Jews was undone by the Roman power under Vespasian and Titus, and not "the kingdom of God." The faithful remnant of the Jewish nation at home and abroad, led by the Chief Apostle after Christ's Ascension, constituted "the kingdom of God" in its limited sense (*vide infra*, p. 199) until the final establishment of the Roman Church. There was no break in the Theocracy, which took Rome in exchange for Jerusalem, and eventually conquered it. Thus the prophetic interpretation of the King's dream included in the words: "And His kingdom shall not be delivered up to another people," contains no provision for the future of that Kingdom, which did not belong to its whole span of existence. As "the kingdom of God" survived and conquered the four monarchies, so is it destined to survive and conquer all powers that oppose it:" in the days of those kingdoms, etc.

For *freedom* (p. 8, l. 17), read Sovereignty. Also on pp. 15 and 22.

For *a limited term of office* (p. 9, l. 22), read a term of office limited by genealogical succession.

After the words *recognised as King* (p. 11, l. 22), add by the nation.

For the sentence *For a portion, etc.* (p. 11, last three lines), read For a portion only of the features or characteristic powers of an order do not constitute that order, which, etc.

For *in right* (p. 27, l. 13), read in fact.

For *secular* (p. 33, l. 21), read profane.

For heading of chapter (p. 81), substitute: The Temporal Power of the Pope : definable or indefinable.

For *what* (p. 91, l. 11), read want.

For paragraph beginning: Allow me (p. 122), read: Allow me again to inquire whether the Roman Pontiff, who now, according to the opinion of some, retains a fraction of the old Papal States, could, if he saw fit, cease to claim the remainder? In other words, could the Roman Pontiff ever see fit to cease to claim the Papal States, as, etc.

For *regnum* (p. 156, l. 2), read regimen.

For East (p. 168, l. 5), read Judea.